Altared Ground

Altared Ground

Levinas, History, and Violence

Brian Schroeder

Routledge
New York and London

Published in 1996 by

Routledge
29 West 35th Street
New York, NY 10001

Published in Great Britain by
Routledge
11 New Fetter Lane
London EC4P 4EE

Printed in the United States of America on acid-free paper.

Library of Congress Cataloging-in-Publication Data

Schroeder, Brian
Altared ground: Levinas, history, and violence / Brian Schroeder.
p. cm.
Includes bibliographical references and index.

ISBN 0-415-91452-3 (cl) — ISBN 0-415-91453-1 (pbk)
1. Philosophy. 2. Religion. 3. History—Philosophy. 4. Violence.
5. Subjectivity. 6. Self (Philosophy). 7. Levinas, Emmanuel. I. Title.

B945.S33A48 1995 95-36343
179'.7 —dc20 CIP

To my parents
Faye and Gary

Avant la guerre, étaient les autels.

– Emmanuel Lévinas

Contents

Acknowledgments

I am appreciative and indebted to the following people for their friendship and astute reading of this book during various stages of its development: David Allison, Jay Cassel, Tamsin Lorraine, Kelly Oliver, and Mary Rawlinson, with special debts of gratitude to Thomas Altizer and Edward Casey. They have been enormously responsive, critical and encouraging throughout this labor. Words cannot be found to express my deep respect and admiration for the work of Emmanuel Levinas which has enriched me both philosophically and personally. The friendship and phenomenological/cultural explorations of Alphonso Lingis have also been of great value and inspiration. I wish to acknowledge my present and former colleagues and students at the University of Southern Maine, the University of Maine, Orono, Rollins College, Rocky Mountain College, and SUNY Stony Brook, as well as the Collegium Phaenomenologicum and the Wisdom Rendezvous, for expanding my intellectual and social horizons. The teachers of my youth, whose profound love of teaching and personal interest continue to affect me to this day, deserve special mention, especially Richard Cristofoletti, Maurice Holloway, and Maureen Sherlock, who introduced me to the way of philosophizing that I embrace today and to the themes of which the present work is comprised. I am grateful to Barb Northrop, Rachel Hill, Jill MacKenzie, and Dan Quan for their friendship, patience, and support during the most trying periods of this writing. Finally, my thanks to Maureen MacGrogan, Kimberly Herald, and the staff at Routledge for their invaluable editorial assistance.

Portland, Maine
May 1995

Abbreviations

Works by Emmanuel Levinas

AE	*Autrement qu'être ou au-delà de l'essence.*
CPP	*Collected Philosophical Papers.*
DEE	*De l'existence à l'existant.*
EDE	*En découvrant l'existence avec Husserl et Heidegger.*
EE	*Existence and Existents.*
EI	*Ethics and Infinity.*
EeI	*Ethique et infini.*
HH	*Humanisme de l'autre homme.*
HS	*Hors Sujet.*
TN	*In the Time of Nations.*
LR	*The Levinas Reader.*
NP	*Noms Propres.*
OB	*Otherwise Than Being or Beyond Essence.*
OS	*Outside the Subject.*
TA	*Le temps et l'autre.*
TO	*Time and the Other.*
TI	*Totality and Infinity: An Essay on Exteriority.*
TeI	*Totalité et infini: essai sur l'exteriorité.*

ForeGround

One of the most pressing concerns for contemporary society is the issue of violence and the factors that promote it. This book stages an engagement between Emmanuel Levinas, one of the leading figures in twentieth century European and Continental philosophy, and Plato, Hegel, Nietzsche, Heidegger, Gadamer, Adorno, Merleau-Ponty, Deleuze, Derrida, and others (in the form of extended notes) in the history of ideas. Not intended to be a mere exposition of Levinas' original and complex ethical thinking, this study is an attempt to reread the history of Western philosophy and religion by extending and going beyond Levinas' alternatives to traditional theories of the self in order to suggest a notion of subjectivity that is not grounded in violence. The aim is to contribute to current discussions of reconceiving subjectivity as intersubjectivity in a postmodern context by taking up such diverse themes as alterity, ground, transcendence, responsibility, language, community, politics, divinity, and futurity in relation to interpersonal violence.

What is proposed is an interrogation into the relation between the philosophical concepts of ground (*Grund*), subjectivity, and violence, with the dual purpose of both assessing the accuracy of Levinas' reading of the history of philosophy and advancing the notions of ethical subjectivity and intersubjectivity in the domain of future social and political relations. This book is thus interdisciplinary in scope, concerned with the interdices between philosophy, religion, theology, literary theory, social-political thought, social psychology, and postmodern theory. It contests, along with Levinas, the claim that peace and totality go hand in hand, that the overcoming of violence necessitates the totalization of subject and object, of self and other, into a metaphysical one or whole expressible as *ground*, despite contentions that such a unity does not preclude the integrity of difference and multiplicity. Traditional metaphysics, in its multiplicity of forms, is marked by a tendency to value unity over multiplicity, identity over difference, sameness over otherness, order over chaos. This work challenges such a hierarchy of terms and seeks to determine an alternative to the tables of thought that have aided and that continue to aid the propagation of intersubjective violence. And, perhaps more importantly, it explores the forceful, surprising, and potentially dangerous claim that it is precisely *conceptuality* itself that is the origin of violence. Specifically, what is at issue is the relation between infinity and alterity, the determination of the origin of ethics, and thus the possibility of a *non-totalizing ground* for the ethical (intersubjective) relation that *preserves the autonomy of the subject*, the principal legacy of the Enlightenment.

Chapter one (BackGround) frames Levinas' thinking within the horizon of Hegelian and post-Hegelian philosophy. The overarching themes of the constitution of *ethical* subjectivity and intersubjectivity and the debate between modernity and postmodernity are introduced and situated in the context of human liberation. Levinas' philosophy is then considered in the light (darkness?) of the death of God, specifically with regard to the questions of atheistic existence, and whether the naming of the Absolute, the Infinite, or the Godhead (depending on one's orientation) predicates the conceptual origin of intersubjective violence. Levinas' conception of religion (not of theology)—which he defines as the practice, not the theory or dogma, of interpersonal or social ethics—is also taken up.

The second chapter (UnderGround) opens with a brief assessment of the history of the early Greek understanding of violence. It then centers on the importance of the imagination (ἐικασία, not φαντασία) in Plato's effort to dialectically grasp the forms. This brings into play the decisive question of Western metaphysics as a whole: namely, the status of "truth." Martin Heidegger's construal of the history of metaphysics is taken up through an analysis of his interpretation of ἀλήθεια as unconcealedness (*Unverborgenheit*) in Presocratic and Platonic thinking. This is of vital importance, as this study is an effort to determine whether violence is rooted in θεωρία—in the conceptual positing and grasping of truth.

In chapter three (HelioGround), the attention turns again to Plato, this time with respect to the idea of the Good posited *beyond* being which plays a pivotal role in determining Levinas' own understanding of the ethical transcendence of alterity. The radical exteriority of the Good and the One, vital for Levinas' conception of the Infinite, is examined with an eye to Hans-Georg Gadamer's interpretation of transcendence via the form of the beautiful. The tension between justice (Levinas) and beauty (Gadamer), as that which makes accessible the Good, underscores the movement of this chapter.

The next four chapters focus on Hegel's philosophy and Levinas' reaction to it. The fourth chapter (IdeoGround) briefly situates Hegel within the context of the history of ideas, and continues the enquiry into the origin of violence by way of examining the concept of the Idea (*Idee*) and its subsequent unfolding as consciousness or Spirit (*Geist*) to its teleological realization as ground (*Grund*).

Chapter five (MiddleGround) takes up Hegel's concepts of action, mediation, and the distinction between individual morality (*Moralität*) and ethical community (*Sittlichkeit*) as they are primarily expressed in the *Phenomenology of Spirit*. Hegel's attempt to demonstrate the ethical or moral efficacy of his philosophy is contested via both Theodor Adorno's assessment of mediation and his negative dialectical interpretation of the subject-object dichotomy, and Levinas' juxtaposition of *proximity* to mediation as the modality of being that best describes the nature of the self-Other relationship.

The thesis of chapter six (WarGround) is that Hegel's project of determining an "absolute knowing" is inherently violent in that, despite his objections to the contrary, it refuses to acknowledge the Other as truly other. Approaching this question primarily through the *Science of Logic*, Levinas' construal of infinity as radical alterity is employed as the locus of this criticism. The relation between symmetry and reciprocity is also examined, in an effort to grasp the subtleties of Levinas' interpretation of *asymmetrical* intersubjectivity.

Chapter seven (MystiGround) concludes the assessment of Hegel's philosophy with the intent of searching for a clue towards the establishment of a ground that refuses the totalizing impetus and structure of previous (including Hegel's expressed own) conceptions of *Grund* that rely, ultimately, on the transparency of rational consciousness to itself. It is argued that, despite Hegel's efforts, he does not fully succeed in overcoming once and for all the *mystery* of being. Focusing on his concepts of *Trieb* (urge, impulse, drive) and *Unendlichkeit* (infinity), this chapter proposes that Hegel prefigures postmodern thinking with its emphasis on radical difference—a difference to which Levinas assigns an ethical significance and, moreover, one that he indicates lies at the earliest beginnings of Western philosophy.

Chapter eight (TransGround) takes us out of Levinas' relation to the idealist tradition and face to face, so to speak, with the thinker that he considers to be the most profound of the twentieth century, namely, Heidegger. But Levinas makes a decided departure from his former teacher, developing much of his philosophy in direct contestation to the early Heideggerian project of grounding a fundamental ontology, which is a partial continuation of Hegel's attempt to ground being in and as history. Their shared, though considerably different, conceptions of the *face to face* are considered. Heidegger's notions of nothingness and letting-be (*Gelassenheit*) are then contrasted to Levinas' ideas of alterity and responsibility in order to more fully grasp the concept of *transcendence.* In addition, the relations between identity and difference, separation and proximity, the ethics of care and responsibility, and finally, the conception of Desire as transcendence in Levinas are assessed.

The question of the use of metaphysical language and the paradoxes that it entails is the topic of chapter nine (DiaGround). Levinas' philosophy is considered in the context of recent French thinking. His theory of language is assessed in relation to Maurice Merleau-Ponty's in an effort to further clarify the meaning of ethical transcendence in the intersubjective relationship. Merleau-Ponty's key concept in his later work, of intertwining, or *chiasm,* and the reversibility implied in such a concept, is examined with an eye to better understanding Levinas' claim that there is a fundamental *irreversibility* in the self-Other relation. This essential intersubjective non-reciprocity is pronounced in Levinas' later writing as the difference between the saying (*le dire*) and the said (*le dit*) which concretizes the asymmetrical character of the self-Other relation. Gilles Deleuze's and Felix Guattari's analysis of faciality and Jacques Derrida's contention that the Levinasian conception of the Other as *alter non-ego,* as a paradoxical conception of alterity that leads one to a non-sensical ground, are also engaged.

The title of the tenth and final chapter (HyperGround) alludes to Merleau-Ponty's concept of *hyperdialectique* advanced in his unfinished ontology *The Visible and Invisible.* Nietzsche's potent rejection of the possibility of establishing *any* metaphysical ground is considered by way of his thoughts on the ontologico-metaphysical primacy of *chaos.* This is taken up with the intention of advancing Levinas' conception of the pre-original, an-archic alterity revealed in the face of the Other. The work concludes by engaging the fundamentally religious thematics with which it commenced, ending (beginning?) with remarks on the difference between eschatological and apocalyptic visions of the future in Hegel, Nietzsche, and Levinas—and beyond.

1

BackGround

If the overriding question of modern philosophy has been the status of the subject, it can equally be said that a central concern of much contemporary European and Continental thinking is that of "the other." Taking the lead from those celebrated hermeneuticians of suspicion—Marx, Nietzsche, and Freud—twentieth century philosophy has called into question the substantiality of the subject-ego, thus bringing into prominence the issue of alterity. Hitherto, philosophy had largely been an attempt to dominate or subsume the object (otherness, difference) under the rubric of identity or selfsameness, which is to say, of *comprehension* by rational consciousness.

Now, if philosophy is in a state of crisis, as postmodernist theory (despite its often *un*theoretical pretensions) claims, then the crisis is over the status of the *subject*. The historical progression of philosophy from its ancient sources to its modern expressions, especially Hegel, has produced, in its quest for a ground of epistemological certitude, a conflation or confusion of the terms "subject" and "object" resulting in various notions of transcendental subjectivity.

One of philosophy's principal concerns has long been epistemology. The status of the relation between thinking and being, first articulated by Parmenides and Heraclitus, remains one of the most celebrated and important *paradoxes* of philosophy. Hegelian dialectics claims to overcome this tension by reconciling, conclusively, the claims of epistemology and metaphysics in the totality of the speculative logic of the *Aufhebung*. But confronted with the philosophically and theologically devastating aftermath of the death of God, of which the loss of the said epistemic ground is one of the greatest casualties, thinking is faced with the task of recovering a viable, tenable notion of subjectivity that does not fall into the totalizing sovereign tendencies of the modern subject.

The death of God and the resulting nihilism challenge most, if not all, classic notions of subjectivity, truth, and meaning. Thus there can be no genuine overcoming (interpreted here to mean primarily an ethical transformation—the *revaluation of values*) without a radical re*vision* of Western thinking. And yet, despite the enormous critical reaction to the totalizing impetus of systematic and dialectical philosophy, of metaphysics, it is not at all certain that Western philosophy escapes the great logico-metaphysical web of Georg Wilhelm Friedrich Hegel.

Few philosophers have provoked such a reaction as has Hegel. His philosophy was challenged almost immediately in the nineteenth century, beginning with Kierkegaard's insistence that the individual existent is lost in the vastness of the System and Marx's contention that Hegel does not truly grasp the concreteness of historical transformation through physical labor, to Nietzsche's repudiation of any metaphysical teleology. More recent critiques include Adorno's criticism of the overly-positivistic stance of speculative dialectics with its "preponderance of the subject," and Deleuze's decidedly anti-Hegelian interpretation of Nietzsche. To be sure, positive interpretations, appraisals, and appropriations of Hegel abound as well—for example, Kojève's and Hyppolite's interpretations of the *Phenomenology of Spirit*, and Derrida's inclusion of dialectical "double play" in the deconstructive method (to name but a few). But whether pro or con in their assessments, the above mentioned all share Hegel's desire to reassess or revaluate the meaning of subjective existence while simultaneously rejecting the truth-claims of traditional notions of the subject. Yet they are also, with the possible exception of Marx, united in rejecting the governance of a universal logic culminating in an absolute knowing by, through, and of Spirit (*Geist*).

The suspicion of the clandestine complicity between the concept of *totality* and social-political totalitarianism belies much of this century's rejection of metaphysics and the subsequent emphasis on revaluating difference and otherness. However, this century finds bequeathed to philosophy an original and powerful reassessment of metaphysics and ontology. Emmanuel Levinas' interpretation, or rather, *deconceptualization* of metaphysics[1] calls upon philosophy to radically reconceive, with a Nietzschean vigor, the relation between the Same (τὸ αὐτόν) and the Other (τὸ ἕτερον), the very ancient dualism posed by Plato in the *Sophist*. Deconceptualization here refers to the attempt not only to decenter onto(theo)logical discourse, but to stress that the metaphysical-ethical (identical terms for Levinas) relation not only precedes determination by selfsame consciousness, but is contingent upon a certain refusal on the part of the selfsame to conceptually totalize the other. Levinas' reformulation of metaphysics emphasizes the radical alterity (*altérité*) and the ethical supremacy of the Other (*l'autrui*),[2] insists on the priority of difference over identity, and contests the logic of Western philosophy, both traditional and Hegelian, at its very core. It is a proto-deconstruction of the metaphysically and ontologically conceived concept of totality and its violent way of being towards otherness in general (*autre*) and the Other in particular.

Levinasian metaphysics is a movement towards the invisible, "towards a pluralism that does not fuse into a unity, [a] break with Parmenides."[3] Parmenidean unity is interpreted here in terms of ontological totality and provides the locus for the criticism and assessment of metaphysics and ethics in, arguably, Levinas' most important work, *Totality and Infinity*. Metaphysics is conceived here as the relation of consciousness with a prior term absolutely exterior to it. Prelinguistic and preconceptual, metaphysics is the relation (ἔρος) with the infinitely other, which is to say, with Another person. The relation with the Other precedes the totality of selfsame consciousness. The other person constitutes the ethical meaning of the self's existence. The face of the Other (*le visage d'autrui*) contests the freedom of the I; at the same time, the wonder of subjectivity, of absolutely *separated* being, is celebrated.

Levinas stands in the forefront of contemporary thinkers who are dissatisfied with the course of the philosophical tradition, but what distinguishes him from many of his contemporaries is that he seeks to find *ethical* meaning in the relation with the Invisible, a "space" that is ontologically (though not metaphysically) nothingness and, therefore, traditionally construed as non-meaningful. Yet he is virtually alone among his peers in his conviction that this seeming void is charged with an overflowing positivity of meaning.

Levinasian ethics is the maintenance of the radical distance or separation that exists between the same and the other, assuming the form of *responsibility* for the Other. The ethical relation is prior to thought, to language, even to Being (*Sein*) itself. Ethics (or metaphysics) is "first philosophy,"[4] the originary signification; it originates in that which is "otherwise than being" (*autrement qu'être*) and not in non-being. Conversely, ontology, preoccupied with the evidences of being, is, as first philosophy, a philosophy of power. Consequently, this reappraisal of ethics requires a reappraisal of the constitution of subjectivity and intersubjectivity.

I

According to Hegel, subjectivity is fully realized in its conceptual dialectical relation with its other. This relation is predicated upon the concept of *totality*, a concept that logically equates otherness with non-being, and being with nothingness. The totality of Spirit is infinite becoming for Hegel. It is precisely the concept of totality as infinite ground against which Levinas directs his polemic. He argues that the dissimulation and reconstruction of the Other into the simulated order of a conceptual totality is violent in that it makes faceless the individual existent and strips away one's primal alterity. Thus are the possibilities of domination, oppression and war laid bare. In the extreme, the ontological totality, manifest as the political State, is that alone which is free and has rights; the individual is subordinate to the rational movement within the totality. In the journey of the *Weltgeist*, the singular and the collective existents become mere pawns, tools, useful only insofar as they serve the purpose of the greater power.

The course of much European and Continental thinking has been a reaction to the Cartesian *cogito* and the Hegelian dialectic. The postmodern question in philosophy is centered largely around the status of the subject. The modern conception of the subject-ego, one of the primary inheritances of the Enlightenment (*Aufklärung*), is rightly characterized as that of a sovereign, totalizing entity, constitutive of itself and its world, including the other. In Hegel's philosophy, for instance, the philosophical concept of substance is identified as subject, and the autogrounding circularity of the dialectic is historically realized in an absolute knowing, culminating in the development of the universal, homogenous sociopolitical state. This is the metaphysical prefiguring of the recent attempts to establish a "new world order" which rests upon the condition of the possibility of conceptually grasping and politically realizing an operative notion of totality or wholeness.

Here the totality or unity of the modern subject is fully manifest in the unity of the state of which the individual is the mirror. Hegel's formula of I=We in the *Phenomenology of Spirit* is the culmination of the Western attempt, commencing with Plato's theory of the tripartite soul in the *Republic*, to identify the particular with the universal, the individual with the communal collective. However, given the rise and proliferation of technologically supported totalitarian, dictatorial regimes this century, is it possible any longer to equate peace and stability with the eventual emergence of a selfsame totality? In other words, has the Western philosophical, theological, and scientific preoccupation with totality resulted in inevitable slides towards social and political totalitarianism?[5]

The modern theories of subjectivity and intersubjectivity are predicated on the knowable unity of the self, a unity that until the end of the nineteenth century was essentially a given. Nietzsche's radical critique of metaphysics and epistemology set the wheels in motion for the current forays into the hitherto largely ignored or suppressed issues of difference and otherness. The debate between modernism and postmodernism hinges on these very concepts. Nietzsche insightfully notes that the history of philosophy is that of an error, an error which he identifies and names as *Platonism*. In so doing, he again raises the question that has enticed and titillated much of Western thinking since the time of its Greek inception—that of the beginning (ἀρχή)—and with it that which has been the decisive, and perhaps most divisive, question in the history of ideas: Is the origin or genesis of being determinable as ground; or is it beyond being, outside the reach of such determination?

With this question the status of being is brought to the fore, and with it a plethora of other queries, both old and new: Why is there something rather than nothing? What is the meaning of being? What is the relation between truth and being? What is the difference between Being (*Sein*; *être*) and beings (*Seiendes*; *étants*)? From whence do we assign value? These questions subtend others: What is the relation between ontology and ethics (metaphysics)? How does this question determine, and how is it determined by, the concepts of totality and infinity? What consequences does this determination hold for the relation between ontology and epistemology? What is the relation between the ethical and the political? How much of this discourse is confined to the structures of modernism? And, in what respects does postmodern discourse reframe the positing of these questions and the mode in which they are taken up?

These questions will be addressed, and an account and a revaluation of the modern conception of the human subject as an ethical and political agent will be offered. Primarily focused on the original ethical philosophy of Levinas, the present work seeks to situate itself within the history of Western thought precisely to forward it in a significant manner, to trace, for the purposes here, the (non?) groundwork of a new interpretation of subjectivity for what has become referred to by many as the "postmodern," which is also to say, the *postmetaphysical* era.

Postmodern theorists claim that modernity is philosophically denoted by an emphasis on *comprehending* formalism, hierarchy, identity, totality, determinacy, and sameness; and subtending these emphases is the concept of transcendence. If this is so, then modernity is indeed the realization and culmination of the ancient quest to grasp the paradox of the One and the Many (or the Dyad), to reconcile the tension between Parmenides and Heraclitus. Postmodernist theory, then, can be characterized, though not defined, as the attempt to *apprehend* certain antiformalist, anarchic tendencies, difference, the non-totalizing (infinity?), indeterminacy, and alterity, in the immanent domain or region of social being.

But does the distinction between modernity and postmodernity hold? Does the postmodern direction or gesture preclude the possibility of a philosophically, religiously, and socially viable and operative concept of transcendence? And if so, what is the subsequent effect on the issues of the constitution of subjectivity, intersubjectivity, and finding a ground for ethical valuation?

II

Since the time of its Mediterranean inception, Western philosophy has essentially presented itself as a philosophy of the *center*. This notion, questioned in various degrees by European thinkers from Hegel to Derrida (though the first credit goes to Nicolas of Küs[6]), concerns itself most profoundly with the concept of spatiality. Philosophy since Socrates and Plato has grown out of the soil of geopolitical space, of the ἀγορά, and consequently defined and extended its "mission" to disseminate the "truth" to regions exterior to the center. The ontology endemic to this philosophy has imposed itself on those peripheral spaces for five centuries since Columbus "discovered" the "new" world and, for all practical purposes, founded the *ego cogito* on the *ego conquiro*.

The emerging liberation philosophies and theologies of this century, whether feminist, Latin American, Asian, African, Native American, African American, or even Eastern European, as movements from the *periphery*, are "postmodern" in the sense that they seek to overcome and transform the modern Western vision of a totalizing and centered "new world order." Still, the language of liberation, despite its movement from the exterior (other), is nonetheless a language of the center. It would not be coherent or effective were it otherwise; indeed, it would not be a language of liberation at all. This does imply, though, the loss or annulment of different individual or cultural identities. Genuine liberation does not seek to dethrone or displace the dominant ideological language of the center merely to consecrate or situate another in lieu of it.

In what respects has the language of European-based philosophy, especially that of the existential-phenomenological tradition, either aided or hindered the development of a postmodern philosophy of liberation, a philosophy that posits justice as the means to freedom? The movement of liberation philosophy has been delineated to some extent, but what is lacking is the truly critical and transformative voice which can only be provided through the praxis of oppressed peoples of the periphery. The legacy of phenomenology is merely the most recent extension of the ontology of the center. European philosopies have for the most part emphasized the person-to-nature relation as the primary mode of understanding, of comprehending Being. A philosophy of liberation, on the other hand, invokes the person-to-person, the "face to face" relation as constitutive of πρᾶξις in the sense defined by Aristotle—enigmatically the first systematic thinker of the center—as the relation between politics and ethics. But πρᾶξις also conveys the critical, dialectical relation between theory and practice in which each term informs and transforms the other. Phenomenology, in this reading, insofar as it attempts to comprehend the question of the meaning of Being, continually finds itself aligned with θεωρία, an imperialistic modality of being-towards-the-other if ascribed preeminence over the pre-conceptual lived experience (ethics). It is for this reason that liberation thinkers, despite particular commitments dictated by their respective contexts, are united in what has come to be identified as the rallying call of liberation thinking: praxis precedes theory.

A philosophy of liberation seeks to transform the status quo and thus decenter the horizon of future possibilities. Enrique Dussel states that this means turning the attention on "the past of the world and on spatiality to detect the origin (archeology) of dependence, weakness, suffering, apparent incapacity, and backwardness."[7] He follows Levinas in focusing on the *an-archic* trace of the Other and the spatiality of proximity in an effort to establish the liberating praxis (ethical metaphysics) of the one who stands outside the law and order of the established system. Responsibility for the Other, responding to the "silent" voice of the oppressed, reveals the *epiphanic* "beyond being" quality of goodness, though not in a naive and uncritical sense. In this way, the liberating act (of gratuitous goodness), inasmuch as it is beyond intrasystemic interest, is and can only be illegal, contrary to present laws which, because they are those of an old order that is now oppressive, are unjust. It is the inevitable position of liberation: subversive illegality.[8] The challenge confronting contemporary liberation thinking is the transformation of this "illegality" into the *justice* of societies.

The history of ontology, with its emphasis on light and theory, has often blinded itself to the darkened faces of those on the periphery, on the margins, whose voices, if not completely reduced to silence, are often dismissed as the garbled utterances of the barbarian (τό βάρβαρον). Silence here does not denote a lack of ability to communicate on the part of the oppressed; instead, it signifies the denial or, at least, the apathy on the part of the dominant center of the self-same to listen to the Other. But as Michel de Certeau notes, Native Americans, for example, have retained in the *silence* of the "tortured body" and "altered earth" the memory of what European culture has largely "forgotten."[9] The voices of liberation form the collective memory of a hitherto silent body crying out to the center for recognition and justice. The risk, as Hegel notes, is that of genuine *reciprocity*, of the spatial though infinitely discontinuous time of proximity (Levinas) prior to any mediation that reveals the totality of the world of sense, of the horizon of horizons.

III

It has often been noted that philosophy arrives on the scene too late; and the frustrated attempts by philosophy to fully grasp and articulate the totality of the lived experience is testimony to the thesis that being's primary mode of relation is not to itself, nor to thinking (as Parmenides and the tradition following him has held), but to that which is *otherwise than being*. According to Levinas, the radical exteriority and transcendence signified by the Infinite or absolutely other is not separate from the finite world of becoming but, paradoxically, is reflected *within* the totality of being or history (*TeI* 7/*TI* 23). The separation of the same from the other, implied in the idea of infinity, is *produced* in the concretized event of interior existence, as a "psychism." But the *paradox* of this separation is apparent only after the event itself, when apprehended in its abstraction (*TeI* 46/*TI* 54). Yet the paradoxes of an absolutely separated being, of an interiority or inner life of a different order than that of the totality of historical time, are "overcome by the psychism," first as fecundity, then as memory.

> Memory recaptures and reverses and suspends what is already accomplished in birth—in nature. Fecundity escapes the punctual instant of death. By memory I *ground myself* after the event, retrospectively: I assume today what in the absolute past of the origin had no subject to receive it and had therefore the weight of a fatality.... Memory as an inversion of historical time is the essence of interiority. (*TeI* 48–49/*TI* 56; italics added)

In other words, "ground" is not the result of self-comprehending Reason, as Hegel would have it, but the product of the interior mnemonic operation of an already separated a-theist being independent in his or her transcendence of the totality of dialectical being which, moreover, is *concretized* in fecundity.

Surely a primary difference between traditional Western thinking and various forms of non-occidental thinking, such as Oriental, Indian, or even Hebraic, revolves around issues of paradox and contradiction—which are not synonymous. For the vast part of its two-millenia-old history, Western philosophy and theology have been hard-pressed to deal with the problem of cognitive paradox. Even the most celebrated theological "mysteries" have generally been construed as hiddenly rational or open only to the "knowledge" that faith can bring. And until recently, philosophy's recourse has been, following Aristotle, either to assert the preeminence of the logic of noncontradiction or, following Hegel, the logic of dialectic. To be sure, contradictions abound; but a contradiction is something that reason can at least grasp, even if it fails to reconcile or fully comprehend it. Is it any wonder therefore that contemporary thinking, in the fallout of the death of God, and rightly suspicious of systematic philosophies, so often takes recourse to what amounts to nothing more than a hermeneutical relativism? Or, just as powerfully (witness in theology the current, though indeed ancient, threats of gnosticism and fundamentalism), to conservatism?

Hegel represents, along with Whitehead, the last great attempt to formulate a systematic metaphysics based on logical principle. In his philosophy one finds the most comprehensive attempt to render all absence, all difference, all otherness, totally manifest or present. There is ultimately no paradox in dialectical metaphysics; contradictions or opposites are reconciled through the logical move of the *Aufhebung*. And yet, again paradoxically, it may be that the very fullness or totality of presence in Hegel repudiates his claim that otherness, difference, and absence are granted a complete ontological status in his philosophy.

IV

The twentieth century is witness to the demise of the deity. The predominant tendency in Western thinking has been to construe the Absolute or Ultimate either as illusion, nothingness, or phantasm, or as radical exteriority. The latter is the position adopted by Levinas. However, the exteriority and irreducible alterity signified by the idea of infinity, while not comprehendable as a cognitive object, *is* apprehendable in its capacity for consciousness as a limit principle for both ethics and epistemology. A critical distinction needs to be drawn here between the powers of *apprehension* and *comprehension* by consciousness. Hegel too distinguishes between these terms.[10] Apprehension refers to the partial, immediate grasp consciousness has on the object; comprehension denotes the total accessibility of the object to cognition. On the ethical level, the apprehension of the absolutely or infinitely other does not occlude the Other's alterity; whereas the comprehension of the Other's otherness negates the primordial alterity of the Other, draws her or him into the totalizing stance of selfsame consciousness, and thus constitutes the violence that Levinas associates with the "imperialism" of θεωρία. The comprehensive negation and reduction of the other to a momentary movement of the same is the instantiation of ethical violence. It marks the transition from the metaphysical to the ontological, that is, from the dimension of the face to face, the lived ethical relation, to that of the conceptual. In this move is effected the implicit relation between the concept of totality and the political and social realization of totalitarianism.

The status of *Grund*, of Reason, of the Absolute or, if one will, of the presence and/or absence of God, hinges on the relation between the concepts of infinity and totality. Subjectivity cannot divorce itself of its relation with these most foundational concerns. But the death of God is at the same time the demise of the subject.[11] Like Nietzsche, Levinas is often construed and dismissed as an enemy of subjectivity, as a threat to the coherent unity of Western philosophy. Yet Levinas (and Nietzsche, for that matter) is a thinker deeply concerned with the preservation of the autonomy of the subject. In their thinking one finds the basis for a new understanding of alterity and, consequently, of subjectivity.

Traditional metaphysical forms up until Hegel, who reintroduces the importance of time back into philosophy, are founded on a conception of the subject as a completed entity and not as a process or becoming. In attempting to retrieve a sense of the dynamism of human existence and of the world in general, Hegel reduces the alterity of the Infinite to the level of pure theory. Otherness serves only as a pole for the self-identification of the same; alterity is a mere moment of Spirit's quest for self-recognition. Levinas' charge against Hegel, and against phenomenology as a whole, is that the Other is not recognized as being genuinely other since in Hegel, for instance, one finds the collapse of alterity in the formulation of the identity of the same and the other. In addition to this denial of the fullness of alterity there is, maintains Levinas, the correlate suppression of the genuine transcendence of subjective being:

> The idea of Infinity implies the separation of the same with regard to the other, but

> this separation cannot rest on an opposition to the other which would be purely antithetical. Thesis and antithesis, in repelling one another, call for one another. They appear in opposition to a synoptic gaze that encompasses them; they already form a totality which, by integrating the metaphysical transcendence expressed by the idea of infinity, relativizes it. An absolute transcendence has to be produced as non-integratable.... *Correlation does not suffice as a category for transcendence.* (*TeI* 45/*TI* 53)

Levinas is remarkable if only for his unrelenting attempt to think ethically in the very *absence* of a rationally retrievable and knowable concept of ground. Yet the problem of the genesis of the divine, whether interpreted as the Idea, the Godhead, the Absolute, or the Infinite, is not shirked by Levinas. It is taken up in a new and innovative way for the modern thinker, but not in the manner of postmodernism which retreats before the face of the question of genesis, repudiating the knowability of a primal beginning as merely the continuation of classical metaphysical and theological interest. Still, this is not the invalidation of the question of the *meaning* of origination.

Levinas is primarily opposed to Hegel in this study as they represent, arguably, two of the most powerful proposals for their respective positions on the question of primordial beginning: origin as creation (Levinas) versus eternal genesis (Hegel). According to Levinas, Being is the *trace* of the passing of an "absolutely heteronomous" and unrecollectable creative past power, namely, the Infinite.[12] But for Hegel, existence is the eternal infinite becoming of finite being, a beginning never temporally located, only logically posited.

Is it possible to ever reconcile these two great tides of Western thinking? Or is the metaphysical project, in its historically multiplicitous guise, at long last defunct?

Levinas' attempt to *revaluate* the metaphysical project, and with it the meaning and constitution of subjectivity, is radical because it commences with the Other and not, as Hegel does, from the selfsame conception of the absolutely other. It is not the logic of ontology, of classic metaphysics, that lays hold of or apprehends the elusive nature of alterity; it is the *surprise* of exteriority which paradoxically arises from the interiority that the face signifies as the trace of the Infinite. The continual revelatory and epiphanic dimension accorded the Other is the heart of Levinas' hermeneutic of the metaphysical (ethical) relation. Subjectivity is not vanquished by the presencing of the absence of the absolutely other in the face of the Other. Subjectivity is constituted in and through this relationship, and moreover, is given meaning prior to its own self-determination. Thus the philosophy espoused by Hegel is actually antagonistic to the "inner life." It subsumes under the rubric of totality both subject and object, self and Other, and consecrates them as substance; and not only that, but as that to which one is, to use Hegel's own term here, *subject.*[13]

V

While the present work understands itself to be philosophical and not theological in nature, Levinas approaches the issues of origin and alterity from a decidedly

Greek-Hebraic standpoint. The religious aspect of Levinas' thinking derives from his Judaic heritage and his extensive grounding in the study of Talmud; however, he breaks with the majority in this tradition insofar as he maintains that the notion of the transcendence of the Good is a fundamentally Western, philosophical insight. But religion is not confined by Levinas to a certain cultural or theological perspective; *religion is universal.*

Now, the theologically minded reader may well wonder whether Levinas is indeed coming from a scriptural as well as a philosophical perspective, but Levinas takes pains to separate his philosophical writings from his religious ones.[14] Still, he is astute in finding parallels regarding, for instance, the transcendence of the Good or absolutely other in both traditions.

There is always a risk in conflating the claims of religion and philosophy; the same is true with religion and theology. Now there is, of course, a huge difference between theology and religion. Theology is essentially the extension of metaphysics into a new linguistic domain, girded with the claims of revelatory knowledge; but theology and classical philosophy are nevertheless united in their mutual quest to lay hold of the Absolute in some, if not the, determinate manner. The very meaning of theology (θεός, λόγος) implies comprehension of the Godhead. Religion, on the other hand, implies for Levinas the non- or pretheoretical relation of the face to face experience. Religion is social ethics, the concrete action of justice. The naming of God, and perhaps even of the death of God, is the attempt to comprehend the absolutely other and thereby lay hold of or dominate the Other. It is a theological, or actually, *the* theological move.

A key question is whether theological knowledge is a possibility. According to Levinas' reading of the history of ontology and metaphysics, theology should be dismissed, along with idealist philosophy and fundamental ontology, as a violent way of thinking. Levinas situates theology and most variants of traditional metaphysical philosophy under the rubric of "ontology," which is opposed to "religion" or "metaphysics." Religion, as ethics, signifies the inability to have any absolutely determinate knowledge of the nature of the Godhead or, to use Hegel's term, Spirit (*Geist*). It is precisely the positing of the knowability of God that constitutes the very essence of theology. Religion, which lacks the audacity of theology, signifies the concrete ethical exchange between the self and the Other in the historical arena of social relations, the lived face to face relation between individuals who speak to one another. The phenomenon of religion is anterior to any philosophical or theological articulation of it. Prior to any affirmative or negative proposition, the idea of the Infinite, the object of religion, awakens that which initiates the very possibility of discourse between self and Other.

Metaphysics is the point of interface between philosophy and religion. As philosophy, metaphysics assumes the form of ontology which takes for its object the Absolute, or in Hegelian terms, the status of the Idea (*Idee*). Thus are philosophy and theology aligned.[15] Religion, in the sense it is used here, is not to be construed as synonymous with theology; it is the relation between the same and the other nonthematizable as a totality. Furthermore, the disjunction between the same and the other is expressed in the infinite difference between time and eternity which, contra Hegel, are not the same for Levinas: "Religion, where relationship subsists between the same and the other despite the impossibility of the Whole—the idea of Infinity—is the ultimate structure" (*TeI* 79/*TI* 80). Transcendence is of the domain of ethics or religion, and not that of the artifices of theology or ontology. The union of theology and philosophy (ontology) is the move to render the Absolute intelligible to thought, which is to say, to name it.

Religion, in Levinas' sense of the term, is the ethical force of a "pre-original saying," the prohibition against murder. Religion is not the attempt to designate the ineffable absolutely other; yet such naming cannot be avoided, though it is effected only through an "abuse" or "betrayal" of language:

> But this pre-original saying does move into a language, in which saying and said are correlative of one another, and the saying is subordinated to its theme.... The correlation of the saying (*le dire*) and the said (*le dit*), that is, the subordination of the saying to the said, to the linguistic system and to ontology, is the price that manifestation demands. In language qua said everything is conveyed before us, be it at the price of a betrayal (*trahison*). Language is ancillary and thus indispensable.... Language permits us to utter, be it by betrayal, this *outside of being*, this *ex-ception* to being, as though being's other were an event of being.[16]

Language, and thus consciousness, falters before the invisible Infinite, before the wholly other (*tout autre*), before an alterity of such passive force that it simultaneously marks the limit and horizon of language.

The question of religion, the relation of the creator or absolutely other to the created or same, is one of paradox or mystery, though this does not signify meaninglessness. While alterity (infinity) permeates being and infuses it with life and meaning, there is an absolute separation that exists between the other and the same. This radical distance forms the boundaries of the ethical relation.

How does one come to know that this separation exists? Why should one not assume that the Other is essentially like, the same as, another self? Just how other (*autre*) is Another (*autrui*)?

The idea of infinity requires the separation of the same and the other. Infinity is produced in human consciousness as a psychism indicating the asymmetrical relation between the same and the other. The idea of the Infinite "overflows" the content of its thought, its *ideatum*; it admits of no other. The apprehension of the transcendence of the Good, of the absolutely other, is possible through the production of the separation or distance between creator and created, other and same. "The distance between me and God, radical and necessary, is produced in being itself" (*TeI* 40/*TI* 48). Goodness is produced in and as sociality, in the ethical interaction between separated beings. The world is not so profane as to refuse admission to the Infinite; but then, neither is it sacred enough to contain the Absolute in its totality.

Religion, ethics, and transcendence are essentially synonymous terms for Levinas, all of which designate the movement of Desire (*désir*) towards and for the absolutely other. The movement that originates from alterity, from the unseen or the invisible, Desire is *prior to* thought. "Desire marks a sort of inversion with regard to the classic notion of substance. In it being becomes goodness..." (*TeI*

57/*TI* 63). Levinas qualifies his understanding of invisibility, particularly regarding its relation to Desire:

> The metaphysical desire does not rest upon any prior kinship. It is a desire that cannot be satisfied.... It is like goodness—the Desired does not fulfill it, but deepens it.... Desire is absolute if the desiring being is mortal and the Desired is invisible. Invisibility does not denote an absence of relation; it implies relations with what is not given, of which there is no idea. Vision is an adequation of the idea with the thing, a comprehension that encompasses. Non-adequation does not denote a simple negation or an obscurity of the idea, but—beyond the light and the night, beyond the knowledge measuring beings—the inordinateness of Desire. Desire is desire for the absolutely other. (*TeI* 22/*TI* 34)

Elsewhere, he says that invisibility is not that which is "invisible to the senses," but to that which is "non-thematizable in thought" (*EeI* 112/*EI* 106).

Desire or religion, the modality of (a) being's relation to a term exterior to it, is effected in the passing of an alterity so other as to be unassimilated in the totalizing movement of thought.

> The void that breaks the totality can be maintained against an inevitably totalizing and synoptic thought only if thought finds itself *faced* with an other refractory to categories. Rather than constituting a totality with this other as with an object, *thought consists in speaking.* We propose to call "religion" the bond that is established between the same and the other without constituting a totality. (*TeI* 30/*TI* 40)

Religion, which is also to say ethics or metaphysics, is effected through the trace of the Infinite in the face of the Other. Yet the alterity of the trace does not consume the subjectivity of the "I." The Other awakens subjectivity and arouses the same to assume responsibility for the self's own freedom *and* for the liberty of the Other. The commencement of speech with the Other is the moment of *justice.* The relation between consciousness and the Good or the absolutely other is the positing of justice before freedom. Religion is the bond of justice between the self and the Other through which the meaning and affirmation of subjective freedom occurs.

The great thesis that permeates Levinas' thinking is the priority of justice over freedom. This runs absolutely counter to the great legacy and ruse of the Western tradition: that the primarily ontological modality of being-in-the-world is that of freedom. But freedom's cost—justice—is not equivalent to the negation of freedom. The inversion of the concept of substance and the metaphysical reversal of freedom and justice point to the inherent paradox of religious being. The ethical bond that religion proposes between the self and the Other is that of speech, of language.

VI

Central to the question of religion, understood in both its Judaic and Christian contexts, is the issue of *kenosis* (derived from κενόω, to empty), the self-emptying or humbling of the Godhead into its opposite, i.e., corporeality. Perhaps a none too insignificant aspect for the theological reader of the present work is that engaging the thinking of Hegel through Levinas renders a reading of Hegel in which the influence of Luther is conspicuously absent—that is to say, a Hegel in which his deep Christian ground is absent. But the question of *Grund* cannot be divorced from the issue of *kenosis* which is clearly central for both Hegel and Luther. Is it possible, then, to maintain a Levinasian understanding of Hegel in the face of this Lutheran-Hegelian category of *kenosis*? In other words, can one truly address Hegel without being open to the possibility that the Hegelian Spirit, in the movement of self-negation, is a co-movement in which the fullness of the Godhead is kenotically released in its own apparent and sensual alterity so that the Godhead itself is actually and truly other, even while simultaneously being identical with its original ground? To put it another way, can one understand Hegelian thinking and simply dissolve or suspend its Christian methodology?[17]

It is not altogether clear in Hegel whether he locates within the Christ-event the actual *kenosis* of the dialectic, or posits that within the person of Jesus, the incarnation and crucifixion are not merely historical expressions, that is, the movement of Spirit cast in a historically contextual theological terminology to express the second stage of the dialectic, the unfolding of the divine Idea within the natural world. One could say that for Hegel, the moment of kenotic incarnation of Christ is actually not the fulfillment of the dialectic, but rather a moment within the overall dialectic of Spirit.

Should one interpret the Hegelian dialectic through the structure of a theologically conceived Trinity, or the Trinity through the *Science of Logic*? If the latter is the case, that the Trinity is merely a moment in the greater dialectic, then the *kenosis* would actually assume for Levinas the form of mere theoretical speculation rather than that of any actual, historical event. But Hegel sees himself as moving *beyond* Christianity. This is textually supported in the corpus of his own writing, namely, at the end of the *Phenomenology of Spirit* where the religious moment of the dialectic is superseded by Absolute Knowing, in what can be construed as a decisively *philosophical* moment.

While Levinas does not follow Hegel's hermeneutic of *kenosis*, pivotal for Hegel's thinking as a whole, neither does he ignore its importance—despite the fact that "there is probably no need, here, to remind ourselves that the idea of divine incarnation is foreign to Jewish spirituality."[18] Levinas locates the kenotic "humility" of God in "the letter and spirit of many verses of the Old Testament, in which "to the attentive reader" (*TN* 119),

> The mastery of *Elohim*, master of all powers, expresses itself in the very act of creation *ex nihilo* of a world, or more precisely a countless number of worlds, and it also expresses itself (as their maintenance in being) by his *association* with these worlds...individual persons, collectivities and ideal realities. In this pluralism there is the possibility of being-toward-being, of alterity (*TN* 123).

Moreover, in this *kenosis* a "hierarchic order" is established, an order that is *ethical* in its scope. This order is a situating of otherness before sameness, of the Other before the self which either "*nourishes*" or "exhausts" the association between the Infinite and the world (*TN* 124–25). This is a principal thought in all of Levinas' work, and like Hegel, dependent upon a certain construal of *kenosis.* And it is surely with Hegel (and Kierkegaard and Sartre, for that matter) in mind that Levinas writes:

> The world *is*, not because it perseveres in being, not because *being* is its own *raison d'être*, but because, through the human enterprise, it can be justified in its being. The human is the possibility of a being-for-the-other. That possibility is the justification of all existing. The world is justified in its being by human dis-inter-estment.... More important than God's omnipotence is the subordination of that power to man's ethical consent. And that, too, is one of the primordial meanings of *kenosis*.... This sudden reversal of human subjectivity, which can no longer be defined as an *in-itself*, or as a *for-itself*, which is defined as a forgetting of self in "fear and trembling" for the other, for the worlds and the other human beings (an abnegation which also expresses a God giving up his omnipotence and finding satisfaction only in the for-the-other) is expressed by...an *offering of oneself*, an outpouring of the soul. (*TN* 127–28)

In *kenosis* there lies the basis for ethical transcendence *concretized* in the *act* of responsibility for the Other to the point of substitution. However, whereas for Hegel the self-emptying of the Godhead is a decisive moment that inaugurates the "path of despair" towards Spirit's self-realization of itself as freedom, *kenosis* is understood by Levinas as the continued proliferation of plurality as alterity. But are Hegel and Levinas really so far apart on this issue? Is not plurality continually generated and preserved by Spirit as Hegel claims? This question, to be developed throughout this work, rests on the status of *infinity.*

Does Levinas' conception of the absolutely other as the Other, deriving from his conception of God, which is a Jewish understanding of the radical alterity of the divine, understand God as the *only* infinite? If so, then does not this necessarily imply a thinking or understanding of all identity as a non-present, non-actual, non-concrete identity whereas in Hegelian thinking, one could argue, with its grounding in self-negation, that is, in the self-alienation of Spirit, a ground is opened so that one is able to comprehend the whole? Would that not mean, all too significantly for Levinas, that every metaphysical category is totally abstract and non-actual including, above all, the category of the infinite? These questions indict Levinas of a certain, if not radical, a- or even, non-historicity of thought. It is the task of the present work to address this charge.

VII

Levinas begins *Totality and Infinity*, the first of his two great works, by posing the question of "whether we are not duped by morality," and thereby sets the stage for his often abstract and obtuse discourse. However, one should not confuse the abstraction of his philosophical voice with the concrete realities that he is continually addressing. This point is driven home in the opening pages where the discourse begins with the very concrete historical theme of physical violence, of *war*, a mode of intersubjective being that Hegel himself admits is unavoidable, and even necessary, in the historical progress of Spirit's self-realization. Spirit is a theodicy.[19]

Much of the force of Levinasian ethics revolves around the premise that violence first arises *conceptually*. In other words, intersubjective violence occurs first as a violence of thought, in the conceptualization of both the absolutely other and the personal Other as objects for consciousness. Violence arises when the self makes prejudgments about the Other before the Other speaks to the self, before the Other reveals the wonder and glory of his or her own uniqueness. By extension, violence also arises in the will to comprehend the Absolute as ground, to name the Infinite. In this regard, Levinas remains fundamentally Jewish.

Levinas is primarily interested in intersubjective violence, the violence associated with human will and volition. The question of natural violence does not concern him whereas for Hegel, the violence of nature, as intrinsic to the unfolding of the Idea, seems to serve as a justification of sorts for the violence of history. To speak of violence in such a manner is to invoke the questions of the origin, of ground, of the Absolute, of the Godhead. Levinas' unique and radical assessment of the foundation of ethics and violence necessarily takes one back to this most obtuse of questions. However, rather than following suit with a certain dominant philosophical tradition, i.e., classical metaphysics or ontotheology, he distances himself from the tradition's invariable tendency to determine or name this ground. The realization of the impossibility of such a project (the radical separation of subject and object, self and Other, eternity and temporality) that the idea of infinity signifies in its non-signifying fashion is the beginning of ethics. Violence is first present in thinking, in the concept, in the naming of the Absolute and the ground of being that reduces alterity to a theoretical moment of selfsame consciousness.

But if the attempt to comprehend the meaning of ground can be characterized as violent, how does one keep separate the constant use of terms that have literary and ethical connotations but are looped over into what may be termed ontological beings or conceptual entities? Is there a claim being made here that in the ontological and metaphysical domains we do best to interpret what is going on in ethical terms? Is there not a huge difference between naming God and seeking a knowable ground? Naming the divine seems to be a religious act while seeking the ground is fundamentally philosophical. Is there a tendency to conflate philosophy and religion in this process of naming the Absolute? What about certain tendencies to move ethical and literary categories over to what has been traditionally seen in philosophy as a different domain? One of the reasons to keep these domains separate is so that one does not become confused and lose sight of the awfulness of concrete violence. Does not the violence that Levinas sees as entailed in the attempt to comprehend the ground result in only a violence towards the self, if in any violence at all? Is it the tendency of this kind of thinking to conflate the realities of concrete and abstract theoretical violence?[20]

Certainly the violence that arises in attempting to conceive the Absolute is different from the violence of hatred and war, and yet the two are interconnected. The most horrific form of violence in recent history, the Holocaust, serves as a prime example. Is not the violence of the Holocaust the result of a prior determination of ground, history, and the Absolute by the Third Reich, which then determined the role or non-role that Jews, Slavs, Gypsies, and other non-Aryans were to play in the formation of the *then* "new world order"? Levinas' thesis rests upon the contention that the two actions, that is, thought and the concrete manifestations of that thought, are inseparably related.

Levinas' abstract language leaves him susceptible to the criticism that the face to face is non-concrete, non-historical. But the horror of war, of the gulags and stalags, not to mention the mass death camps, should be alone enough to delegitimize the very possibility of such a question. Yet these examples do not serve as totally unique moments or examples in history or consciousness. Such horrors can surely occur again. Violence is not equivalent to the errors or mistakes that inevitably occur in the field of social relations. While interpersonal relations entail a certain economy of violence, the force of Levinas' position is best seen when applied to violence at its most engorged level: to war and the techno-political machines that engender it. And to the criticism that the face is not a concrete face, that the violence of history is not a concrete violence, that the Other is not a genuinely existential other, Levinas offers this remarkably succinct and profound statement: "The absolutely other is the other person [*L'absolument autre, c'est l'autrui*]" (*TeI* 28/*TI* 39). The distinction between the absolutely other and the Other person collapses in the ethical significance of the face.

So in the wake of God's death, is it possible, or even desirable, to think in terms of ground? This is the crux of the postmodern dilemma. The task that Levinas lays out is to move beyond, in a significant, decidedly non-dialectical way, the sovereign totalizing tendencies of the modern conception of the subject, while at the same time preserving subjectivity's autonomous bearing in the *groundlessness* of absolute differential alterity.

2

UnderGround

The origin and locus of violence has been traditionally defined as the *separation* or non-union of subject and object, and thus, of self and other. The poet Hesiod's account of the myth of the castration of Ouranus by Cronos in the *Theogony*, which results in the separation (χωρίσμος) of Ouranus and Gaia, is perhaps the first reference to this violence in Western literature. This theme enters philosophy with the Dark One of Ephesus' conclusion that violence, as strife or war (πόλεμος), is the ruler of all and the δύναμις of all becoming.[1] But then, "we do not need obscure fragments of Heraclitus to prove that being reveals itself as war to philosophical thought, that war does not only affect it as the most patent fact, but as the very patency, or the truth, of the real" (*TeI* 5/*TI* 21).

In the *Symposium* Plato will consider the essence of conflict, of violence, in terms of separation, as the non-harmony of parts within the whole. And though he rejects Aristophanes' myth of primordial androgynous being, he retains the notion of harmony (ἁρμονία), of the creative and dynamic tension of opposites. The importance of this concept extends into the Enlightenment. But it is the Aristophanean perspective that influences the development of metaphysics from Augustine to Aquinas. Sin or evil, the cause and locus of all violence, is henceforth construed as the non-union or non-participation (μή μέθεξις) with God or the Absolute.

The identification of thinking and being by Parmenides of Elea inaugurates the history of metaphysics. This thought finds full expression in Aristotle's positing of the Good as the highest idea or concept of being,[2] and is extended in scholastic theology and philosophy. The conflation of these two key concepts demarcates the point of departure from the Platonic thought of the Good as beyond being and determines the decisive dualism within which the history of Western thought moves. For all of its multifarious manifestations, metaphysics is, with but very few exceptions, unified under the thesis of *adaequatio rei et intellectus.*

It is the medieval epistemological concept of *adaequatio* that eventually unifies metaphysics and later gives rise to the correspondence theory of truth. The hierarchical order of being reflected in Aristotelian and medieval metaphysics rests upon the concepts of unity and totality. Aristotle's reduction in the *Ethics* of the transcendence of the Good to merely the highest concept of Being, and his interpretation of λόγος as *ratio*, begins the ontology of totality, the dominant philosophical tendency of Western thought. This move, combined with Augustine's definition of God as the conflation of the Good and Being, constitutes the actual beginning of onto-theological metaphysics.[3]

Thus it is that God or Being proper becomes the ground or stratum of which all beings (nature) are the mirror (*reflectio*). Rather than the creative tension associated with ἁρμονία, a static conception of λόγος prevails. Perfection becomes defined in terms of fixed points; meaning is understood in terms of knowing the place of things, of objects and entities, in the given order of the cosmos. Knowledge is henceforth interpreted in terms of grasping the universal logos structure of reality by the intellect. This metaphysic is reflected not only in the thought of Aristotle and his interpreters, but in much of Neoplatonism as well.

One cannot adequately approach the issue of ground in modern thinking without situating it within the greater context of the history of ideas. In Plato's philosophy, for instance, living wholly, i.e., embodying one's thinking, occurs as much within the *descent* back into the cave as it does in the emergence from it. This chapter descends into the history of philosophy to engage in a metaphysical spelunking to further determine the roots of the various philosophically and theologically articulated notions of ground. And since Plato is one of the primal grounds in Western thinking, the questions of truth, justice, imagination and transcendence will be situated within the context of his philosophy. The "logic" behind much of Levinas' position on the ethical transcendence of the Other is more Platonic than Hegelian, even though Hegel's thinking serves as the backdrop for most twentieth century Continental philosophy, especially phenomenology, the tradition that Levinas is most closely associated with. Levinas alludes numerous times to Platonic motifs in his writing though he never fully develops the connection between his thinking and Plato's; the burden is left to the reader. It is the aim here to take up this burden, attempting to demonstrate in the process that contemporary advances in thinking need not necessarily hinge upon a total rejection of the ancient foundations of thought, as is often argued in many recent postmodern analyses.

Any consideration of the Platonic idea of the Good (τοῦ ἀγαθοῦ ἰδεάν) and the theory of forms (εἶδη) of necessity brings one to the question of the status of "truth." Heidegger sheds light on this important question through his controversial interpretation of ἀλήθεια. He contests traditional metaphysics and locates the origin of the metaphysics of presence, of the shift in the meaning of truth, at the heart of Greek thinking. The question for Heidegger is the reification of the Presocratic notion of οὐσία (essence; being) as ὑποκείμενον (primordial substratum) and *substantia* (substance) in the history of thought.

I

Returning to the origins of Western thinking, most notably to Plato, is not commensurate with the attempt to delineate or demonstrate the truth of the closed circularity of the system of concepts of which Hegel, for instance, sees himself as the culmination. The operative trope or metaphor for Plato's epistemology and ontology is the unclosed or open circle which, as unending, necessarily evolves in a spiral-like fashion. The completion of knowing, the aim of modern philosophy, is denied by Plato as a possibility since the Good remains forever elusive as an *adequate* object or concept for cognition, contra Aristotle. It is perhaps this one aspect of Plato's thinking that distinguishes him most from the train of thinking that follows him until the nineteenth-century breakdown of metaphysics. The remarkable formulation of the transcendence of the Good espoused in the *Republic* almost immediately acquires the status of an anathema thought beginning with Aristotle and culminating in the modernism of Hegel, Nietzsche, and Heidegger. Assessing the historical connection of ideas, especially the relations between the finite and the infinite and between transcendence and the categories of ground and the Absolute, is fundamental for evaluating the underpinnings of Levinas' thinking.

Now, the history of philosophy is famously said by Whitehead to be nothing more than a series of footnotes to Plato. Nevertheless, the historical developments of Platonism and Neoplatonism do not necessarily reflect the philosophy of their namesake. Is Plato to be construed then as the West's founding father? Certainly he never thought of himself (as Nietzsche seems to have at times) as the seed, the progenitor, of an entirely new civilization, of a new metaphysic. He himself refers to "my father Parmenides." Be that as it may, Western thinking is the inheritor of a Platonist—though not necessarily *Platonic*—legacy.

The modern critique of Platonism, first hinted at in Hegel's philosophy, finds its full force in Nietzsche's thinking when he declares that the history of philosophy is the "history of an error,"[4] and that God is dead. But does the celebrated error begin with Plato or with his interpreters? Are we the progeny of his "error"? Does the postmodern discourse about the cultural aftermath of the death of God, construed by Heidegger and others as the end of philosophy and the advent of thinking (*Denken*), mean the demise of all meaningful discourse on a metaphysical scale; or does it just signify the cessation of a particular discourse?[5] Are we to negate (Hegel) or forget (Nietzsche) so as to forge ahead anew? Or should we return to the cavern to begin the process once again? If a return, a retrieval, must be undertaken, then one should commence with Plato. But where should one begin? Is there any text or group of texts that is most representative of Plato's philosophy as a whole?

The cosmological treatise *Timaeus* shaped the development of Platonism through the Middle Ages to the present day; but it may also be contended that the *Republic* lies at the heart of the Platonic corpus of writing. While both works are exercises in speculative philosophy, the *Republic* differs from the *Timaeus* in that it is essentially pragmatic and praxis oriented in its character (as a strategy for a theory of education and ethico-political behavior). The *Timaeus*, on the other hand, is purely hypothetical, without any real applicability; it is speculative philosophy on a cosmological-metaphysical scale.

Whether Plato actually holds Timaeus' views regarding cosmology is open to debate. The *Timaeus* may be merely an exercise in the use of the imagination, as is much of the *Republic*, and nothing more. Or it may be that the *Timaeus* is an assessment and further development of a cosmology already present within certain circles of Pythagorean thought, an influence found throughout the dialogue.

Whatever the case, there is a tension that exists between the metaphysics of the *Republic* and that of the *Timaeus*, though this difference does not negate the validity or the possible contemporary relevance of Plato's philosophical positions.[6] This tension revolves around the issue of *transcendence*.

II

There is a subterranean theme in Plato that suggests a metaphysics of originary difference, a difference Levinas understands as the difference signified by the absolute alterity of the wholly other. This metaphysic is not to be identified with traditional identity oriented substance-philosophy which begins in Aristotelian philosophy and is advanced in Augustinian theology. It is Aristotle's and certain Aristotelian-influenced Neoplatonist's interpretations of the Good as circumscribed within the totality of being that enable the Patristic tradition to formulate the groundwork for the classic metaphysics of the West. The metaphysics of light and later of substance becomes in modernity the will toward the comprehension of the ground (*essentia*) of being. The god of the philosophers, that is, ground knowable in its essence as ground, is able to be comprehended only if it is Being or Substance itself.

Levinas' thinking represents, along with Hegel's though in a radically different way, a continuation of the speculative enterprise. The modern realization of the death of God, which reaches its philosophical acme in the thinking of Hegel and Nietzsche, does not preclude speculative philosophy; it just dethrones such activity as φιλοσοθία πρώτη. Speculation, as Plato and Aristotle know all too well, is the product of the imagination (εἰκασία), of the creative activity of the mind. Still, in itself, speculation or pure theory is nothing. The descent after the "upward path" is the bittersweet realization of this truth. For Plato, the upward movement towards understanding (νόησις), exemplified in the famous line drawn and divided by Socrates at the end of *Republic* Book VI, is first and foremost an activity that finds its completion (τέλος) in ethical-political activity (πρᾶξις) rather than in subjective intellection (θεώρειν) or the universal totality of thought (νοῦς).

The significance of Plato's speculation that the Good lies *beyond* being obviously stands outside the boundaries of general rational inquiry. Nevertheless, this enigmatic formulation is of vital importance, not only for understanding the Levinasian construal of infinity and alterity, but for situating the movement of the Western metaphysical tradition as a whole. This question will be taken up in this chapter by first examining Plato's theory of forms in order to determine the difference between the idea of the Good (ἰδέα τοῦ ἀγαθοῦ) and the forms in general (εἶδη).

At the heart of Levinas' philosophy is the insistence that the meaning of being's relation to that which is otherwise than it (infinity; the absolutely other; God) is justice and not freedom, contra Hegel. This theme recurs throughout the early so-called Socratic dialogues. And in the later *Republic*, Socrates searches in vain for the proper definition of justice. That is because the essence of justice does not lie solely in its conceptual form, its look, but in its sensibility, actualization, or embodiment, which, it is argued here, is what Plato means by εἶδος. For example, it means nothing to say what justice is and not practice it; its form would be hollow, one-sided. The meaning of justice lies in the visible activity of justice. "Form," has *two* aspects: that of the invisible conceptual image (ἰδέα) and the visible sensible image (εἶδος). The form of justice is only fully apprehended by being just. The *ambiguity* present in the notion of εἶδος lies at the very core of Platonic thinking as a whole.

Though unengaged as an issue for Levinas, the difference between εἶδος and ἰδέα is informative for his thinking as it serves to historically underpin his distinction between "idea" and "concept," which is crucial for his distancing from the idealism and later from phenomenology. Though etymologically similar, it is not at all clear or certain that the two terms (εἶδος and ἰδέα) are identical and thus interchangeable in their meaning. There is a critical distinction between the terms that, even if he is not fully aware of, Levinas is picking up on. The forms (εἶδη), while suprasensible, are nevertheless also tangibly or visibly manifest, albeit imperfectly via participation (μέθεξις). For example, the form of justice is the enactment or embodiment of justice and not its mere concept or idea, no matter how exalted. This is why Socrates' numerous inquiries into the genuine nature of its form are left unanswered. Socrates is frustrated by his own desire to purely theoretically grasp the "truth" of the forms. Thought is able to merely apprehend, not comprehend, the invisible aspect of the forms. Socrates is stymied precisely because thought is inadequate with regard to comprehending not only the idea of the Good, since it is beyond being, but also the totality of the being (οὐσία) of the forms (εἶδη). The philosopher-rulers, after their many years of dialectical training come to this realization and then, far from acquiring the status of perfected minds, grasp ever more clearly the limited capabilities of human cognition.

Plato's polemic against the poets is contained in this thought. The poets' yarns about the gods are dismissed not only on the basis that they are demonstrably untrue or internally contradictory, but also on the contention that they can then never be employed in a concrete visible manner by mortal beings. Even if this is never specifically stated by Plato/Socrates, it is implied in the very logic of the argument.

Levinas is, in some sense, doing what Plato himself tried to do in the allegory of the cave and the schema of the so-called divided line, that is, bring together the conceptual and perceptual natures of reality, the invisible and the visible aspects of existence, into a meaningful dialectical relation (in the non-Hegelian sense) that still allows for some sort of transcendence. For Plato, it is the transcendence of the Good; for Levinas, it is the transcendence signified by the ethical superiority of the Other over the selfsame.

III

Certainly Heidegger is the great thinker of *ontological* transcendence this century, a transcendence made possible only by the rejection of presence and the projection (*Entwurf*) of Dasein into nothing. Heidegger finds himself opposed to the

Platonic thesis of the transcendence of the Good. In this regard his thinking is greatly affected by Nietzsche whom he construes as the "unfettered Platonist," "since to him all wisdom starts from the metaphysical origin of 'value.'"[7] Insofar as Nietzsche sees truth as a kind of error, maintains Heidegger, he remains tied to the traditional essence of truth as *adaequatio*. The reason for this is that the exposition of τὸ ἀγαθον as ἰδέα in Plato paves the way for the subsequent valuation of the Good as a moral term and thus "as an inner consequence of the modern comprehension of 'truth,' a concept that came into fashion in the nineteenth century...."[8] In Heidegger's eyes, Nietzsche is the last metaphysician of the West.

The problem of much classic philosophy, says Heidegger, has been the overdetermination of the Greek concept of ἰδέα (form; outward appearance) as "presence." This has resulted in a history of truth defined as *adaequatio rei et intellectus* and in an understanding of οὐσία (essence; being) as ὑποκείμενον (substance).[9] So when Plato, and especially Aristotle, turn from Being to beings as the central concern of metaphysics, Being is separated from beings or, more precisely, the *meaning* of Being is concealed in beings. The question therefore becomes that of the status of οὐσία ("permanent presence").[10] The original Presocratic conception of ἀλήθεια as unconcealment or unhiddenness (*Unverborgenheit*) is covered up in the course of the tradition.

At one point, Heidegger will argue that there is effected a shift in meaning of the term ἀλήθεια from unhiddeness to ὀρθότης (correctness of apprehension).[11] This is demonstrated by the unfettered prisoner who is turned around, and in ascending out of the cave continually engages in the process of making his glance or vision "more correct." This turning around or "orienting or reorienting of human nature into the realm respectively designated for it is the essence of what Plato calls παιδεία," which Heidegger claims is untranslatable but which is generally rendered as education.[12] The liberated prisoner encounters and names at every transition or stage in the ascent from the shadowy cave the unhidden ἀλήθές. Once out of the cavern "'the most unhidden' is so named because it makes its appearance first of all in everything phenomenal and makes the phenomenal accessible."[13] Heidegger determines that ἀλήθεια in Plato is primarily oriented toward the what (*quidditas*) of things, toward essence (*essentia*) and away from existence (*existentia*).

The transition from one situation to another consists in making one's glance more correct. Everything depends on ὀρθότης, the correctness of the glance. Through this correctness, seeing and recognizing become something right, so that it (this correctness) can eventually be directed straight ahead to the highest Idea and made fast in this "straightening out." In this directing of itself, perceiving is compared to what is supposed to be sighted. That is, the "outward appearance" of beings. In consequence of this assimilation of perceiving as an ἰδεῖν into an ἰδέα, a ὁμοίωσις subsists, that is, an agreement between the recognizing of the thing and the thing itself. And so, before ἀλήθεια a change in the essence of truth springs forth out of the front ranks of the ἰδέα and the ἰδεῖν. Truth becomes ὀρθότης, the "correctness of the ability to perceive and to declare something."[14] In other words, the *what* of the phenomenon that is apprehended is actually the essence or presence of the *idea* of the thing and not the thing's actual existence.

The act of knowing (γιγνώσκειν) is supplanted in importance by that which is known (γιγνώσκόμενον), that is, by the *idea*, says Heidegger, and

> Only in this shift do νοεῖν and νοῦς (perception) preserve according to Plato, their essential relation to the "idea." The adjustment involved in thus directing oneself to the ideas defines the essence of perception and consequently the essence of "reason."[15]

This interpretation is contested by Paul Friedländer who maintains that a balanced dialectic exists for Plato regarding the relation between ἀλήθεια and ὀρθότης,

> ...an equilibrium between the revealing truth, the unhidden reality, and the truthfulness which measures that reality by this truth. Plato did not corrupt the concept of ἀλήθεια as Heidegger claims. Plato sharpened the concept, systematized it, and heightened it.[16]

Friedländer contends that Heidegger's basic mistake is that he reads Plato as subordinating ἀλήθεια to ἰδέα in general, not locating the shift in the meaning of "truth" in Plato's thought. According to Friedländer, the correct interpretation should be the subordination of ἀλήθεια to the highest ἰδέα, that is, the highest *concept* of the Good. But as John Sallis points out, both Heidegger and Friedländer modify their positions with regard to each other:[17] Heidegger, in his later acknowledgement that for the Presocratic and Homeric Greeks ἀλήθεια did not mean *Unverborgenheit*, and that the Greeks before Plato grasped ἀλήθεια as correctness; and Friedländer, in that he retracts his opposition to the interpretation of ἀλήθεια as unhiddenness among the early Greeks, though continuing to insist that there is a pre-Platonic determination of ἀλήθεια as correctness. So it is that this famous debate, spanning decades, sharpens the meaning of ἀλήθεια to the crucial point that what is truly at stake and decisive for metaphysics is the *ambiguity* in ἀλήθεια between correctness and unconcealment.[18] This ambiguity Heidegger locates in the end of Book VI and at the beginning of Book VII of the *Republic* where ἀλήθεια falls under the "yoke" of ἰδέα leading to the determination of being (οὐσία) as presence.

IV

The Presocratic view of φύσις (nature; process) as "abiding-emergence" implies a sense of balance and stability.[19] However, φύσις is not a static state but rather, an ec-static process. The conception of φύσις as abiding presence is a revelatory process in which what is hidden becomes revealed, that is, brought forth from concealment and yet, still able to stand in itself.[20] Φύσις is simultaneously present and absent; being and becoming are inextricably tied together and not separate. Heidegger's early philosophy is an attempt to recapture the original sense of wonder and awe of the Presocratic view of the world.

Plato primarily incorporates the emerging or "standing forth" aspect of φύσις (nature) into his notion of ἰδέα, but in so doing, Heidegger maintains, he detaches the emerging sense of presence from its original background of φύσις as abiding-emergence and its interplay with ἀλήθεια. This results in a removal of truth from the world and a subsequent historical situating of it in a suprasensible, intelligible world of forms. The ἰδέα, as an absolute universal form, therefore betrays the original meaning of φύσις which in turn functions as a modality of οὐσία. Being becomes interpreted in terms of static presence by substance-metaphysics and the Presocratic conception of the world/cosmos as flux is either ignored or systematically downplayed as, for example, in Plato's *Theatetus* or in Aristotle's view of αἰσθέσις (sensation; perception).

It is actually Aristotle who remains truer to the spirit of the Presocratics than does Plato in his interpretations of φύσις, ἀλήθεια, and λόγος and, at first, to the original essence of being in his interpretation of ἐνέργεια (activity of being). Yet even he remains under the sway of his former mentor and so inaugurates the articulation of the essentially Platonist theory of forms, that is, of pure archetypal conceptual structures. Instead of emphasizing the individual being standing within the presence of Being, Aristotle reconceives ἐνέργεια as the individual existent standing within the vision of the ἰδέα, thus effecting a movement away from the dynamic ἐνέργεια to a presence stabilized in the recurrence of eternal essences.

The history of metaphysics henceforth begins to lose the dynamism of φύσις and comes to reveal itself as a binary structure privileging one term (essence) over the other (existence) in the guise of a unitary Being. The double stance of οὐσία, the revealing of something that is and the what that stands and appears, loses its Presocratic sense in Aristotle and its meaning is reified as ὑποκείμενον. The "gathering up" process of the λόγος stops; the dialectic ceases between Being and beings. The meaning of Being, says Heidegger, is forgotten, a forgetting due to the exposition of Being as ἰδέα resulting from a change in the meaning of ἀλήθεια.

V

The Platonic ἰδέα comes to form the Aristotelian ground of Being; οὐσία takes on the meaning of essence and paves the way for the medieval notion of *substantia*. The two modes comprising οὐσία (ἐνέργεια and ἰδέα) form the groundwork for what later becomes the scholastic distinction between *esse* (existence) and *essentia* (essence). The abiding and emerging characteristics of φύσις separate and correspond to the two modes or aspects of οὐσία accordingly: the abiding, the "standing back," becomes the ἰδέα and the emerging, the "standing forth," correlates with ἐνέργεια. "Platonism" finds its true beginning not in Plato but in the philosophy of Aristotle.

What now needs assessment is the status of the relation between εἶδος and ἰδέα. Following suit with the tradition, Heidegger seems to essentially equate the two terms as if they had univocal or at least interchangeable meanings: "In Greek 'outward appearance' is εἶδος or ἰδέα."[21] While this is justified in some respects, Heidegger does acknowledge a distinction between the terms. Still, a strong etymological case can be made that what distinguishes idea from εἶδος is the fundamentally conceptual nature of idea as opposed to the essentially perceptual quality of εἶδος. Originally a non-philosophical term given further philosophical status by Plato, εἶδος comes to mean that which is seen and/or is made visible, the "look" that the thing has about it; in other words, that which has and/or is given form or shape.[22] In Plato, εἶδος takes on the sense of being both a noun and a verb. Plato does not mark the closure of the Presocratic ontology of becoming, as Heidegger claims, but rather, lifts the previous ineffability of Heraclitean flux to the level of philosophical articulability.

The bringing into play of the terms εἶδος and ἰδέα, a highly intuitive and imaginative move on Plato's part, is not to be construed as an absolute conflation of the meaning of the two terms. Neither is there an absolute separation or difference between the two signifiers. The terms find their fullness of meaning in the relation that they have with one another. However, though they are similar and mutually informative in many respects, there exists a fundamental difference between the two terms that must be acknowledged if one is to correctly understand the meaning of the cave and line imageries.

The examples of the cave and line demonstrate the dialectic that exists within being between εἶδος and ἰδέα, between sensibility (visibility) and intelligibility (invisibility). The descent back into the cave (dialectic), and correspondingly, down the line, is the making visible of the conceptual forms or ideas. For Plato this is possible only through the continued application of the imagination (εἰκασία) at every stage or division of the line/cave. The progress from the shadowy vagueness of reflected images at the base or lower end of the line (if one follows convention by drawing the line in a vertical manner, which by the way, Plato never says one is to do) to the clear forms apprehended by dialectic at the other end proceeds in its course from dogmatic opinion (δόξα) to knowing (ἐπιστήμη) via the power of eikastic image-making. The process of bringing images into the fullness of their being, into their "form," is precisely the aim of knowing. Imagination is accorded a pivotal role by Plato in the quest for the attainment of understanding (νόησις), the apprehension and realization of the forms through the proper and judicious use of dialectic. Εἰκασία is not mere mental image making; it is also that which in-forms sensuous reality (ὑλή). Sallis defines εἰκασια, as "apprehending images (εἰκόν) *as* images in such a way that one sees through them to the originals which they image."[23] Genuine understanding is the ability to create, the full utilization of dialectic, to bring the conceptual forms into physical being, into visibility (ὁρατόν), that is, to understand and realize the full potential of the imagination (εἰκασία).

Now the history of metaphysics has tended, for the most part, to denigrate the role of the imagination, subordinating it to cognition or reason in an attempt to separate or distance itself from it. This is clearly not Plato's intention. Reason or cognition (διάνοια), he says, is not the apex of thought and hence, is unable in itself to grasp the truth of the forms. Dialectic is not only a cognitive operation; as discourse or conversation it is also sensible. Still, while the journey towards truth and the Good (not the same) necessarily employs the power of εἰκασία to propel its ascent, Sallis points out that

> the taking of distance from imagination belongs structurally to the metaphysical project no less than does the appropriation of imagination.... Such is, in briefest out-

> line, the dynamics that governs the relation between imagination and metaphysics in the Platonic texts: Imagination both empowers and inhibits the metaphysical drive to presence, and metaphysics must, accordingly, both appropriate and take distance from imagination. The metaphysical theory regarding imagination is not only a matter of metaphysical self-understanding but also one of distinguishing metaphysics from an other from which, as from the sophist, it can never free itself once and for all.[24]

Continuing this thought, Sallis notes that in the time between Plato and Pico della Mirandola's text "On the Imagination" (1500) there occurred "several shifts" affecting the relation between imagination and metaphysics, most notably, that of the predominant meaning of imagination itself from εἰκασία to φαντασία. This, in turn, gives rise to the Latin terms *imaginatio* and *phantasia* which have determined the general signification of the imagination to this day. "Remarkably," says Sallis, "εἰκασια goes virtually untranslated." This is pointed out to emphasize Plato's radical insight into the power of the imagination and its inaugurating effect on the history of metaphysics.

VI

Plato's images of the line and the cave are merely different ways of saying the same thing.[25] The two analogies focus, respectively, on the epistemological and ontological aspects of knowledge. Although the line analogy represents his theory of knowledge and the allegory of the cave his theory of reality, there is within each example an epistemic and ontic distinction to be made. While it is the convention to label the portion of the line above the horizontal division that gives the analogy its nomenclature the realm of intelligibility and truth, the labelling of the visible and invisible is also applicable on the sides of the *vertical* division of the *initial* line drawn.[26]

The reading of the line is not accomplished through a purely linear progression. Each step or stage of the divisions draws upon and carries with it the previous stages, giving additional form and clarity (εἰκασία) to that which was previously obscure. Thus, the culmination of the ascent, the realization of the form through dialectic, is nothing but the uplifting of the power of the imagination (εἰκασία), that is, the ability to create images, into the stage of realizing the unity of the visible with the invisible image.

Only the allegory of the cave provides the reader with the clue that the reading of the line is to be done in a spiral-like fashion. The prisoner, once outside the cavern, turns around (παιδεία), either by the force of persuasion or, unfortunately, according to Plato, by coercion and returns to the shadows to teach others (παιδεία). In fact, the ascent out of the cave involves a similar return to the shadows, though motivated purely by self-interest and not altruism, in order to recover or recollect the past knowledge so that the process of dialectic can continue. True, Plato does not say that the prisoner physically returns to his or her seat after each stage of the journey out; but surely there is a continual mulling over and mental returning to the relative tranquility of the shadows until the eventual emergence.

The descent back into the cave is the decisive clue as to how one should read the line. One need only superimpose the diagram of the line on the image of the cave to see that this is so. Why else would Plato offer the two examples back to back if not to demonstrate their mutual informability? Still, the metaphors of the cave and the line are not offered by Plato as *decisive* models for the attainment of "truth." Like the Good, absolute truth is forever beyond the bounds of human comprehension, of totalization by rationality. Plato does not abandon the Presocratic sense of ἀλήθεια so much as he renders its dialectical interplay of presence and absence *somewhat* accessible to thinking. The beginning of understanding (νόησις) lies in the recognition of the *limited* scope of human reason (διάνοια). Plato, one can venture to say, is fundamentally a speculative hermeneutician. He allows for the very possibility of hermeneutic multiplicity precisely by leaving the division between visibility and invisibility *ambiguous* in the text.

Plato is not the pure idealist that an essentially onto-theological tradition has generally portrayed him as. Knowledge that does not ultimately return to its visible home is useless. Certainly, Plato entertains the notion that the forms were suprasensible; but the crux of this teaching lies in the theory of participation (μέθεξις) apart from which the forms are meaningless. The theory of recollection is contingent upon the reincarnation of the immortal soul. The vertical unilinear interpretation of the line, i.e., knowledge as pure ascendency without return to the sensible, fundamentally exclusive of the bodhisattvian allegory of the cave, is only intelligible with the theory of the soul proffered by Hellenistic philosophy, Gnosticism, Pauline-Patristic Christianity, and some variants of Pharisaic Judaism and Islam. An older tradition, one with which Plato may have indeed been familiar, out of which sprang the wisdom of the *Upanishads* and the *Bhagavad Gita*, describes participation (μέθεξις) as *embodiment.* But the lenses of cultural, and therefore philosophical prejudice are thick and murky. The West has inherited an interpretation of Plato that is essentially theological, that remains increasingly speculative and fantastically idealist to the modern consciousness. Even Nietzsche, for all his insightfulness into the nature of Platonism, and Levinas, who disavows any "orientalism" attached to the Platonic thesis of the Good, cannot see past the halographic Plato still so fervently cherished and preserved in the steadfastness of Western tradition. However, as Levinas points out, with regard to the transcendence of the Good, "it matters little that Plato made of it an idea and a light source" (*AE* 36/*OB* 19).

3

HelioGround

Levinas, while often critical of Plato as an idealist, offers a new perspective for interpreting the Platonic text, and a reading of philosophy that does not reflect the Western penchant for totalizing intellection. Levinas' primary connection to the philosophy of Plato rests on the status of the ἐπέκεινα τῆς οὐσίας: "The place of the Good above every essence is the most profound teaching, above every teaching, the definitive teaching, not of theology, but of philosophy" (*TeI* 106/*TI* 103). The essentially onto-theological tradition that issues from Aristotle and Augustine is the rejection of such a transcendence and not its affirmation. Being is not transcendence; indeed, it is incapable of transcendence in classic philosophy and theology as it remains circumscribed within the totality of existence and is unable to break free of the totality on its own accord or power.

The transcendence signified by the Good is that of irreducible alterity. The impossibility of thought to grasp the Good as an object of thought testifies to the "glory of the Infinite" (*AE* 220–38/*OB* 140–52) and to the recognition of ethics as first philosophy (*TeI* 340/*TI* 304). It invokes the themes of justice, freedom, and responsibility. Levinas contends that situating the ontological concept of totality (same) before the metaphysical idea of the infinity (difference) results in a violence towards the Other at the level of intersubjectivity in that it reduces personal alterity to the level of a selfsame concept. Plato's assertion of the fundamental unknowability of the Good on the grounds that it is exterior to being and *inadequate* to its concept thought[1] is critical for Levinas since

> Every "comprehension" of transcendence leaves the transcendent outside, and is enacted before its face. If the notions of totality and being are notions that cover one another, the notion of the transcendent places us beyond the categories of being. We thus encounter, in our own way, the Platonic idea of the Good beyond being. (*TeI* 326/*TI* 293)

This important formulation of the Good exterior to every essence is not only determinative for Levinas' (de)conception of the absolutely other as the Infinite and the role that it plays in paving the way for the autonomy of the subject; it is also crucial in determining the philosophy of Levinas on the crucial question of the constitution of the ethical subject.

On the other hand, responding to an intellectual tradition almost exclusively bound by the quest for truth and knowledge as its highest aspiration, Nietzsche, Heidegger, and Gadamer either reject or ignore the Platonic thesis of radical transcendence. In *this* regard they remain, in their respective interpretations, within a totalizing modality of philosophy which betrays the original Platonic intention, as this chapter will attempt to demonstrate.

I

As the cause and object of knowledge and truth, the Good retains its original Greek meaning as that which is of use to something and that which makes something useful.[2] The Good itself is not a mere object for cognition, nor is it a form among the other forms. Any attempt to grasp its essence in a comprehensive manner ultimately fails as it is beyond being in "dignity and surpassing power."[3] The reality of the Good itself (αὐτό τοῦ ἀγαθοῦ) is not comprehended in its general idea or concept. As ἐπέκεινα τῆς οὐσίας, the Good is beyond its concept since the concept is only meaningful through its representation of being. Thus the Good is present or *revealed* in being only as the *idea* of the Good (τοῦ ἀγαθοῦ ἰδέαν). The idea of the Good is not, despite Aristotle's reading, or even more recently, as will be elaborated later, Gadamer's analysis, a form (εἶδον) in the same sense as are the other forms (εἶδη); it is the condition of being for the rest of the forms. Plato never refers to the Good as εἶδον, only as ἰδέα. Paradoxically, the Good functions as both the limit principle for knowledge and truth and as the open horizon of possibilities. Transcending being, the Good is invisible both to the eye and to the mind.

The dialectic between the Good καθ'αὐτό and being is of an asymmetrical modality. Being is infused with the Good but is not itself the totality or wholeness of the Good. The Good is beyond comprehension though it is able to be continually apprehended in the forms. Beyond reason or cognition, it is essentially irrational or chaotic, that is, if chaos is defined as that which defies ordering or definition from without. Wisdom or understanding (νόησις) is precisely the recognition of the impossibility of absolute knowledge.

Heidegger's early claim of an "unwritten" shift in the meaning of ἀλήθεια in the Platonic text that determines the Platonist tradition of onto-theological metaphysics may indeed be true, at least to a partial degree. But there is another key moment of non-inscription in Plato's writing that Heidegger, for the most part, systematically downplays, namely, that concerning the exact status or definition of the Good. Plato is only able to approach Glaucon's question of the nature of the Good obliquely, by way of analogy. This is necessary if he is to maintain the integrity of his essentially *hermeneutical* project.

As a speculative philosopher, Plato is willing to entertain a plurality of perspectives on any given issue. Though Socrates' voice is often construed as totalizing and domineering, this does not contradict the above statement. Socrates continually searches for the form of truth (among other forms) in the dialogues, but he is constantly confronted with the realization that there is no single truth to be found within being, or at least none that cognition or intellection is able to lay hold of. The essential meaning or truth of the forms is hermeneutically open, for Plato, on account of the limitless horizon of the Good.

Quite often in the dialogues what is important is not the position of Socrates but rather, the dialectical engagement with others. Plato's inconsistency on various issues (for instance, the immortality of the soul) testifies to this. The will to totalization or systematization reveals itself for Plato as dogmatic opinion (δόξα). Socrates never tires of playing the gadfly, of deconstructing the opinionated "arguments" of the other. In Nietzsche's view, for instance, the voice of Socrates, the voice of reason, seeks to negate all other voices. Those who find Plato confusing or frustrating often do so because they try to systematize his thought. As a speculative philosopher Plato remains at the head of the class, but as a systematic thinker he falls short of the mark.

Genuine understanding, for Plato, is the recognition of the limitation of human knowledge where questions of the status and meaning of the cosmos are concerned. Heidegger interprets the Good in an Aristotelian manner, that is, as the highest *concept*, and also adopts the Nietzschean perspective that positing the Good beyond being devalues existence in the here and now, resulting in an existential nihilism. Both Nietzsche and Heidegger fail to see, however, the genuine radicalness and overarching importance of the Good beyond being for Plato and how it actually determines for him the meaning of ἀλήθεια. The Platonic Good is not an object for thinking in the sense that it is for Aristotle, who reduces it to happiness (εὐδαιμονία) and political science (λόγον πολιτικόν). The Good is not the Being (*Sein*) of beings (*Seiendes*), nor is it the most exalted of concepts. The Good signifies a difference exceeding the ontico-ontological difference. The concepts of Good and Being are not synonymous; they do not form a totality. Nor is the Good the self-generative (*sui generis*) principle of Being. Like the Timaeic receptacle, the Good instantiates and partakes in the generative process in a "mysterious" way that is not open to the scrutiny of rationalization.[4] Truth, for Plato, remains an open hermeneutic horizon which is continually determined and redetermined dialectically. The original meaning of ἀλήθεια as the flux of unconcealment is not negated by Plato, nor is it relegated to the level of pure subjective (θεώρειν) or universal (νοῦς) mind. Plato retains the dialectical interplay of presence and absence found in the conceptions of both nature (φύσις) and ἀλήθεια and insures this aspect by placing the Good exterior to being.

It is actually Aristotle who inaugurates the tradition of logocentric metaphysics, of Platonism, as it is he who first *totalizes* the Good *within* being as the highest of ideals. Heidegger, inasmuch as he asserts that Plato's ἰδέα τοῦ ἀγαθοῦ corresponds with Aristotle's notion of the Godhead (τό θεῖον), equates the "idea" with Being (τὸ ὄν) and thus steadfastly ignores the transcendence of the Good. *This* is what is unwritten in Heidegger's own text, and what determines his own interpretation.

II

Ever since Plotinus' celebrated tractate "Concerning the Beautiful" (Περί τοι καλόν),[5] philosophy has been at odds where to place the realm of aesthetic inquiry with respect to the question of "truth." The Beautiful (τό καλόν) is only sometimes affirmed as a transcendental on the same plane as are the One, the Good, and the True. The distrust shown aesthetics belies the latent positivism that much of philosophy has long harbored. Yet, there are those who maintain that the surest, and perhaps only, access to the Absolute is through the ontological modality of beauty that participates in the metaphysical vision of the One True Good.

Hans-Georg Gadamer's hermeneutic philosophy is the product of an extensive background in theology, German idealism, and phenomenology; but even more so, it is a thought that grounds itself in ancient Greek and medieval philosophy. He attempts to recover and remain faithful to the dialectical enterprise inaugurated by Plato, and in many ways he succeeds.

Gadamer maintains that for Plato access to the Good is possible through the mediation of the beautiful. This form provides the clue for grasping the "speculative unity" of language that enables understanding in the hermeneutic event. Gadamer's interpretation is a virtual wedding of Platonic and Aristotelian philosophy. The enigmatic formula of the Good as ἐπέκεινα τῆς οὐσίας found in the *Republic* undergoes a substantial change in the *Philebus*, thus changing the role of Aristotle from a critic to a sympathetic interpreter of Plato on this point. Gadamer interprets the positions of Plato and Aristotle as ultimately congruous with regard to the Good. This "shift" in Plato's thought enables Gadamer to make a case for the accessibility of the Good in itself through the metaphysical modality or form of the beautiful.[6]

Wishing to avoid the metaphysics of Greek philosophy and the dualistic legacy of Cartesianism, Gadamer strives to remain within the philosophical tradition while simultaneously breaking free of it. The seductiveness of his thought lies in the way that it retains the classic metaphysical and ontological concepts of unity and totality, while striving for a non-hierarchical, non-Hegelian dialectic between unity and multiplicity. His appropriation of the Platonic-Plotinian metaphysical concept of the beautiful, as that which reveals the Good and hence truth, is the focus of the present query. Gadamer's position here contests that of Levinas, which maintains that access to the Good occurs through ethics and not aesthetics.

Echoing Heidegger's famous dictum that "language is the house of Being,"[7] Gadamer claims that "Being which can be understood is language."[8] The constitution of the "original unity" occurs in and through the medium of language, the ground or central point whereby the world and the I meet. This unity is speculative in nature. Following the lead of idealist philosophy, what is sought is the establishment of a dialectical (in the Greek sense of the term) *play* between unity and multiplicity that does not fall prey to the abstraction of traditional metaphysical theories. The finite speculative character of linguistic unity underscores Gadamer's emphasis on the history of concepts.

Deriving much from the medieval christological notion of the center of language and its focus on the function of the verbs *imago* and *reflectio*, Gadamer attempts to deduce the common element in this concept for metaphysical and hermeneutic dialectic. Though the term speculative refers to the mirror relation, the speculative center is a movement away from the notion of language as the reflection of a pregiven *forma*.[9] Language is the emergence of a "totality of meaning."[10]

In hermeneutics, priority is assigned to the activity of the object over that of the subject. The "game" receives priority in the ontological scheme of things as truth emerges only out of its being played.[11] Borrowing heavily on Heidegger's analyses of ἀλήθεια and φύσις, hermeneutics hopes to free itself from the relativism of much contemporary thought or, at the other extreme, modern scientific methodology, by employing the ancient insight of the nature of the beautiful.

The object or thing itself, he says, takes hold of the speaker and is the active partner in the process of understanding. Thought "suffers" this activity of the game which is the real speculative moment. The activity of the thing points to a "universal ontological structure" present in play which, in turn, reflects the speculative unity expressed in language.

In play, the subjectivity of the player becomes indissoluble with the activity of the game, i.e., the thing itself. This testifies to the relational status of truth. We do not play with language so much as language plays with us. The totality of meaning that is brought to presence in the play of the game reflects (in the medieval sense) the speculative unity or wholeness of the λόγος. Even that which is unsaid carries with it this totality of signification. The occasionality or imperfection of human speech is maintained despite the thesis of an indivisible metaphysical unity graspable by consciousness through the hermeneutic experience.[12] Play reflects not only our hermeneutic experience of the world, but our experience of the beautiful, the true, and the Good.

The sense of presence evoked in play differs from the traditional notions of presence criticized by Heidegger and others. There is no pre-given that stands before language or that conditions the linguistic event. Language receives its own definition in its manifestation or coming-to-be. Being (*Sein*) is self-presentation and intelligible precisely because of its fundamentally linguistic nature. In the hermeneutical event, the thing in itself (not καθ'αὐτό) transmits its own truth and so disturbs the subject's horizon. Inasmuch as the world (object) gives itself over to the receiving party (subject), there is the possibility for genuine, reciprocal communication, that is, speech.

Truth, like language, is based on the ontological view of being as self-presenatation. Traditional metaphysics has, at times, linked the concept of the beautiful with that of the Good, thus transferring upon it transcendental qualities. Paralleling certain theological formulae that hold that the obtainment of the Good is the loss of desire (e.g., the beatific vision), the beautiful is that in which desire comes to rest (*cuius ipsa apprehensio placet*). Gadamer's recourse to Platonic thinking signals an attempt to free the notion of the loss of desire from its metaphysical context of the doctrine of substance (*forma*). This is accomplished in the appeal to "truth" (ἀλήθεια) as the essential element of the beautiful.

III

Hermeneutics is aided by the metaphysics of light. Light is the first creation of God, or to use Plotinus' terminology, the first necessity or emanation (ἀνάγκης) of the One (τὸ ἕν).[13] Gadamer aligns himself with the Augustinian position that before the advent of creation and differentiation, light was needed, "according to which the multiplicity of what is thought proceeds only from the unity of the word. The metaphysics of light brings out a side of the classical concept of the beautiful that is justified apart from the context of substance metaphysics and the metaphysical relation to the infinite divine mind."[14] Light alone is created without the Word of God (*verbum Dei*). It is this light that makes the linguistic phenomenon a possibility and allows for the emergence of multiplicity and differentiation in the world.

But it is precisely the retention of heliotropes or light metaphors to describe the beautiful that reveals Gadamer's dogged insistence on remaining within the flow of traditional metaphysical discourse. The light of the mind (νοῦς) is the point or site where true beauty and the Good are brought to presence. The concept of νοῦς as developed by Aristotle not only enlightens the intelligible, it also drives deeper the wedge between the sensible and the non-sensible. The Greek metaphysics of light serves as the philosophical ground for the Christian doctrine of the Word (*verbum creans*). The light of the Word (Λόγος) causes everything to emerge (ἀλήθεια) and manifest itself in a comprehensible manner. The hierarchical binary structure[15] that characterizes traditional thought reaches its fruition at this point.

The interpretations of the Platonic εἶδη and of the question of ἀλήθεια rest upon the pivotal function of the beautiful since the relation between the ideas of the Good, the beautiful (τό καλόν), and beauty (καλλονή) are sometimes so close as to be a "confusion."[16] This indivisibility of the Good and the beautiful is due to the fact that the beautiful in itself is (con)*fused* with the one, uniform, and boundless.[17] But despite the fact that there is a confusing relation between the good, the beautiful, and beauty, there is still a fundamental difference between the terms, within which lies the beautiful's specific advantage, says Gadamer. Access to the Good is possible only through the beautiful which is revealed or disclosed in the search for the Good. This is so because part of the nature of the beautiful is to be visibly manifest. This aspect of the beautiful renders it accessible to thought. As the beautiful distinguishes itself from the Good in that of itself it presents itself, its most important function is revealed: the mediation between the intelligible (ἰδέα) and the appearance (εἶδος). This is the "metaphysical crux of Platonism."[18]

The concept of participation (μέθεξις) mediates the form of the beautiful.[19] Through this key concept, Plato seeks to overcome the logical difficulties of being and becoming. The participation of the beautiful within the finite world as mediation relegates the sensible world to a secondary level of importance, that is, if one interprets Plato in the orthodox manner of traditional philosophy, thus giving rise to the alleged dualism of Platonic thought. Since the ἰδέα of the beautiful is fully present in what is deemed beautiful, it serves as the "hiatus" between the world of the senses and the realm of the ideas. The classical dualism of the invisible and the visible is avoided by conflating the two terms under a common denominator which overcomes the difference between them. The beautiful is the reflection of the ontological ordering of the world and being.

The metaphysics of the beautiful helps to establish "the ontological background of the hermeneutical expereince of the world."[20] The concern is not so much with the construction of a hermeneutical method that reveals an already established ontological structure, but with the establishment of an ontology that *grounds* our fundamental hermeneutic experience of the world.

The metaphysical mark of the beautiful is the closing of the gap between the sensible and the intelligible. Focusing on the concept of the beautiful, an "undercurrent" in Platonic philosophy, Gadamer hopes to bypass the logical pitfalls of epistemological and metaphysical dualism. The closing (μέθεξις) of the separation (χωρίσμος) between the visible and the invisible, appearance and idea, accident and substance, finite and infinite, subject and object, and same and other by the beautiful is not an attempt to deny the dualistic character of existence.[21] The doctrine of the forms, argues Gadamer, is not negated by the mediation of the beautiful which constitutes the ontological speculative unity.

IV

Gadamer's appeal to the concept or form of the beautiful is contested here, however, on the grounds that it allows for a false interpretive optimism that paves the way for a social conservatism (non-transformational). Unlike the form of justice, the beautiful is essentially a-moral and, secondarily, a-social. And unlike the ethical metaphysics proposed by Levinas, that of the beautiful does not allow for the complete transcendence of the Infinite, of difference itself, of the absolutely other. Such a metaphysic, which tries to establish or ground a non-hierarchical dialectic between unity and multiplicity, inevitably slides back into a philosophy of totality or identity.

Hermeneutics reveals a disturbing potential conservatism in that there is little or no room left for negation. The beautiful and the true are products of mediation, a form of synthesis reminiscent of Hegelian idealism. Gadamer's overly optimistic stance regarding "prejudice" does not adequately deal with the potential distortions of such prejudgments. Gadamer is essentially conservative insofar as his thought, while appreciating the positive aspects of the tradition (with all of its prejudices), does not deal with the "revolutionary potential" involved with hermeneutical or metaphorical thinking.[22] In other words, he does not deal with how to change the tradition. Praxis never emerges as a true concern.

The appropriation of the beautiful as the clue for truth betrays itself as a totalizing metaphysics in its movement toward a speculative unity. The beautiful manifests itself in the conflation (μέθεξις) of the visible and the invisible. However, since it is not the beautiful in itself but rather, the beautiful καθ'αὐτό that is manifest in the event, hermeneutics hopes to avoid the dualistic pitfalls of substance-metaphysics.

Gadamerian hermeneutics rests upon an ontological privileging of the whole or totality over that of a metaphysical difference. The rejection of the ἐπέκεινα τῆς οὐσίας is necessary for the position that the Good is to be found *only* in the beautiful.[23] But what does this mean for the ethical relation? The infinity signified by the Good is not something in itself, though Gadamer insists, like Hegel, on its equiprimordiality with the finite. But infinity is certainly not to be construed as radical alterity in hermeneutics. The beautiful, as that which discloses the Good, closes via participation (μέθεξις) the hermeneutic circle and thus reveals (ἀλήθεια) truth.

Hermeneutics thus understood places the interpreter in the role of a panoptic observer (much in the manner of Schleiermacher's pyschologizing of the author), despite Gadamer's contrary contentions that the interpreting agent is fully bound in the play of the game and thus freed from the perspective of objectivism. The hermeneutical phenomenon is a purely finite event. The move to collapse the intelligible and the sensible neutralizes the primordiality of difference or alterity. Given this non-valuative stance, truth runs the risk of absolutization, of dogmatization. The question of truth is not decided on the basis of an objective, prior knowledge of the object. The hermeneutic experience of beauty and truth is a temporal event. The finitude of historical existence refutes the attempt by logical positivism to categorize knowledge or truth in any definitive fashion. The presentation of the world as truth does not signify the presencing of an absolute, permanent substratum of meaning in nature. Truth both presents and absents itself in a dialectical intercourse of disclosure and concealment, of play.

Does this dialectic (in the Platonic sense) necessarily require the presence of interlocutors? The speculative structure of language is confirmed insofar as being, as language, "of itself offers itself to be understood"; but there is no necessity that language must be dialogical. Despite the insistence on the priority of the to-and-fro movement of play, Gadamer reflects his bias for the metaphysics of unity, of monological language, when he states that "to be expressed in language does not mean that a second being is acquired."[24] Play is thus similar to the Greek notion of διάνοια, the "soul in dialogue with itself," as Plato states. The dialectic of the totality of meaning, it would seem, does not necessarily require interlocutors, which is to say, the "face to face."

V

If one follows Levinas' lead, then the thought of the Good beyond being signifies a radical generative alterity. This otherness, however, is not a negation of Being or a movement of selfsame consciousness as it is, for example, in Hegelian dialectics. The alterity of the Good is within being, within the totality that is history, but it is more than this totality. As such it is *different* or *otherwise* than being. Though Plato never refers to it as such, the Good is the Infinite insofar as it is both the same (in[the]finite) and other than being.

Ancient Greek language lacks the capacity to express the thought of infinity; for most Greeks, and especially for Aristotle, it is simply the most barbaric of thoughts. The terms ἀπείρον (indefinite) and ἀίδιος (everlasting) are often mistakenly translated as "infinite." The fact of the matter is that there is simply no word available in the Attic language to signify this most other of thoughts. That is why Glaucon remains incredulous about Socrates' claims regarding the transcendence of the Good. It is simply incomprehensible, precisely the point that Plato was trying to make.

Knowledge, or rather, reason, ultimately fails when confronted with the Absolute. Truth, or absolute knowledge, is faced with the task of maintaining the other being καθ'αὐτό, a position totally dependent upon the continual and complete self-revelation of the other (object) independent of all initiative or intentionality on the part of the selfsame. Rather, the other being is disclosed as that which is relative to the consciousness of the same.

This relative manifestation of other being Gadamer terms "in itself" (*an sich*). Employing a distinction between the in-itself and καθ'αὑτό, a distinction that Derrida (and perhaps Levinas) fails to make,[25] he seeks to provide an outlet for the genuine experience of the Good via the form of the beautiful:

> [The] idea of being-in-itself is only the apparent equivalent of the Greek concept of καθ'αὑτό. The latter means primarily the ontological difference between what an existent object is in its substance and its essence and what can exist in it and is subject to change.... What exists "in-itself" in the sense of modern science has nothing to do with this ontological difference between the essential and the inessential; rather, it is determined as certain knowledge, which permits us to control things.... What exists in-itself...is relative to a particular way of knowing and willing.[26]

Viewed from the center of language, he says, the concept of being-in-itself is an abstraction and as such cannot serve as a model for truth. Such abstractions categorize the world in such a way as to render the infinity present in the object susceptible to a notion of totality which attempts to strip away the veil of a (pre?) primordial alterity. This totalizing way of relating to the world is the way of the modern scientific approach and of totalitarian politics. An idealistic objective stance such as that espoused by Hegel is an impossibility given our linguistic enrootedness in the world. Gadamer will reject all attempts at forming an infinite metaphysics as "idealistic spiritualism."[27] However, not all metaphysics of infinity need be dismissed thus, as Levinas demonstrates. The hermeneutic conception of infinity remains a concept bound within the framework of totality. The infinite is speculative; it mirrors the whole and thus opens itself to understanding or comprehension. Formulated as such, infinity in Levinas' interpretation loses its privileged status as the thought that thinks more than itself, that is, as preoriginary difference itself.

The fundamental emphasis of Platonic thought implies the presence of interlocutors and interpersonal relations. Levinas joins Plato in rejecting any relation with the Absolute or infinitely other as καθ'αὑτό:

> The disclosed being is relative to us and not καθ'αὑτό.... Knowledge in the absolute sense of the term, the pure experience of the other being, would have to maintain the other being καθ'αὑτό.... Manifestation καθ'αὑτό consists in a being telling itself to us independently of every position we would have taken in its regard, *expressing itself.* (*TeI* 60–611/*TI* 64–65).

A relation with a being or mode of being (for example, with the beautiful) καθ'αὑτό would be a solitary, impersonal relation characterized as reason (διάνοια). The relation with the other καθ'αὑτό as expressed above is dismissed by Levinas as it is by Plato on the grounds of its fundamentally non-social character. Truth is the movement towards the absolutely other; it is not the grasping of the Absolute, the Infinite, the Good, or the other by reason or the understanding.

VI

Even though Plato insists that the Good refuses conceptualization of itself as an object, he nevertheless holds that one can come into a certain knowledge of it, albeit inadequately, through its ἰδέα. Similarly, in the *Meditations*, Descartes forwards the thesis of the innate idea of infinity or perfection, of the idea of God "put in us."[28] These supraontological insights are placed by Levinas alongside the Aristotelian theory of the agent intellect, Dionysius the Areopagite's doctrine of *via eminentia*, Kant's notion of the unity of apperception, and Bergson's concept of *durée* (to name a few) as great moments in the history of thought insofar as they signify the presence in thinking of an idea whose content or *ideatum* exceeds the capacity of thought to contain it.[29]

The congruency of Plato's and Descartes' positions forms much of the basis for Levinas' radical and innovative reconsideration of the concepts of infinity, goodness, alterity, and difference. His interpretation imports a qualitative sense of meaning to these terms as opposed to a merely quantitative signification. The possibility of ethics lies in the recognition of the limitation of knowledge with regard to the absolutely other. But how does a being come to know goodness, that is, ethical difference, if the Good, which is to say, the One, the absolutely other, is removed from all experience? The ethical relation is announced in the epiphany of the face that takes the form of prelinguistic signification. This meaning, the idea of the Infinite, situates the primacy of the Other over the selfsame and privileges, contra Aristotle, ethical πρᾶξις over θεωρία.

Levinas significantly and radically advances the ancient insights regarding the Good and the One. A metaphor for the Infinite or the absolutely other, the One is both the transcendental condition for the unity of being and simultaneously that which is superseded by the social multiplicity. The transcendent God is not preserved in Levinas' conception of religion; transcendence is historically determined or produced as Desire within being (totality) as the ethical intersubjective relation. The "wholly otherwise" quality signified by the Platonic Good and the Levinasian recasting of it does not imply the imposition of an imperialistic ordering will. The difference between the other (creator) and the same (creation) signifies total separation and thus, the non-coercive, persuasive agency that Plato alludes to in his cosmological treatise *Timaeus*.

Still, Levinas parts company with the Platonic and Plotinian conceptions of the One and extends the notion of the Good beyond being to not only include the immanent, but to make immanence, i.e., social plurality, the locus of truth. In this he follows, for example, Nietzsche's, Hegel's, and Whitehead's[30] reversal of the terms of the dialectic between the one and the many and their assertion that "truth" is not an object but a process. But whereas the above mentioned remain tied to the concept of totality, Levinas recognizes

> the very overflowing of infinity, or, to speak concretely, the very overflowing of all the

> surplus over being—all the Good—that is produced in the social relation. The negativeness of the finite is to be understood on the basis of this Good. The social relation engenders this surplus of the Good over being, multiplicity over the One. (*TeI* 325/*TI* 292)[31]

Levinas' aim is the metaphysical privileging of multiplicity over unity, difference (infinity) over sameness (totality), without compromising ethics in the ontic-existential realm. The trace of the other, the idea of infinity present in the face of the Other, compels one towards ethical responsibility; it is not the manipulation, coercion, or ordering of the created universe. But the primary question in the history of metaphysics is that of "truth." It is with this theme that Levinas must come to grips. Is truth rational and thus knowable, or is it of a different "order," that of ethics? Put another way, is ethics, as goodness itself, beyond even truth (reason), knowable to consciousness only through the *trace* of the passing of an infinite alterity? Leave aside for the moment the postmodern suspicion to the following question: What is the highest, the True or the Good?[32]

4

IdeoGround

The quest for truth, for a knowable ground, is not without struggle and thus a certain violence. But what is the origin of violence? Is not being and thus subjectivity implicated, initially and continually, in violence merely by virtue of its inherent relationality? The mark or trace of absolute violence (e.g., death, total negation or annihilation) is paradoxically the closure of all forms of violence. But surely peace does not stand on the same level as nothingness. Does the cessation of intersubjective violence lie therefore in a positivity that emerges from the great *Ursprung* of the Negative itself?

Such is the conviction that grounds Hegel's philosophy, which rests upon the presupposition of the metaphysically and ontologically conceived concept of totality.[1] Subjectivity, absolute knowing, and consequently, all ethical, social, and political development is predicated upon this concept. In many respects, Hegel represents both the culmination and overcoming of Western philosophy. But how much is he implicated in the metaphysics of light, the legacy of Greek and Christian thought? Is the said metaphysic identical or inseparably related to substance-metaphysics? Hegel certainly does share or retain elements of both perspectives. Still, how much does he either advance or break away from this thought? Does the closure of the metaphysical and epistemological circle by the logic of speculative dialectics signal the overcoming of the tradition or its fulfillment?

Modern European thinking reaches its epitome in the logico-metaphysical system of Hegel. Philosophy to this day falls under his great shadow. But how does truth, which is to say light, cast a shadow? If truth is the movement of Spirit, then it is the luminous itself.[2] According to Hegel, "the System" does not block the sun (to use Plato's metaphor); rather, it "reflects" it.[3] The "doubling"[4] structure characteristic of the dialectic is explained by Hegel through the image of reflected light. However, dialectical metaphysics not only reflects; it *refracts* the light of truth as well.

Whereas classic metaphysics employs the imagery of a mirror (*reflectio*; *imago*) to describe the relation between the One and the Many, Hegelian metaphysics can be said to resemble a prism. Unity is not the transcendent source of emanation; it is the totality of difference itself. Just as the single beam of (white) light, which is diffused in the prism and refracted as the multiplicity of the color spectrum, remains the same (source of) light, so too is the difference that is Spirit but a refraction of the unity of the divine Idea (*Idee*).

The concept of the Absolute Idea is complicit with Aristotle's notion of νόησις νόησεως, of thought continually thinking itself (*Metaphysics* 1074b34). "Νοῦς, simplicity, is substance."[5] Still, Hegel seeks to free himself from the overly optimistic metaphysics of light whose essential trait is the total intelligibility of οὐσία (essence; being). He professes to be as concerned with darkness (error, falsity, evil, death) as he is with light (correctness, truth, goodness, life). From his earliest writings on, he is certain that light or reason will break free of the darkness. But unlike Aristotle, and to some extent Plato, Hegel does not hold that the truth of Being or essence is purely and simply disclosed. The *Science of Logic* is the demonstration that truth or light is not continuous from the start. Light slowly peeks through Indra's net, "unfolding" itself (non-temporally) until the darkness, the veil of ignorance, is either torn or unraveled.

Hegel does not see himself merely as the culmination of Greek-Christian metaphysics; in his eyes, he is the overcoming (*aufheben*) of the naive immediacy of previous forms of the metaphysics of unity and identity. The new unity of speculative dialectics not only recovers but preserves the integrity of difference at its very core. Yet this preservation is founded upon and necessitates a metaphysical economy of violence. Derrida poignantly and succinctly points out that "Metaphysics is *economy*: violence against violence, light against light: philosophy (in general)."[6] And in a further consideration of the relation between light and totality, Levinas states:

> The very idea of totality or of a whole is only intelligible where there is a being that can embrace it. There is a totality because it relates to an inwardness in the light. Here we come to recognize the profundity of Kant's views about the role of the synthesis of apperception and of its unity in the constitution of the world—on condition that we understand it as a synthesis of intuition, sight, or light.[7]

In other words, Levinas' concern is precisely the issue he takes up with Hegel, among others—that is, the preservation of a subjective interiority that does not collapse under the exteriority of a synthetic totality or unity of comprehension, of an absolute knowing.

For all of the insistence that Spirit is the historical unfolding of freedom, the prism remains a veritable prison of sorts. But does Hegel participate, as Derrida puts it, in "the ancient clandestine friendship between light and power, the ancient complicity between theoretical objectivity and techno-political possession?"[8] That is to say, does Hegelian metaphysics inevitably result in a technological and political domination? This rests on the question that permeates this study: does the concept of totality carry with it the specter of totalitarianism?

I

The philosophy of totality and its practical application, the political State, contains an inherent contradictory violence. Ontology posits unification and, presumably, peace as its goal; yet, it condones the use of violence to bring about non-violence. So justified have nation-states perpetually sanctioned their wars, churches their theodicies, and capitalism its "third-world" and environmental exploitation.

In his lectures on the philosophy of history, Hegel suggests that violence is largely the result of human stupidity or ignorance since it is "the seal of the absolute and sublime destiny" of humanity that we ascertain what is good and what is evil, and that it is an error to equate innocence with the ignorance or unconsciousness of evil.[9] While violence of some sort is inevitable and necessary in the System, particularly in the fight or struggle that must occur in consciousness's quest for recognition, this violence is ultimately overcome in the concrete historical act of forgiveness, that is, in Spirit's self-realization actualized in and as history as community.

How is Hegel exonerated from his own indictment that violence is the result of ignorance if the τέλος of the System, present within its very foundation, reveals itself to thought as violent and imperialistic, and so undoes itself? What if he is correct? What if peace is founded or predicated only on the basis of a prior relation of the violent to the violent, of the negation to the negation? Would this not refute the conclusion of his own position, or at least indict him in some bizarre twist of logic and fate of his own condemnation? Is it possible to break free of, to transcend or overcome (*aufheben*), the economy of violence which is the very essence of becoming itself? If it is not, then does not Hegel's philosophy amount to the greatest and most dangerous ruse of human thought?

In his *Concluding Unscientific Postscript*, Kierkegaard will state in a thought later echoed by Georges Bataille that Hegel would be the greatest and most profound of thinkers if only when he had completed the system, he had had a good laugh. But he did not. He took the System, *his* system, all too seriously. Hence, so did most everyone else who read him. No god of the dance, of celebration for the sake of celebration, of desire for the sake of desire, is Spirit. It is the seriousness with which Hegel took himself and his work that has perhaps revealed itself as the most dangerous element of his speculative metaphysics. Perhaps the danger lies in taking philosophy too seriously. The "spirit of gravity," which is conveyed most acutely as *ressentiment* and manifest as the knowledge or belief that human reason (which, for Hegel, is ultimately divine) could encompass the vicissitudes of difference and otherness, is indeed one of the greatest detriments to the development of human existence as Nietzsche warns us.

II

Hegel prefigures and, to some extent, represents the end of a certain ordered philosophical and theological discourse in the formulation of the death of God, a theme first formulated by his friend Friedrich Hölderlin and given additional expression in the heretical mystical poetry of William Blake. But most would agree that the death of God finds its most famous and forceful expression in the thinking of Nietzsche. Still, Hegel's conception of this greatest of events is unique. Unlike Nietzsche, who asserts the impossibility of absolute knowing, Hegel sees such knowledge (that is, the realization of substance as subject) as signifying only the death of the transcendent deity. Consciousness, in attaining self-consciousness, becomes the divine consciousness of Spirit.

But if history and humanity assume the heavenly purple, does God ever truly die? Is violence necessitated in any way prior to its historical instantiation by Hegelian logic?[10] Is intersubjective historical violence the result of a non-historical or co-historical (since the end is implicit in the beginning) conceptual violence that grounds all other violence? That is to say, is there a moment in the unfolding of the Idea where the concept (*Begriff*) is prior to any historical instantiation or manifestation of the divine Logos? Being is becoming and knows no other than itself since it is both in-itself and for-itself. Is it possible then for an ethical transcendence, a "non-allergic" (Levinas) relation with alterity, to occur? Does not the system perpetuate itself eternally, constantly forgiving and redeeming itself only because it first commits a violence for which it must atone?

Spirit or genuine subjectivity is possible only within a totality of conceptual relations. This systematic, totalizing mode of philosophy has been criticized since Hegel's death as anything from a "lack of integrity"[11] to a "visage of being that shows itself in war" (*TeI* 5/*TI* 21). Hegel is often criticized for perpetrating systemic violence. But his critics have not located the said violence within the logical structures of his philosophy.

The shell of the Hegelian framework is thick enough to withstand an explosion; an *implosion* is necessary. Too often Hegel has been and is still attacked from the outside, from the relatively safe and ineffectual standpoint of historical distance and retrospection. The alleged violence of Hegel's system of concepts must be demonstrated on its own grounds. What needs to be exposed are those elements within his thought that in and of themselves resist the conceptual totalization of the System. To point out isolated examples that are not specifically covered by Hegel does not constitute a refutation of his philosophy. These are easily dismissed as "contingent" and are absorbed into the system as such. Only when one uncovers or unveils those fundamental concepts that resist the totalization of Absolute Reason is it possible to look Hegel in the eye and deny consciousness its claim to panoramic vision and knowledge.

III

One of the great stumbling blocks in interpreting Hegel's phenomenological system is that of the question of teleology. Is the τέλος present in the *Science of Logic* historical, that is, actualized in the transformation of cultural, social, and political institutions and forms as the emergence of a collective consciousness; or is it merely conceptually realized in the individual consciousness? The goal of Spirit is the realization of freedom in and as history. Freedom and the Absolute are identical says Hegel. History is a "slaughter bench"[12] and the unfolding of the concept in nature and history is, as Schelling first realizes, a theodicy. Such freedom invariably carries with it the specter of violence. Here Hegel sides with Hume regarding the mutual compatibility of freedom and necessity.[13] The necessity of freedom and the freedom of necessity are founded upon an economy of violence.

It is precisely in the questioning of the ontological primacy of freedom that Levinas locates the ethical moment, the metaphysical moment prior to even truth itself (which is itself the product of reason). Contemporary thinking finds itself in the position of reevaluating the relation between subjectivity and constitution in such a way as to preserve the autonomy of the subject, the principal legacy of the Enlightenment, while avoiding conceptual and concrete violence towards the Other.

An alterity that is able to be absorbed or consumed under the synoptic gaze of a comprehending Reason is not an absolute alterity. The question is whether one can name the absolutely other, or whether it is ineffable. Hegel explicitly states that the concept (*Begriff*) must be articulated and determined if indeed there is to be meaning at all, since "what is called the unutterable is nothing else than the untrue, the irrational, what is merely meant (but is not actually expressed)."[14] Elsewhere, in discussing the relation between naming and meaning, he says:

> We only know our thoughts, only have definite actual thoughts, when we give them the form of objectivity, of a being distinct from our inwardness, and therefore the shape of externality, and of an externality too that bears the stamp of the highest inwardness. The articulated sound, the *word*, is alone such an inward externality.... But it is also ridiculous to regard as a defect of thought and a misfortune, the fact that it is tied to a word; for although the common opinion is that it is just the *ineffable* that is the most excellent, yet this opinion, cherished by conceit, is unfounded, since what is ineffable is, in truth, only something obscure, fermenting, something which gains clarity only when it is able to put itself in words. Accordingly, the words give to thoughts their highest and truest existence.[15]

This position is adamantly opposed by Levinas in a thesis that permeates all his work, namely, that alterity is meaningful prior to the selfsame's identification of that meaning with and for itself through language. The Other teaches the self about his or her destitution, vulnerability, and defenselessness in the primary frankness of revelation that only the face can convey, opened up in consciousness by the separation implied in the idea of infinity. According to Levinas, it is *prior to* the institution of language, that is, the rationally constructed system of signs.[16] Meaning is conveyed in the infinity of the face prior to signs emerging from it. The Infinite is present only as the trace of an absolute alterity; the search for a knowable ground or for the true name of the Godhead is abandoned by Levinas as a futile and violent enterprise. Speech enters in the effort to give some (it is never complete) shape or form to the revelation of the ineffable other whose trace is in the face.

The ground (*Grund*) of being, for Hegel, is both originary and teleological; it is knowable as Absolute Spirit which is immanent in all reality and which is, in actuality, prior to being. That is because the concept of Being (and Nothingness), as it stands alone, is merely an empty abstraction. Ground is the principle on which all existence depends; it is the divine Idea. As ground, the Idea is "first in nature," as Aristotle initially observes. It is not first in us, in subjective human consciousness. Dialectical logic cannot begin with the concept of ground since such a beginning would be unintelligible. The Absolute, ground, is a result, a becoming; it results from what it is mediated by.[17] Mediation cannot serve as a starting point because it demands examination of that which it presupposes. This is why the *Science of Logic* begins with pure, simple, indeterminate immediacy, that is, with the concept of Being.

But if the Idea is already saturated or pregnant with meaning prior to its historical instantiation, then what is the difference between this conception of signification and Levinas' contention that the Infinite is already present in the face in the fullness of the ethical command prior to the predication in being of the *cogito*? The question is one of the retrieval of originary meaning. For Hegel, the truth of being is the comprehension of the objective Idea in history as Spirit by subjective human consciousness; for Levinas, it is the subjective response to the ethical appeal in the face of the Other, a response that immediately and irrevocably calls into question the stance or comportment of subjective being that Hegel's philosophy promotes. Yet despite this significant difference they are, interestingly enough, in agreement with regard to the modality of existence that constitutes the intersubjective relation—Desire—though their approaches to it differ profoundly.

IV

Continental philosophy has tended to center its analyses on the *Phenomenology of Spirit* even to the point of presenting it as the heart of the Hegelian project. Along with the *Philosophy of Right*,[18] this work forms the nexus for the majority of Hegel studies in the Anglo-American, French, and Continental traditions. While the attention given to the *Phenomenology* can be and has been justified, particularly given the concerns of existential phenomenology and Western Marxism, in order to understand the Hegelian enterprise as a whole the earlier *Phenomenology* must be interpreted through the categories of the later *Logic*. However, as Jean Hyppolite makes clear, the relation between these cornerstone texts of Hegel's philosophy is far from being clearly resolved. Hyppolite deals with this question at both the beginning and the conclusion of his massive study on Hegel, but acknowledges that

> it is a problem which fundamentally will remain insoluble because it will lead us to ask whether Hegel's philosophy is itself a phenomenology or an ontology. It is both, no doubt, but which is the authentic proceeding, which is the source of Hegelianism? Is Hegel's logic independent of all phenomenology?[19]

Still, in the opening passages of the introduction to the *Logic* it is stated that the dialectic of the *Phenomenology* is no different than that of the *Logic*. The earlier existential or humanistic moorings of the System, it would seem, undergird its logic.

The question that opens the *Science of Logic* is whether the beginning of logic should be a mediated statement of the principle or an unmediated postulate.[20] In other words, with what must philosophical science begin? Hegel attempts to construct, through a universal logic, truth (the mind of God prior to determinate creation) as absolute knowing much in the same manner as the ancient and medieval concepts of νοῦς and *intellectus agens.* This signals a return to the λόγος metaphysics of light and substance but in a manner that goes beyond or transcends previous metaphysical forms. Gadamer notes that Hegel rejects Plato's dialectic as being only negative since Plato does not recognize that

> there are no single ideas, and it is the purpose of dialectic to dispel the untruth of their separateness...[since] the λόγος is always a complex of ideas, i.e., the relation of ideas to each other. And to this extent, the first truth of Hegel's *Logic* is a Platonic one which is to be perceived even in the *Meno*, when it said that all of nature is interrelated and that therefore the path of recollection of one thing is the path of recollection of all things.[21]

Levinas will take issue with this last point, namely, that the idea of infinity does not assume a unique and privileged position. In a nutshell, this is the crux of Levinas' entire polemic against Hegelian and other ontologies of totality.

V

According to Hegel, pure being is implicitly (*an sich*) the Idea. Logic proceeds from the realization of the inseparable unity of subject and object. Hegel's "objective" logic is to be distinguished from formal logic, which takes for its object an external and independent reality. Formal logic is characterized by understanding which stays at the level of difference. The philosophy of Immanuel Kant never gets past this stage, that is, it does not advance from the concept of the understanding (*Verstand*) to that of philosophical or speculative reason (*Vernunft*).[22] This is because formal logic denies the mutual interdependence of form and content. It claims to be abstract from form and content without detriment to either term. Since the understanding operates on the purely reflective level which makes hard and fast distinctions, it fails to elevate (*aufheben*) the respective terms into the unity of the whole or totality. Only dialectical reason (*Vernunft*) can accomplish this.

Though it is not within the scope of this work to develop Kant's philosophy with regard to Levinas' thinking, it is important to situate Kant within the context of the primary issue at hand, namely, the possibility of philosophically, i.e., rationally, determining the concept of *Grund* and then applying it within the context of the everyday.[23] Kant's principle task is to find a ground for ethical valuation and polity decision making that avoids the oppressive heteronomous structure of previous metaphysical forms. He remains an Enlightenment thinker, for all of his criticism of such thinking, insofar as he advocates the free use of reason in formulating the concept of pure practical reason (*reine praktische Vernunft*). By taking recourse to this essentially intuitive modality of reason he seeks to ground subjective autonomy as the ultimate principle in ethical and moral determination. Having abandoned transcendental intellection, Kant turns towards the will in order to solve the dilemma of whether some sort of objective knowledge is possible.

Kant's questioning of the cosmologically and ontologically based rationality of scholastic metaphysics, through the demonstration of the antinomies of pure reason, hammers the first nail in the lid of the coffin, first built by Cusanus, of the philosophical deity.[24] This is accomplished by positing God, not through an act of pure or transcendental reason, but through practical reason via the notion of duty (*Pflicht*). While this does not amount to the formation of a theologically based ethics, Kant's moral theory remains traditionally Christian in its character. He is firm in his conviction that morality invariably leads to religion (which is not to say to theology). Religious claims are ultimately confined "within the limits of reason alone." Moral obligation is independent of any prior knowledge of the Absolute. Kant's thought grows out of the tension between pietism and the Enlightenment. Insofar as he places considerable importance on the role of conscience in determining moral judgment, he remains true to the legacy of Luther.[25] Kant represents a serious break with that tradition inasmuch as he places human autonomy beyond even the supernatural powers of God. This radical autonomy that Kant tries so desperately to preserve is precisely what is lost in Hegelian dialectic.

The Protestant reformation inaugurated by Luther was not only a reaction against the corruption of Roman ecclesiastics, but also a reactionary response to the other rebellion of the day against Rome—the Enlightenment (*Aufklärung*).[26] The principle claim and legacy of the Enlightenment, that is, the immanent self-justification of the foundations of reason, rests on the paradoxical notion that thought must demand and accept these grounds even though it cannot think (through) them. Enlightenment rationality contests the foundations of traditional metaphysical reason or logic, whether in the form of revelation, authority, or innate ideas, on the basis of the essentially contradictory or unjustifiable epistemological ground upon which these claims are made. Human experience is limited to finite appearances; the infinite or noumenal remains a transcendental unknown. Questions about the status of subjectivity and objectivity remain on the side of the subject. The problem is whether objective knowledge is possible.

The metaphysical transition from theology to science marks the advent of the modern age of thought. Previously, knowledge was uncritically grounded in unconditionals. The formulation of the infinite in the finite begins to turn the metaphysical wheels of the modern period, from the Renaissance and Reformation through the Enlightenment systems of Spinoza, Leibniz, Malebranche, and Hegel, and their subsequent criticism by Nietzsche, Heidegger, Adorno, Rosenzweig, Levinas, and others. Modern philosophy, which culminates in the metaphysics of Hegel, brings together the infinite and the finite in terms of totality. The totalization of the infinite as finite becoming, which Hegel considers to be the death of God, is that which Levinas contends is the locus and origin of all intersubjective violence.

Hegel sees his task as completing that which Kant and Fichte left unfinished. Though Fichte is the first to recognize the systematic implications of Kant's transcendental philosophy, Hegel maintains that Fichte does not go far enough in developing the project of human knowledge out of self-consciousness. In other words, Fichte does not extend his critical analysis to the starting point, that is, to the "I." The presupposition of an unmediated subjective origin does not guarantee any definite understanding of what the self is in a transcendental sense.

VI

The logic of speculative dialectics is the thinking study of thought; it is coincidental with metaphysics. The categories of the understanding are not separate or external to the things they signify. Thought strives to construct concepts of the things themselves and to grasp their universal or essential nature. This is what Hegel means by objective.

The unity of the Idea, that of Being and Nothing, is Becoming which is essentially an unending activity, an "infinite restlessness," the "absolute unrest of pure self-movement."[27] The object of the *Science of Logic* is the unfolding of the Idea in its quest to know itself as Spirit, as Totality. The Idea is the truth of the concept which is the unity of the subjective and the objective. Speculative reason realizes this essential unity. From the vantage of the Idea, reason (*Vernunft*) is a critique of the understanding (*Verstand*) from the point of view of the concept; but from the standpoint of reason, the Idea proceeds from the development of the understanding which it holds as one of its moments.

The relation of the Idea to consciousness, that is, the world as ideal, as subjective and objective unity, is therefore of central concern. The Idea is present to consciousness as the embodied mind or soul, as life. This embodiment is the objectified subject, that is, the concept. It is expressed in several ways: The concept is the mind or soul of the corporeal organism; it is its life, its universal organizing principle.[28] But the body is also the particularization of the universal which, though mutually differentiated, is functionally interrelated in a reciprocal manner as ends and means. However, this unity is only immediate; it is still at the level of the sensuous and not yet free being for-itself (*für sich*). This is the deficiency in ancient dialectic which Hegel characterizes as being only negatively objective. Even Plato's *Parmenides*, which he considers to be the "greatest masterpiece of ancient dialectic," remains submerged in substance (in the concept only in itself); it has not yet attained the level of subjectivity (being for itself).

VII

The advance from the *Phenomenology* to the *Logic* in Hegel's chronology of writing (the present work primarily considers the inverse transition from the *Logic* to the *Phenomenology*) rests on the dialectic of belief and knowledge.[29] The end of the *Phenomenology* marks the sublative shift (*Aufhebung*) when there is no longer any difference between belief and what is believed.[30] Depending on one's perspective, Hegel either fulfills or overcomes what Kant terms onto-theology.[31] Belief is no longer separate from the content of the belief. The transition is one from private subjectivity to objective subjectivity, from an "'I' that is 'We' and 'We' that is 'I.'"[32] Intersubjectivity is constituted as historical Spirit.

So are we already in history, or is there a more authentic, truer history to arrive on the scene, a "kingdom come," so to speak? One can only speculate whether

Hegel's teleology is merely formal, that is, logical, realized in the individual who goes through the moves of the *Phenomenology* and the *Logic*; or whether it is objective, that is, realized in some form of collective consciousness.

"Natural," as opposed to "philosophical," consciousness (the terms Hegel employs in the *Phenomenology*) is already at the historical stage where it is present, though not recognized, as subjectivity. Natural consciousness is the certainty of the Cartesian *cogito*. Subjectivity is not a mere philosophical stance or position; it is also historical, that is, culturally contextual. It represents a certain frame of mind. Natural consciousness takes its subjectivity for granted. Not content with Descartes' conclusions on the nature of the epistemological certainty of the *cogito*, Hegel throws the entire Cartesian enterprise into question in the *Phenomenology* and embarks upon the arduous trek on the "pathway of despair." What most characterizes this path is the opacity of its finish, its telos, to natural consciousness. The despair arises in consciousness when what initially appeared to be so close (the I) is, upon closer inspection, realized to be far away (the We).

What is new in the Hegelian system is something linguistic or conceptual. The *Phenomenology* is preeminently a treatise on education.[33] Hyppolite refers to Hegel's text as an educational novel (*Bildungsroman*). Hegel sees the whole project of the *Aufklärung* as educational or pedagogical, as its primary aim is to help overcome the alienation between the self and culture. Inasmuch as this is true, Hegel not only represents an attempted overcoming of the Enlightenment but a continuation of that enterprise.

The dialectical progression of the *Phenomenology* is the development of language, the ability to express that which was previously unarticulable, that is, the immediacy of sense-certainty. What is unspeakable is not true; therefore, it is devoid of significance. The immediacy of individual sense certainty is an ontological deficiency. That is not to say that the immediate or the given is unknowable, but it is only so by way of the mediation of a linguistic framework as Kant is the first to recognize.

Language leads one to speculative dialectical logic because there is a natural logical instinct to language of which the transcendental logic of the *Science of Logic* is the unfolding. According to Gadamer, "here lies Hegel's great relevance for today: the speculative statement is not so much a statement as it is language.... Dialectic must retrieve itself in hermeneutics."[34] The question, as Schelling initially notes, is how the system of concepts developed in the *Logic* can continue to move when the natural logic of language is exhausted in the realization of philosophical consciousness by Spirit?[35]

Now for Hegel, the truth of the pure "I" is Spirit, that is, absolute knowing. In reading or going through the conceptual moves of the *Phenomenology*, the I or individual (natural consciousness) realizes that, prior to this endeavor, it has no identity that constitutes it as a unity. The process of reading the text, of advancing though the various *Gedankenbestimmungen* (thought-configurations), reveals to the I its essential nature as a We, as a collectivity, as an identity in process. Consciousness knows nothing more of itself in its realization of itself as thinking self-consciousness. Philosophical consciousness is the ability to express and communicate this awareness to ourselves and to others. The realization of the collectivity of the I in philosophical consciousness constitutes the telos of Spirit. The meaning of the ontological formula "Substance is Subject" is existential. That is to say, subjectivity is indistinguishable from intersubjectivity. This leads one to examine more closely the status of the Other in Hegelian metaphysics.

5

MiddleGround

The problem of otherness in Hegelian philosophy is overcome existentially in the dialectic of confession and forgiveness that reconciles the alienation first presented in the dialectic of lordship and bondage. This in turn gives rise to the concepts of *Moralität* (personal morality) and *Sittlichkeit* (communal ethics). These concepts are figurative as one finds here the beginning of the apocalyptic realization in Hegel's thought, that is, the unity (totality) of freedom and nature as the universal State that is the concretization of *Grund.* But Hegel's attempt to demonstrate the ethical or moral efficacy of his philosophy is contested via Theodor Adorno's assessment of mediation and his reinterpretation of the subject-object dichotomy and Levinas' juxtaposition of proximity to mediation as the modality of being that best describes the nature of the intersubjective relationship. The problem of the *Aufhebung* emerges here as crucial in the questions of mediation, reconciliation, and the relation between the constitution of the epistemologically determined subject-object relation and the metaphysically determined self-other relation (ethics). Adorno and Levinas converge at this point, regarding the relation between the object and the other in a decidedly non-Hegelian fashion.

I

In the dialectic of confession and forgiveness, Hegelian Spirit is concretized or brought into actuality (*Wirklichkeit*). Subjective action is the locus of this transformation which overcomes the clash of consciousnesses, the result of the "law of the heart" (the transformation of desire and/or pleasure into an act of the will).[1] During this phase of the dialectic the slave discovers his or her freedom through the activity of work. This is the realization, produced in determinate negation, of the particular as the universal I, that is, the We. The work produces embodied action, "the very heart of the matter" (*die Sache selbst*).[2]

But whether work is interpreted socially, politically, or as the act of writing, the being of action is always the activity of an individual for itself and for others. "Action divides [Spirit] into substance."[3] And Spirit is the *actuality* of ethical substance:

> Spirit, being the *substance* and the universal, self-identical, and abiding essence, is the

> unmoved solid *ground* and *starting-point* for the action of all, and it is their purpose and goal, the in-itself of every self-consciousness expressed in thought. This substance is equally the universal *work* produced by the action of all and each as their unity and identity, for it is the *being-for-self*, the self, action.[4]

The first instantiation of universal action is the universal I that tests and institutes laws. The problem, however, is that the law is only *formal* at this point (in the sense that Kant postulates the categorical imperative). It remains tautological in that it is the identification of law and truth and as such opens a door to both intellectual and political totalitarianism. Law does not ensure the actual embodiment of the universal I. The dialectical progression to Spirit is the actualization (historical) of this formal, abstract freedom which is accomplished by mediating such freedom with nature.[5]

The mutual recognition between the self and the other as thinking and acting self-consciousnesses moves Spirit or subjectivity proper from the realm of morality (*Moralität*) to that of ethical substance (*Sittlichkeit*).[6] This move is important as it will help clarify the distinction between morality and ethics. Furthermore, this distinction has been made before in the history of thought; the difference that Hegel posits between *Sittlichkeit* and *Moralität* in order to further separate his project from Kant's critical philosophy is a shining example.

In an interview, the published translation of which he reviewed, Levinas also draws a "very important" distinction between the moral and the ethical:

> By morality I mean a series of rules relating to social behavior and civic duty. But while morality thus operates in the socio-political order of organizing and improving our human survival, it is ultimately founded on an ethical responsibility towards the Other. As *prima philosophia*, ethics cannot itself legislate for society or produce rules of conduct whereby society might be revolutionized or transformed.... Morality is what governs the world of political "inter-estedness," the social exchanges between citizens in a society. Ethics, as the extreme exposure and sensitivity of one subjectivity to another, becomes morality and hardens its skin as soon as we move into the political world of the "impersonal" third—the world of government, institutions, tribunals, prisons, schools, committees, and so on.... *If the moral-political order totally relinquishes its ethical foundation, it must accept all forms of society, including the fascist and totalitarian, for it can no longer evaluate between them.*[7]

Levinas' conception of morality encompasses the individual life, as it does for Hegel (*Moralität*), but it also embraces the fuller sense of communal interaction signified by *Sittlichkeit*. Levinas goes beyond Hegel, whose morality/ethics are in the end utilitarian and pragmatic, in positing the ethical as the *necessary* condition for a *non*-totalizing moral life that recognizes the difference between justice and fascist totalitarianism.

Hegel's notion of justice is the maintenance, though not the foundation, of the social order through the institutional structures of law and politics. The allergy or alienation between the self and the Other is overcome in forgiveness. Ethical responsibility is fulfilled at this stage. Politics tends to suppress the face to face relation. Its ultimate aim is the realization of universal freedom (reason). Individual subjectivity means nothing, is abstract and formal, without a sense of the greater communal obligation (*Sittlichkeit*).

Morality, for Hegel, is essentially concerned with self-determination; its bonds are instituted, that is, they present themselves in the form of social, religious, and legal institutions. Morality's basic concern is with the subjectivity of freedom. The tension here is between the ought (*Sollen*) and the is (*Sein*). Morality refers to the relation between the *individual* subjective will and volition, that is, inward action. It is the realization of the will in-itself as the *reasonable* will.[8]

Moralität is Hegel's coinage for Kant's conception of ethics. Kant himself used the more common term *Sittlichkeit*, a term to which Hegel assigns new meaning. The problem with Kantian moralism is its empty, formal sense of moral obligation that ultimately opposes freedom to nature. In morality freedom is aware of itself as such. Morality is not to be construed as synonymous with the Good. There is, says Charles Taylor, a tendency "to think of *Moralität* as more fundamental because we see the moral man as being ever in danger of being asked by his community to do the unconscionable. And particularly so in an age of nationalism."[9] Action derived from the moral order does not always serve the communal needs. An internal relation of the self to its will, the moral life does not embody the universal, the rational will as such.

Sittlichkeit, on the other hand, is bound by natural bonds, e.g., the family, the spirit of the nation (*Volksgeist*).[10] In the ethical substance, the truth of abstract right and individual morality coincide as sociality or intersubjectivity. The tension between *Sollen* and *Sein* is reconciled. The ethical life is characterized as the union of the subjective will with the idea of the good. The *Logic* does not begin but concludes with a consideration of the Good which for Hegel, like Kant, is the good will, albeit universal and not individual. Like his contemporary Schelling, Hegel too finds a distinction between morality and religion. Kant, borrowing from Pietism as well as Lutheran orthodoxy, locates the source of religion, which is to say ethics, in the will rather than in the understanding.

It is at this stage that the reality of the State is encountered in its concept (*Begriff*). The State, as the realization of freedom itself, is the substance of individuals even though it does not, admittedly, exist for the sake of the individual.[11] Morality is fulfilled as *Sittlichkeit*; the circular movement of the logical dialectic is existentially concretized. The autonomous will becomes objective or absolute will.[12] The good will appears as custom (*Sitte*), as natural, habitual practice and not as a set of principles. Substance, according to Hegel, is for the first time truly present as subject, as *Geist*, as freedom in history.

In the mediated reconciliation of the ethical order, which produces the legal status of subjective being and of culture (*Kultur*),[13] and which in turn produces the revolutionary self, the moral consciousness (*das moralische Bewusstsein*, not *Gewissen*) that characterizes Spirit and paves the way for statehood is realized. Nature and morality, indifferent to one another, are synthesized. Nature is revealed as dependent on the moral order, though the contrapositive is not so.

II

Neither law nor personal commitment will establish the universal moral consciousness. Only a transgression of the law, which the historical act of forgiveness represents, enables the realization of this consciousness. In the act of forgiveness, the law is both suspended and transcended (*aufheben*). In this act the self gives back the Other's freedom and thus absolves him or her of all guilt.[14] In this action, the I forgives itself and frees itself from guilt, that is, from the divine or feminine dimension of the ethical substance characterized by the institution of the family and personified as Antigone.[15] This mediated reconciliation is the redemption of the world.

To act is, in some manner or another, to commit violence; guilt is always tied to action. In the act of confession and forgiveness the self no longer acts as judge, but resides in communion with the Other. This is the great moment of mutual recognition, the realization of Spirit, and the emergence of genuine intersubjectivity.[16] Spirit is the recognition that redemption occurs on the universal dimension as much as it does on the particular. The action that forgiveness represents is the unity of being and thought. The end (τέλος) is the beginning (ἀρχή). In the System, Hegel is the re-Incarnate Logos.[17]

Now, the dialectic of confession and forgiveness initially expressed in the section on "Lordship and Bondage" in the *Phenomenology* does vent some ontological violence, but then so do ritual sacrifice and mimetic substitution.[18] But for Levinas, mediation always carries with it the specter of violence though, at times, it is an effective means of accomplishing some reconciliation.[19] Mediation is the power of politics proper. It cannot serve as the power (passivity) of ethics (not morality) construed in the Levinasian sense. The ethical signifies goodness itself; it is first with regard to knowledge (philosophy). Mediation is the product of thought; but thought is always second to ethics. Ontology attends metaphysics. The self always responds to the other, even if it is with the (non) voice of silence.

A subjecthood constituted in and by contact with alterity is not egolatrous and domineering. Levinas never claims to overcome the subjectivism of modern philosophy; rather, his aim is to promote the ethical means by which subjectivity can flourish as the wonder of existence that it is. One cannot disengage oneself from the political aspect of existence; but one can revaluate the relation between ethics and politics and begin the concrete reformation (and here negation plays its truly pivotal role) of institutions and governments.

The end or completion of history is neither the denial of human praxis nor the dismissal of history as illusory. History cannot serve as the arbitrating judge of the ethical relation. If it does, it assumes the role of objective law-giver and moral legislator; it invariably takes away personal freedom rather than bestows it. The totality that is history is denied in this function by Levinas precisely in order that it may be a homeland for all. The violence endemic to sexism, racism, classism, nationalism, etc. is the denial of the totality of being as the *trace* of the infinitely other.

III

One of the strongest and most substantial criticisms of Hegelianism and Marxism has been that of the Frankfort School of critical social theory. The thinking of Theodor Adorno, a first-generation critical theorist, threatens to disrupt the flow of philosophical discourse. His last and arguably most important work, *Negative Dialectics*, parallels many of the moves that Levinas makes in his treatment of the metaphysical or ethical relation.[20] Adorno can be considered a proto-deconstructionist along the same lines as Nietzsche and Levinas.[21]

Adorno's dialectical reversal (negative) of the subject-object relation gives Kant's variant of the Copernican Revolution an axial turn.[22] This is necessary in order to release thought from the tyranny of identity logic, but as Adorno himself admits, such a turn at this stage of history only theoretically negates. Such a philosophical reversal must be actualized, that is, become non-philosophy. This is possible only through an ethical move in the field of social relations that does not permit the reification of the Other into an immutable substance for cognitive reflection. This move allows not only for the letting-be (*Gelassenheit*) of the Other, but for the active responsibility which is justice *for* the Other's freedom.

According to Adorno, philosophy in the West has consisted of an over-accentuation of subjectivity or consciousness. This elevation of the subject reaches its apex in various forms of idealism and positivism. The ascription of being to consciousness in the Hegelian system merely objectifies the subject, raising it in the process to a transcendental status.[23] The privileging of the subject over the object is merely disguised in the quasi-theological or religious term *Geist*. The development of the practical and active side of subjectivity by Hegel is accomplished, as Marx first realizes, only at the level of an abstract transcendental subjectivity. Positivism fails to recognize the active, constitutive power of subjectivity in creating history, culture, and politics and instead gives rise to a passive notion of the subject which sees the world as a completed entity to be contemplated and analyzed. Both of these polar positions are unacceptable. What is needed is a bypassing of the positivistic subject and the transindividual subjectivity both of transcendental and absolute idealism and of some forms of Marxism.

Negative dialectics has often been criticized as pessimistic, if not nihilistic. This is due largely to the use of the Hegelian category of negation without the resulting positivity of meaning afforded in the totalizing activity of the *Aufhebung*. A transformed philosophy, says Adorno, would have to cancel the claim of traditional philosophy, which

> thinks of itself as possessing an infinite object, and in that belief it becomes a finite, conclusive philosophy. A changed philosophy would have to cancel that claim, to cease persuading others and itself that it has the infinite at its disposal...the changed philosophy itself would be infinite in the sense of scorning solidification in a body of enumerable theorems.[24]

The often associated pessimism of Adorno's thought is a direct result of his conception of infinity and of the object of knowledege. Epistemologically construed, it is not the subject that is constitutive of the object of reflection. The subject is constituted by the object; it is the object's agent. There is a "preponderance of the object" that requires of the subject a "total self-relinquishment."[25] But this giving up or giving over is not the same as Hegelian self-negation. Such a move signifies the impossibility of either adopting an objective view of the world and history, an absolute distancing of the subject from the object, or of collapsing the object under the rubric of subjectivity.

The notion of subject is ambiguous for it refers not only to the particular existent but to "consciousness in general," to use Kant's term.[26] The two meanings have reciprocal need of each other. One cannot think of the individual apart from the concept of the subject, for the term would then lose all meaning. To reflect on the particular existent in the form of a concept is to universalize the individual. Defining the two terms to avoid this confusion only lands one in an aporia. Any attempt made by epistemology to equate the concept with the world necessarily falls short because the world and the concept are not adequate to each other. The "antidote of philosophy," Adorno will claim, lies with the "disenchantment of the concept."[27]

This disenchantment or demythologization begins with the realization that the "separation of the subject and the object is both real and illusory."[28] This separation has been a major presupposition of philosophy since Descartes. The truth of the matter is that the subject and the object are "mutually mediated" by one another. "Once radically parted from the object, the subject reduces it to its own measure; the subject swallows the object, forgetting how much it is an object itself."[29] Separation without mediation results in ideology, thus creating a false hypostatization which invariably assigns preeminence to the role of the subject. The question for Levinas is whether this hypostatization occurs in the absolute separation between the same and other despite the claim that an ethical preeminence is to be given to the Other.

IV

Levinas expounds his deeply radical suspicion towards Hegelian claims regarding the role of mediation: "To illuminate is to remove from being its resistance because light opens a horizon and empties space—delivers being out of nothingness. Mediation (characteristic of philosophy) is meaningful only if it is not limited to distances" (*TeI* 34/*TI* 44). Levinas counters the concept of mediation with that of *proximity*, a non-mediated intersubjective positioning (*AE* 129–56/*OB* 81–98; *EDE* 217–36/*CPP* 109–26). The paradox of the notion of proximity lies precisely in that it signifies both the concrete personal nature of the face to face while simultaneously signifying the absolute distance or separation that remains between the self and Other. In addition, the notion of proximity resists the comprehension via mediation that is characteristic of classic and Hegelian metaphysics (ontology).

In Hegel's conception of mediation, metaphysics and epistemology collapse into an absolute speculative unity. It is a myth of modern philosophy (particularly that of Kant) that the relation between metaphysics and epistemology has been severed. On the contrary, both must be mutually informative if the fullest sense of praxis is to be achieved. In this regard, Hegel is fundamentally correct. But do epistemology and metaphysics ever truly coincide? For both Levinas and Adorno, the problem with dialectical metaphysics is that it thinks of itself as possessing the infinite as a higher object while maintaining the finitude of its own speculative operation.

Epistemology, the way in which we come to know the world and the Other, cannot be absolved of its tie with ethics. The proper function of epistemology is to provide a methodology for philosophy. For example, Husserlian phenomenology primarily serves as an epistemological methodology rather than an ontology, though it is certainly promoted to an ontological status in the works of Heidegger, Sartre, and Merleau-Ponty. Epistemology does not constitute the fulfillment of being; it is not synonymous with metaphysical truth as Hegel contends. It is a method that reflects the proper relation of being with its other. To be otherwise would result either in an empty metaphysics, a theory of knowledge without ethical orientation, or, in the case of Heidegger's fundamental ontology, in a theory of reality without morals. The great synthesizing activity of absolute idealism is the conflation of metaphysics and epistemology. Levinas' work is a demonstration that epistemology is subservient to metaphysics, which is to say, to ethics.

In negative dialectics, epistemology concretizes metaphysics. One could say that it makes Levinas' construal of the metaphysical relation, irrational to consciousness being prior to consciousness' self-awareness, graspable or apprehensible in some sort of cognitive fashion. But in Levinasian terminology, it is metaphysics (ethics) that concretizes epistemology (theory). In any case, it would be a mistake to construe Adorno's project as epistemology per se; rather, it is a "metacritique of epistemology" (borrowed from the original title of Adorno's work on Husserl).[30] This term signifies a movement of going beyond philosophy for its own sake as a theoretical discipline into its historic-social foundations "without, however, reducing it to them in the manner of a vulgar sociology of knowledge."[31] The recognition of the preponderance of the object and the insistence on the ethical primacy of the Other pave the way for this concretization of philosophy. A philosophy that does not become non-philosophy is useless, as Marx points out in his *Theses on Feuerbach.* But the opposition of philosophy to non-philosophy, says Derrida, "opens history" in a "violent way."[32]

Reconciliation is always possible epistemologically (though not necessarily metaphysically) between the subject and object because the subject is always an object itself. Adorno's non-synthesizing negative dialectics reveals a movement similar to Hegel's dialectic. The problem with Hegelian metaphysics is that it thinks of itself as possessing the infinite as a higher object while maintaining the finitude of its own speculative operation. The point of difference between them is precisely over the status of difference (infinity; object).

Unlike the positive dialectics of Hegelian philosophy, negative dialectics begins with the object and returns to the object, mediated, though unsynthesized. Higher forms occur without the necessity of an ultimately positive sublation. Here Adorno's link with Nietzsche is most evident. The chaos of existence refuses the positivity of epistemological and metaphysical closure. The element of chance in

Adorno's philosophy leaves him open to the same charges of nihilism that have often plagued Nietzsche's thought.

Given Levinas' and Adorno's analyses of the (non) logic of Desire and its relation to violence, the realization of Spirit, historically actualized in the formation of community through the concrete act of forgiveness and recognition on the part of the self, appears to be not the formation of community but instead, just the opposite. Spirit is actually the denial of true communion with the Other. The road to autonomy is paved with the blood of the Other. Spirit, after all, is a theodicy.

To be in communion is not to be "one" in any transcendent or quasi-mystical sense, nor is it subjection to the greater will of the State. It is the ability to accept the radical difference of the other and to coexist in spite of the infinite distance or separation that will always remain between the same and other.

To be is to be economically; it is to exist within a complex web of relations. Economy implies tension and at times violence. To be in relation is to be confronted by another face. But is this engagement initially and invariably conflictual? Is the face to face relationship possible non-economically? If it were, then absolute peace would be the solution. However, if peace is a relation with that which is beyond the totality of the logic of desire and war, then is it a relation at all? The locating of war as a relation outside the totality would amount to the same criticism. And who would deny that war is a reality? Peace can only be accomplished by beings capable of war. On some levels violence is, arguably, if not justifiable, at least necessary at times. As Nietzsche so poignantly reminds us, creation and destruction go hand in hand. But does this not merely repeat what has been Hegel's position all along?

6

WarGround

In Hegel's philosophy, substance is both subject and the union of totality and infinity, and the aim of Spirit is to realize its own inherent freedom. In fact, he says:

> To this end all the sacrifices have been offered on the vast *altar of the earth* throughout the long lapse of ages. Freedom alone is the purpose which realizes and fulfills itself, the only enduring pole in the change of events and conditions, the only truly efficient principle that pervades the whole. This final aim is God's purpose with the world.[1]

Now it is surely just such a passage that prompts Levinas to respond:

> Hegel's great meditation on freedom permits us to understand that the good will by itself is not a true freedom as long as it does not dispose of the means to realize itself. To proclaim the universality of God in consciousness, to think that everything is consummated while the peoples that tear one another to pieces belie this universality...is to shock reason itself. Interiority cannot replace universality. (*TeI* 269/*TI* 241)

How does the concept of infinity affect an understanding of the nature of alterity? What is the relation of this question to the origin (ἀρχή) of violence and war? The question of the infinite is inseparable from the status of *Grund* and of the teleology of Spirit. Ever since Alexandre Kojève's celebrated lectures on Hegel, European (especially French) and Continental philosophers have often focused their attention on the theme of *desire* and its relation to the question of intersubjectivity. Levinas is central in this regard as he radically reconceives the relation between intersubjectivity and desire. But unlike most interpretations which focus on the *Phenomenology of Spirit*, here the thematic of desire will be addressed primarily through the perspective of the *Science of Logic.* Of issue is the negative quality that desire assumes in Hegel's thought. Desire, as construed by Levinas, is the modality of subjective being that brings us into a genuine relation with otherness while preserving the integrity of the Other's alterity. Does the negativity (i.e., otherness) that Hegelian desire negates in its movement as Spirit render the relation with the Other obsolete; or does it bring one into a genuine relation with the Other? The status of the extreme manifestation of intersubjective violence—

war—hinges upon this question. And in assessing the logic that connects the relation between desire and violence, the epistemological correlate of intersubjectivity, that is, the subject-object relation, must be taken up.

I

Hegel's claim that there is a retrievable or knowable origin (ἀρχή) of identity is countered by Levinas with the reverse thesis of a "past that was never present,"[2] an absolute passivity more passive than passivity itself. This irreducible alterity, present as the lapse of time, as *an-archy*, is meaningful in itself. It is an eschatological "signification without a context" (*TeI* 7/*TI* 23) even though intentionality does not present it to consciousness as an object for reflection.

Early in his writing, Levinas argues for the absolute alterity of each instant which enters history through the Other and not by means of production or constitution by the identity of the same (*DEE* 25–51/*EE* 21–36).[3] Neither Bergson nor Heidegger, both of whom exercise an enormous influence on Levinas' thought, anticipate this move. The radical alterity of time is situated not in the instant (though the importance of the instant as an inaugurating commencement, as the possibility of beginning anew, is never renounced), but in an unrecoverable past. This an-archic past "signals a lapse of time that does not return, a diachrony refractory to all synchronization, a transcending dichotomy" (*AE* 23/*OB* 9). "Absolutely heteronomous," this infinite past cannot be, contra Hegel, recollected (*er-innern*)[4] or remembered as in Plato.

The refusal to situate an absolute exteriority, an irreducible difference (infinity) beyond the totality that is history results in a formal conceptual violence that grounds all other human violence. Representational thought is implicated, along with the anonymity of being in general or the *il y a*, as the primordial scene of violence (*DEE* 93–105/*EE* 57–64; *EeI* 45–51/*EI* 45–52). It consists in a reduction of the Other to a moment of selfsame consciousness. This results in a denial of the Other's alterity and so functions as the origin and locus of violence.

Violence is always directed towards the Other and thus towards a face, but its first instantiation is conceptual, even if it appears that the violence perpetrated is the result of passion or emotion and fundamentally non-conceptual. The face signifies prior to any concept of it; its meaning is expressed anarchically prior to subjective representation. The signification of the face is ethical. Violence, even to the point of war, is the refusal of this position which, in turn, is the instantiation of ontology (philosophy) which thematizes the face and displaces its signification under the theme of comprehension, that is, of individual subjective freedom.

The enrootedness of violence in the conceptual aspect of being lies within the attempt to comprehend the totality of being and thus alterity and infinity. Hegel aims at such totalization by introducing a third term (mediation) to the concepts of same and other, subject and object. But how adequate is infinity to its concept? Can infinity be approached as are other objects for cognition? Is not infinity that thought which presents itself as the most other of thoughts to consciousness? And if infinity is accessible in some manner to consciousness, as both Hegel and Levinas maintain, what exactly is the modality of its disclosure?

II

Hegel asserts that freedom (and presumably peace) are possible only if some sort of transcendental subjectivity, an absolute knowing, is realizable. The subjectivity that comes to know itself as freedom is political subjecthood. Spirit is the actualization of citizenry in the homogenous State. The universal citizen is not only the cornerstone of community; it is the (non) face of Spirit as well. Self-consciousness is manifest as the totality of social relations. The *telos* of Spirit, aside from being the recognition that the individual existent has no meaning apart from the collective social totality and that history is the unfolding of freedom, is also the realization by consciousness of what Parmenides espoused so long ago, namely, that being and thinking are virtually indistinguishable in their relational unity.

Spirit, as the process and goal of absolute knowing, is not the imposition of any new thought-configurations (*Gedankenbestimmungen*); it is the recognition of what is already given to consciousness in the immediacy of sense-certainty. Hegel maintains the paradoxical position that, on the one hand, the Absolute is sheer self-immediacy (selfsameness) and, on the other, that it is self-differentiation (self-sundering and return from otherness). The power or "labor of the negative,"[5] as contradiction itself, both compels (via desire) and propels (via negation) the dialectic. It is "the principle of all self-movement,"[6] and the "*void* as the principle of motion."[7]

The infinite return of consciousness to itself mediated by otherness demonstrates the priority that is assigned to the subject, that is, to selfsameness. Subject is the truth of substance and so transcends (*aufheben*) what is just the object even though the difference between subject and object is maintained in the unity of the Idea. It is the relation of the Idea to consciousness, of the world as ideal, as subjective and objective unity, which is of central concern here as it is within this move that the parameters for understanding the trajectory of intersubjective desire and the relation between war and peace are established.

The Idea manifests itself to consciousness as the concept. This is taken up in the *Phenomenology*, which is preeminently concerned with the relation between concepts, with thought-configurations. The aim of Spirit, the transformation of consciousness into self-consciousness, is achieved only after all the possible shapes that "natural consciousness" can assume have been exhausted. This occurs in the move to "philosophical consciousness" which takes immediate natural consciousness as its object. Natural consciousness is deficient in that it is aware only of the immediacy of its own existence. It takes as its object those things that are outside itself. Philosophical consciousness, on the other hand, takes the concept (or itself *qua* thing or substance) for its object. Seeking knowledge of knowledge, it aims to close the gap between the *an sich* (being; truth) and the *für sich* (knowing). This is accomplished via the acquisition of the *adequate* concept, the thought-determination that knows no other than itself: Totality.

In Hegelian dialectics, otherness has no meaning apart from its relation with sameness and vice-versa. This holds true for every dialectical opposition. While each dyadic term is distinct and knowable as such, its truth value lies in the holistic relation that it has with its opposite. Absolute knowing is the process of consciousness arriving at this truth since "everything turns on grasping and expressing the True, not only as *Substance*, but equally as *Subject*."[8] In the *Phenomenology* and in the *Logic* the problem of otherness is reconciled in the dialectics of the *Aufhebung*. Substance is realized as Subject only by virtue of its having been mediated by the object of its reflection, that is, by alterity.

III

Does Hegel lack an adequate (rather, a *non*-adequate) understanding of alterity? What he construes as "other" is actually a projection of selfsameness onto the object of reflection on the part of consciousness. The Hegelian concept of the other does not signify an irreducible otherness, that is, irreducible to the concept of the same. This absolute irreducible alterity Levinas terms the Infinite; but it is precisely such an infinity that Hegel terms "spurious," recalling the problematic infinite regress rejected by an earlier Aristotelian-substance metaphysics.[9]

Levinas maintains that Western philosophy (a tautology) is dominated by the concept of totality which "suspends morality" and renders in its "visage of being" the very advent of the violence which is war (*TeI* 5–6/*TI* 21). In opposition to this totalizing ontology that has dominated since Aristotle, he posits a redefined notion of metaphysics as the non-theoretical ethical or social relation. This relation is characterized as the movement of Desire (*désir*)[10] towards and for the infinitely other (*l'autre*), which is to say, the Other (*l'autrui*). Metaphysics is the relation of consciousness with a prior term absolutely exterior to it, a term prelinguistic and pre-conceptual.

Seeking to be free of the confining syntax of Hegelian metaphysics, this movement beyond the totality is designated as non-negative. Infinity does not confine itself outside the totality of being as in a vacuum or as a mere concept; rather, infinity is found in the face of the Other, "reflected *within* the totality and history, *within* experience" (*TeI* 7/*TI* 23). Infinity is a surplus in the sense that the Platonic Good is a plentitude. This surplus or ethical transcendence is metaphysical Desire, the manifestation and expression of the excess that the absolute goodness of otherness signifies. Desire (*désir*) is not to be described negatively, nor is it to be construed as a purely positive movement (*TeI* 32/*TI* 42). Here is a split with speculative (*begreifende*) dialectics which maintains that "self-consciousness is *desire* in general."[11] In Spirit's quest for recognition, desire (*Begierde*) is a negative movement since in order for Spirit to become certain of itself, it must negate its alterity. Hegelian desire does not respect the Other as other; its impetus is actually that of need (*besoin*).

Desire (*désir*) seeks to maintain the radical separation that exists between the same and other without fusing into a rational unity or logic. The metaphysical relation with the Other, Desire as transcendence, occurs without the benefit of an intermediary. The luminous concept of mediation is replaced in the Levinasian analysis by that of *proximity*, a position that maintains the separation of subject and object, of self and Other, without compromising the integrity of the relation or theoretically encapsulating it, since it is enigmatic (*EDE* 207–209f/*CPP* 64–66f). Yet Derrida warns that "despite his anti-Kierkegaardian protests, Levinas here returns to the themes of *Fear and Trembling*: the movement of desire can be what it is only paradoxically, as the renunciation of desire."[12]

Just how other is the Other for Levinas? Is there a truly genuine other in Hegel's thought? To be other is to be, by its very definition, *other than*...just as consciousness is *consciousness of*..., at least in its Husserlian formulation. Absolute alterity is other than the concept or thought of otherness and not just the polar opposite of the concept of the same. Hegel maintains that universality is simple selfsameness mediated by alterity. In other words, self-consciousness consists in being recognized as self-consciousness by another self-consciousness. But is this a recognition by a truly other; or is it merely a self-recognition by the same?

The assertion of the equiprimordiality of each term of every dialectical opposition renders the Absolute as Totality, as the identity of identity and difference, the unity of unity and multiplicity, the sameness of sameness and otherness.[13] The synthesizing activity of the *Aufhebung* (negation, preservation, supersession) always returns to the beginning, to the sheer immediacy of identity present in and to natural consciousness, that is, of sense-certainty. The totality is identical with itself (and thus with its other) from the beginning. Philosophical consciousness is the recognition of this simple yet complex point.

IV

The concept of the *Aufhebung* is the cornerstone of Hegel's thought. However, it can be argued that it denies the full status of the Other as other insofar as the supersession is actually a self-mediation of consciousness by its own alterity of thought. Hegel admits this, though he holds that it does not preclude the integrity of the other in its alterity or of the Other in her or his alterity.

Does the concept of the *Aufhebung* conceal a latent *meta*violence upon which all other violence is predicated? If so, then as the absolute move of the absolute Idea, this condemns historical progress to the impetus of a necessary violence or conflict. But what founds the violence of history? Is it the commencement of the relation with the Other (*l'autrui*) through speech-action? Is the negation of the other (*l'autre*) a necessary dialectical stage in the self-realization of Spirit? Or is there is a pre-temporal originary violence that precedes any concrete historical violence, a violence whose essence lies in the logic of the Idea?

Violence, by Hegel's own admission, is unavoidable in the historical progression of Spirit. The concept itself contains the seed of violence insofar as it is primordially self-identical and always returns to itself as such.[14] And what is violence if not that which is directed towards the suppression or the negation of that which is other? If desire, as the manifestation of the power of the negative, is that which overcomes the separation between self and other, between the for-itself and the in-itself, is it not the very movement of violence? Here is questioned the claim of preserving the integrity of the difference of the other. Does Hegelian philosophy constitute an actual recognition of alterity at all?

The epistemological and metaphysical circularity of the concept reveals itself as a form of conceptual imperialism. Violence is done to Another not in the sense of negating the other (which is actually only an auto-negation), but in that the

Other is not recognized as being genuinely other. Consciousness' quest for recognition reveals itself as a narcissistic longing and self-fulfilling aggrandizement.

The apocalyptic vision of Spirit rests on the establishment of the total, universal State, no matter what the cost says Hegel, even the extreme violence of war. "War is the Spirit.... [W]hile, on the one hand, war makes the individual...feel the power of the negative, on the other hand, this negativity is prominent in war as that which preserves the whole."[15] Toward this one goal, posited as freedom itself, all becoming is subject. Is this the actual, albeit disguised, meaning of Hegel's dictum that Substance is Subject? Does Subject here truly denote subjectivity? Is the judgment that properly belongs to ethics that of history? These questions rest essentially on the status of the Absolute. Is it present in history as history; or, is it necessarily trans-historical? And if the latter is the case, does this imply a non-involved, non-praxis oriented theory of politics, or even the impossibility of such a project? On the metaphysical level, the question is that of the status of infinity. Is it recoverable in its totality as an object for thought? Or does the very impossibility of such a closure (on one level meaninglessness itself) convey a signification whose meaning is ethical and perfect? If there is no real distinction between the finite and the infinite as Hegel claims, then is he not correct in arguing for the inevitable perfection of history as politics?

V

Hegelian infinity is equiprimordial with the finite. The two terms cannot be thought separately as they derive meaning from their dialectical relation with each other. The two terms are also fundamentally different from the very outset. Were Hegel able to respond to the idea of infinity as it is proposed by Levinas, it might be: "In the very act of keeping the infinite pure and aloof from the finite, the infinite is only made finite."[16] But is it possible to assert an adequate correlation between a fundamentally ahistorical term (the idea of infinity) and a term that is steeped in historicity (finitude)? The alleged equiprimordiality of the two terms is the question here.

Hegel and Levinas are united in the essentially Greek position that holds the co-determination of metaphysical and political concepts. The definition of metaphysics as the non-conceptual mode of relation with the other in all its manifestations shifts the ancient complicity to that between ontology and politics. Levinasian metaphysics, the non-theoretical movement of Desire characterized as speech (dialectic in the Platonic sense) and not vision (Hegelian dialectic; phenomenology as ontology), is ethics. The opposition of ethics and politics opens *Totality and Infinity* and underscores its entire reading. Philosophy's task, says Levinas, is to avoid being deceived by morality, that is, to avoid conflating ethics and politics. But is that not to deny the very intersection of ideas that will bring peace? Is not the very separation of these fundamental terms the root of violence? What is the danger of such a union?

The theme of war is introduced in the opening pages of *Totality and Infinity* and the reader suspects that this theme will be continued throughout the remainder of the work. Curiously enough, the topic is not engaged again until the final sections of the study, and then only briefly. Rather, what follows in the first section of the work is an analysis of the ontological structures that foster such systematic violence. The thematic of the violence that is war subtends the entire work. Yet war does not need to be proved. "Does not lucidity, the mind's openness upon the true, consist in catching sight of the permanent possibility of war?...The visage of being that shows itself in war is fixed in the concept of *totality* which dominates Western philosophy" (*TeI* 5/*TI* 21). War issues forth in a totalizing order in which all existents are implicated. To be is to be in conflict. Nietzsche's thesis that being is will to power is not denied. History is invariably violent; an absolute peace can only be an eschatology—a relationship with radical alterity.

The respect for and maintenance of plurality constitutes the essence of the ethical relation since, with the introduction of the enigmatic term *illeity* (*EDE* 199f), of the third party, justice enters the world. Illeity signifies the "way of leaving the alternatives of Being" (*EDE* 214/*CPP* 71) via the trace of the absolutely other. Plurality is alterity itself; the metaphysical One is social (historical) multiplicity. Hegelian philosophy, with its supreme insistence on *uni*versality, subordinates all to the achievement of the homogeneous State. According to Levinas:

> Idealism completely carried out reduces all ethics to politics. The Other and the I function as elements of an ideal calculus, receive from this calculus their real being, and approach one another under the dominion of ideal necessities which traverse them from all sides. They play the role of moments in a system, and not that of origin. Political society appears as a plurality that expresses the multiplicity of the articulation of a system.... [This] multiplicity rests in fact only on the hope of happiness [which] maintains pluralism in the society of minds. In this world without multiplicity language loses all social significance; interlocutors renounce their unicity not in desiring one another but in desiring the universal. (*TeI* 239/*TI* 216–17)

Levinas' assessment is born out in Hegel's own words. In the chapter on "Being-for-self" in the *Science of Logic*, plurality is an "inessential" moment that does not designate the other and hence, is not accorded a full measure of reality:

> Thus plurality appears not as an *otherness*, but as a determination completely external to the one. The one, in repelling itself, remains self-related, like that which to begin with is taken as repelled. That the ones are related to one another as *others*, are brought together into the determinateness of plurality, does not therefore concern the ones. If plurality were a relation of the ones themselves to one another then they would limit one another and there would be affirmatively present in them a being-for-other. Their relation—and this they have through their *implicit* unity—as here *posited* is determined as none: it is again the previously posited *void*.[17]

The concrete reality of this logic, for Hegel, is that social plurality, the stuff of ethics, is subsumed in his system under the thematic of citizenry in the universal homogeneous political State.

Yet the origin and function of politics is necessary and inescapable. Neither Hegel nor Levinas would deny this. If politics is opposed to ethics, if freedom is superordinate to justice, does this not deny the *pre*-ontological signification of the face to face, the very relation that opens the possibility, not only of political discourse, but of all discourse? Levinas claims that the face to face relation escapes comprehension by either formal or dialectical logic. Such reason manifests itself in the ontological concept of unity, "an ancient privilege...affirmed from Parmenides to Spinoza and Hegel" (*TeI* 105/*TI* 102). Formal or traditional logic is based on the law of non-contradiction whereas dialectical logic is understood as the coordination or interrelation of terms into a comprehensible totality. Dialectical logic purports to maintain the separation and identity of each term in the relation while simultaneously asserting the mutual co-identity of each term. Dialectical logic does not merely negate the truth content of formal logic; it surpasses (*aufgehoben*) the ability of formal logic to affirm the wholeness of the relation. Both formal and dialectical logic are inadequate or deficient in their attempt to grasp the nature of alterity. They are both logics of the *same*.

The unity that is the legacy of Western ontology is manifest as two similar yet separate movements of thought. The first, to use terms employed by Levinas in *Totality and Infinity*, is the "way of the same" and the second is the "ontology of totality." They are not synonymous. The question here is whether Hegel effects a move in his system from the former to the latter term. If so, then this is the origin and locus of the violence of the concept that Levinas claims grounds concrete intersubjective violence. To use the language of the *Phenomenology*, this movement would be that of desire, the modality of becoming that closes the gap between the for-itself and the in-itself thus supplying consciousness with the necessary adequate concept (totality) requisite for the transition to self-consciousness or Spirit.

Though implicated in the very ontological structure that fosters war, the logic that belongs to sameness is decidedly different from the dominating concept of totality that, says Levinas, "engenders war at its most primordial level." The logic of the same does not found the violence of war.[18] Subjectivity is the way of the same; and Levinas will present his philosophy as a "defense of subjectivity" (*TeI* 11/*TI* 26). This is not to promote the way of the same (freedom) as the highest of ideals, the tendency of Western thinking from Socrates to Hegel. The enemy here is not the freedom of the individual. There is a prior, more elevated position with regard to the Other that precedes freedom—the unconditional responsibility of *justice*. War actually "destroys the identity of the same" rather than ensuring its survival (*TeI* 6/*TI* 21).

VI

The structures of intentionality[19] and representation[20] also belong to the category of the same (esp. *TeI* 127–51/*TI* 122–42). Representation masks the truth that it dissimulates, that being is conflictual. It does not found the violence that is war. Representation is the yea-sayer of πόλεμος. It does not question; it merely obeys. Representation, which is founded on the concept of totality, bestows meaning for individual existents. It assumes the form of the State and promises full freedom for its constituents.

Opposed to the philosophical concept of representation is the non-philosophical modality of enjoyment (*jouissance*) (*TeI* 111f/*TI* 109f). This is what truly measures the dimension of interiority and of subjectivity, and not the theoretical way of representation. Now it is not within the scope of the present work to offer an extended assessment of Levinas' views on enjoyment; the preeminent concern here is with the critique of the self-proclaimed ability of theory or reason to comprehend the Absolute. Both ethics and politics are predicated upon this endeavor, or on the lack thereof. The argument with the philosophers of light is that of the relation between eternity and time; it is the old debate between the Jew and the Greek.

War presupposes the transcendence that the face signifies; it is actually founded on the same structure that makes peace a possibility.

> The exclusion of violence by beings susceptible of being integrated into a totality is not equivalent to peace. Totality absorbs the multiplicity of beings, which peace implies. Only beings capable of war can rise to peace. War like peace presupposes beings structured otherwise than as parts of a totality. War therefore is to be distinguished from the logical opposition of the *one* and the *other* by which both are defined within a totality open to a panoramic view, to which they would owe their very opposition (*TeI* 245/*TI* 222).

This sentiment is echoed by Buber who said that "the great peace is not merely the absence of war."[21] In both war and peace, there is a refusal of the totalizing structure of the State as law-giving community. War is not the entering into the totality; it is the willful rejection of the totality (community) by the I or ego—though not of relationship, says Levinas, "since in war the adversaries seek out one another" (*TeI* 246/*TI* 223). In war the self seeks to transcend the totality as separate, that is, by claiming to be infinite. This is the origin of violence. In attempting to recover infinity as a concept for consciousness, the Other is in turn conceptualized as an object thus denying the basis for any true mutual recognition to occur. Hegelian recognition is therefore essentially solipsistic. Peace, on the other hand, rejects the totality as a means of unification. The whole, if it is to be ethical, can only be a differential social multiplicity, in which case, it is also a refusal of the sameness of totality. Until the ἔσχατον, the State is a necessary evil.[22]

VII

The idea of infinity is the idea of metaphysics, the movement of Desire. It is a *revealed* idea, though not in the sense of natural religion. Infinity is not a concept; it is found in the face of the Other, the desired, which arouses the movement of Desire, "a measure through the very impossibility of measure" (*TeI* 56/*TI* 62). Infinity is not an object (though certainly such parallels can be drawn, as will be seen in Adorno's analysis).

Desire originates from its object; need arises from the subject (*TeI* 56/*TI* 62). The absolutely other, the Other, is desired precisely because alterity transcends every category of thought. Need, on the other hand, implies a lack or deficiency on the part of the selfsame. The object of Desire, the infinitely other, is unattainable by possession. Desire does not seek to fill the void of the soul as does need. There is no emptiness or lack to which Desire is correlate. Desire is the movement towards the Infinite, a response to Others.

Perhaps the most profound expression of Desire in Levinas is to be found in the movement of ἔρος delineated in the third section of *Totality and Infinity*. Ἔρος is not desire in the sense that the two shall become one but rather in that one desires the beloved precisely because the beloved is different than the self. Thus is interest perpetually aroused, as it were, since the Other is always the embodiment of surprise. Even the sexual union, coitus, the supreme erotic act, does not produce a union or totality of the being of the self and the Other. It may produce a third, and this is the wonder of fecundity: that the parents are able to produce beings which, though a part of them are, nevertheless, completely independent in their will from them. In fecundity the originary relationship between the same and the other, that is, atheism, is perpetually renewed and reenacted as "an ipseity, in the fundamental phenomenon of enjoyment. One can call atheism this separation so complete that the separated being maintains itself in existence all by itself, without participating in the Being from which it is separated…" (*TeI* 52/*TI* 58). And putting it in terms of the relation to the absolutely other, Levinas continues:

> By atheism we thus understand a postion prior to both the negation and the affirmation of the divine, the breaking with participation by which the I posits itself as the same and as I. It is certainly a great glory for the creator to have set up a being capable of atheism, a being which, without having been *causa sui*, has an independent view and word and is at home with itself (*TeI* 52/*TI* 58–59).

Levinas' atheism signifies not the disbelief in the divine but rather, the a-theistic *will*, the wonder of the truly unique and subjective creating will, a notion to which Nietzsche has contributed much. Religion and atheism go hand in hand for Levinas. The absolutely other nowise resembles for Levinas the theistic deity of ontotheological metaphysics. The desire for God is not the desire for unity with the divine, for the collapse of our subjectivity into a greater subjectivity. Subjectivity is what it is precisely because it is not the eternally infinite. Yet, by the very fact that there is subjectivity, the trace of the Infinite is present in the face, even in its absence as a total presence. The eternal is infinitely separate from the temporal; eternality and temporality do not form a totality as they do in Hegel who, in a sense, baptizes human consciousness as divine consciousness.

The movement of Desire is not commensurate with the fulfillment or attainment of desire in the Hegelian sense of the term. As with Hegel, desire is the language that bridges the distance or separation between self and other. The self and the Other are paradoxically absolutely separated and absolutely proximate to each other. This is the "miracle" of finite, atheistic existence.

Such a conception of infinity is not to be construed as synonymous with the concept (*Begriff*), nor as resembling the Idea (*Idee*). The idea of infinity contains no pre-coded logic of which it is the seed. Its "logos" is non-teleological, non-grounding, and non-totalizing. Its signification lies precisely in its inability to be comprehended. The idea of infinity is non-constituted and makes possible the non-violent, passive receptivity of relationships between free individuals. But such an infinity, Hegel would assert, is only an empty and abstract concept. Genuine or true infinity is able to be interiorized (*er-innern*), superseding (*aufgehoben*) the distance or separation between its form and content. Accordingly, Levinas' conception of Desire as the desire for the Infinite would be dismissed as spurious by Hegel inasmuch as he would interpret such a conception of infinity as the mere positing of the infinite over against the finite.

Still, Levinas claims that the infinite exceeds the totality of finite existence, "overflows the thought that thinks it [*déborde la pensée qui le pense*]" (*TeI* 10/*TI* 25). An historical infinite, that is, an infinite recoverable in history as and by thought, is a (non) conception of infinity which remains forever incomprehensible. The conflation of subject and object, self and Other, into a unitary theoretical structure (*Begriff*) is the objectification and subsequent elevation of subjectivity as a transcendent ideal. The self-proclaimed sovereignty of the subject as Spirit results in the violent imperialism of theory. The subordination of infinity to the concept thought prioritizes the subject (*ego cogitans*) and minimizes the function or status of the object (other). Infinity, thought as absolutely separated alterity, assigns a certain (negative? non? pre?) dialectical primacy to the object over that of the subject.

VIII

Hegelian metaphysics defines the Absolute as the simultaneously total and infinite. The two terms are not mutually exclusive (the fault of previous metaphysical forms). The opposite term of infinity is finitude, and not totality. This difference in interpretation is the focus of Levinas' criticism. Infinity is accessible to consciousness because it is temporally present in a non-theoretical manner. Infinity is revealed in the face of the Other and is produced within consciousness as the idea (not concept) of infinity. The collapse of infinity and finitude into a speculative unity betrays the transcendence that infinity implies and so constitutes the initial intersubjective violence. The content of the Infinite overflows or surpasses the form of its concept thus signifying the irreducible difference or distance that exists within being between the same (*la même*) and the other (*l'autre*). "The distance that separates *ideatum* and idea here constitutes the content of the *ideatum* itself.... The transcendent is the sole *ideatum* of which there can only be an idea within us; it is infinitely removed from its idea, that is, exterior, because it is infinite" (*TeI* 40–41/*TI* 49). The question is whether consciousness is able to comprehend, and not merely to apprehend, infinity.

The absolute totality, claims Hegel, is the universal simple selfsameness of identity and difference. But if infinity and totality are mutually inclusive, does this not mean that infinity essentially belongs to the order of the same and does not present itself to thought as its other? That is, if infinity is the thought that thought itself cannot contain (Spirit is, after all, only real in its actualization in historical self-consciousness, a finitude), is not the Infinite alterity itself and not the same?

Or are the two terms truly reciprocal, and the above questions true and false simultaneously?

In the *Logic*, reciprocity is understood in terms of the causal nexus. The parts and the whole of the Idea are co-determining. This principle applies also to the nature of the State and the functions of the social totality. Hegel's position on causality, like that espoused by the Buddha, is circular in form. Unlike his Indian predecessor, however, Hegel understands such a relation to be graspable by thought if understood in terms of the concept (*Begriff*). This is where Hegel claims to surpass all previous metaphysical and religious forms. The infinite circularity of cause and effect repeals the infinite regress of the past and constitutes the true infinite as a self-determining totality. Reciprocal cause and effect does not mean that the effect is also the cause of the cause. It means that in every causal relation each term acts as both cause and effect for other relational terms. The causal reciprocity is the element of necessity in Hegelian dialectics. Without such reciprocity, absolute knowing would be an impossibility.

Are reciprocity and symmetry synonymous terms? The teleology of Spirit reveals an asymmetry of terms in that the subject/self is accorded a privileged position with regard to the object/other. Adorno's analysis in *Negative Dialectics* demonstrates this to be the case. Levinas maintains that the ethical relation must be acknowledged as *asymmetrical* if it is to remain ethical. Hegel's violence, therefore, consists of a double violence. Not only is the fundamental asymmetry of terms denied in an alleged totality of meaning, but the asymmetry is weighted in favor of a preponderance of the *subject* (to invert Adorno's phrase). The violence of totality lies in its simulated order; and on top of that, as an order that sees itself as primordial and as ground.

The reciprocity that is founded and necessitated both logically and existentially (and for Hegel, the terms are not contradictory) between the terms "subject-self" and "object-other" does not contain the symmetry that dialectical thought supposes it does in the Levinasian analysis. The constitution of intersubjectivity does not lie in the mere mutual recognition of self and other, a relation predicated upon a presumed identity of terms. It is founded on the asymmetrical relation between being and the Absolute (other). First alluded to by Plato in his formulation of the transcendence of the Good, this asymmetry "should have served as a foundation for a pluralist philosophy in which the plurality of being would not disappear into the unity of number nor be integrated into a totality" (*TeI* 79/*TI* 80). Subjectivity is not a mutually shared experience; if it were, it would no longer be subjective, unique. The essence of subjectivity lies in the promotion and maintenance of distance or separation that exists between the self and the Other. Desire is the mode of relation between the self and the Other that assures this separation. Desire does not suffice as the adequate concept or the means to that concept that closes the distance.

Hegel and Levinas, however, are united in their conviction that the meaning of subjectivity lies in intersubjectivity. It has been argued by Kojève that the essence of subjectivity and intersubjectivity lies in the dialectic of lordship and bondage.[23] Now, Hegel claims in the *Phenomenology* that desire ends in the action, the *work*, of mutual recognition and forgiveness. Desire (*Begierde*) is a negation in that it wishes to fill a lack or void. This gap is being-for-another and is the origin of the "thingish I" of desire. Once the subject (self) appropriates the object (other), the desire is eradicated and the self becomes complacent. Says Hegel:

> Desire has reserved to itself the pure negating of the object and thereby its unalloyed feeling of self. But that is the reason why this satisfaction is itself only a fleeting one, for it lacks the side of objectivity and permanence. Work, on the other hand, is desire held in check, fleetingness staved off; in other words, work forms and shapes the thing.[24]

To this Kojève maintains that the only way the alterity of the object can avoid extinction is to replace the desire for the object with the desire for another desire which is not consumable. This desire is within the self and, since the other is merely another self, within the other as well. The dialectic of desire, which culminates in mutual forgiveness, is a double process.

The violence which shows itself in war is able to be overcome, if not actually, at least theoretically in the Hegelian framework. Transcendence occurs in and through the reciprocal action of confession and forgiveness.[25] Since this dialectic must be enacted in order to be fully manifest, it appears that Hegel has at last reconciled the divisive dualism between action and thought and between the self and the other. But is Hegel's philosophy violent insofar as the system is predicated upon the concept of totality which, even though it resembles the way of the same, is not identical with it and thus gives rise to war at its most foundational level, that of the concept? The logic of the same is an internal logic; violence arises in its externalization as the ontology of totality. But how is the metaphysical asymmetry of the ethical relation to be maintained along with the reciprocity requisite for the legal working of justice?[26] This is the problem facing the legal and political application of Levinas' social ethics.

IX

Perhaps even more pressing for Levinas is the question of historical concreteness. Levinas is open to criticism for an alleged a-historicism of thought—that is, for taking recourse to what is admittedly (in many but not all respects) an essentially *trans*historical term. The "glory of the Infinite" lies in its absolute separation from the same, from the totality of history. Still, "one wonders," says Derrida, "whether history itself does not begin with this relationship to the other which Levinas places beyond history."[27]

The question of history cannot be divorced from the status of politics, as Hegel so brilliantly demonstrates. Levinas' alleged ahistoricity rests upon the radical and absolute separation or distinction he draws between the ego and the non-ego, the same and the other. On this difference Derrida says:

> Now, in *Totality and Infinity*, where the categories of the same and the other return in force, the *vis demonstrandi* and the very energy of the break with tradition is precisely the adequation of ego to the same, and of Others to the other. Without using

> these terms himself, Levinas often warned us against confusing *identity* and *ipseity*, same and ego: *idem* and *ipse*. This confusion, which, in a certain way, is immediately practiced by the Greek concept of αὐτός and the German concept of *selbst*, does not occur as spontaneously in French; nevertheless, it returns as a kind of silent axiom in *Totality and Infinity*.[28]

The question here is whether, and if so, how, the difference between the above mentioned terms manifests itself in the difference between the ethical and the political.

Separation, which is difference itself, is "better" than unity claims Levinas. The (logically) inevitable outcome of the political agenda of idealism, which reduces all ethics to politics, is not only the centralization of government and, possibly, of the reserves of capital (Europe today bears witness to this event); it is also the leveling[29] of the diversity of cultures and languages. In short, it negates the very aspects of human existence that make it interesting. Ontological order, in its assertion that it is the cosmic and worldly order, denies difference its full measure. In so doing, and in realizing itself politically and socially (and can the two terms be thought separately anymore?), it leads to war and, eventually, to nihilism.

Are we not already at this stage of nihilism, as Nietzsche so forcefully reminds us? Is the only road to peace that of war? Are our Alexanders, Caesars, Napoleons, and Hitlers essentially correct, having lacked only the wisdom of a world philosopher as grand vizier to counsel them? If Hegel means only the formation of nation-states when he speaks of universal (global) citizenry, then does this not perpetually condemn humanity to the economy of violence that is war?[30]

Hegel, of course, would answer the above questions decidedly in the negative. The "cunning of reason," a central concept taken up and given fuller expression by Marx, prohibits such blatantly fascist or totalitarian tendencies from becoming *permanently* manifest. Human consciousness is not the only agency that brings about the freedom that is the telos of history. The self-conscious activity of Spirit operates according to its own agenda; human consciousness is but a moment of that greater consciousness. The whole purpose of the Hegelian project is precisely to make the consciousness that both subtends and is Spirit (which is to say, the transcendence of the *Aufhebung*) graspable by human consciousness. If this is possible, then the violence endemic to intersubjective being can be realized as what it is (a theodicy), and the effort to overcome it can finally commence with the whole of history to provide the necessary impetus.

But an ethical metaphysics is not a moral theory to which politics can conform. The moment the ethical relation, the face to face, is joined by the third party, illeity, ethics enters the domain of politics and becomes morality. Ethics is defined as the relation between the self and the Other that precedes categorization by thought. Morality, on the other hand, is the creation of values by the self (individual or collective), for the self. Morality sits at the feet of ethics for Levinas. Only when morality, as politics, asserts itself as ethical, as absolute, does the violence towards the other come fully into play. Morality must always remain free in order to avoid the totalizing domination of the State and other forms of the same. This is why Nietzsche, for instance, insists upon the revaluation of all values; why he designates himself an *immoralist.* The self-creation of morality, that is, freedom par excellence, is the essence of subjective existence. It is this very liberty that Levinas seeks to preserve in the ethical relation.

7

MystiGround

Hegel's philosophy, in line with that of modernity, can be characterized as the effort to bring to light all that has been previously held to be shrouded in the darkness of metaphysical mystery. But does he accomplish this in the end? This question rests on the status of the concept of *Trieb* (drive, impulse, urge) and its relation to the concept of *Unendlichkeit* (infinity). To what extent does the concept of *Trieb* and its kenotic process of self-revealing alterity as identity prefigure contemporary or postmodern philosophical concerns with radical difference and otherness? How does Hegel's conception of infinity serve as a preparation for contemporary assessments of otherness as they affect the determination of a ground (*Grund*) for ethical subjectivity and intersubjectivity? In other words, what are the contributions that Hegel makes to more recent interrogations into the ethical possibilities of absolute alterity, non-closure, and a radical "universal difference [*allegemein Unterscheid*]"?[1]

I

The attempt to break free of what is often construed as the limiting, totalizing framework of the dialectic expresses itself in the language of existential phenomenology as the question of the other. In the progression of Spirit's quest for self-consciousness and absolute knowing, substance is (determined as) subject, and the otherness that is continually encountered by the self in this movement reveals itself in the end as the projection of selfsame consciousness upon the object of reflection, though the alterity of the object remains intact or preserved. This realization is necessitated upon the mediation of the intersubjective relation by alterity through the other's recognition of the self as another self-consciousness. Hegel concludes that the meaning of individual existence is inseparable from that of the collective social totality, or as Husserl later expresses it, following the critiques of Heidegger and Sartre, that transcendental subjectivity is intersubjectivity.[2]

It is beginning with Hegel that the relation between the self and the other is truly on the brink of being philosophically comprehended and not merely posited through faith, intuition, or duty. Hegel's aim is to arrive at a presuppositionless starting-point. He is arguably the most profound modern thinker of non-mystery and identity; and yet, he is also a precursor to postmodernity with its insistence on the priority of difference, chaos, and non-closure; and with that, the possibility of an absolute alterity. This differential prehension is found in the unfathomable notion of *Trieb*, the source from which the Idea derives its very power and existence. Rarely explicated by philosophers, most likely due to its religious or theological implications, the metaphysical significance of *Trieb*, for Hegel, connects the inexplicable with the domain of rational thinking that denotes philosophy even in its postmodern vestiges.

Hegel is rightly construed, perhaps most forcibly so by Heidegger, as that thinker who brings Western metaphysics both to its completion and to the brink of its own self-destruction or self-overcoming. This dual distinction, however, is not enigmatic but dialectical and, ultimately, revolves around the status of the relation between the finite and the infinite. Hegel fulfills the metaphysical project originated by the classical Greeks by advancing the notion of speculative rational thinking connected with the ideas of the infinite and the unconditioned. Yet he also stands at the very threshold of modernity's closure in his insistence that metaphysics from Plato to Kant has erred in its continual opposition to the unity and totality of the infinite and the finite. However, despite the fact that Hegel is largely responsible for bringing European and Continental thinking to their current positions, he does not cross over into the rhizomatic subterranean corridors of postmodernity precisely because he refuses to abandon the overarching thesis of his work, namely, the sovereignty of reason.

The rejection of universal reason and the affirmation of originary genetic difference (will to power) signals Nietzsche's role as perhaps the first truly *post*-modern thinker, but he would not have come to this point had it not been for Hegel and the pursuant climate of thinking Hegel inaugurated. The celebrated death of God and the consequential end of philosophy (Heidegger) does not lay to rest the question of the status of infinity. Buddha's cavernous shadow and the sepulchral edifices of European civilization linger still. The relation between the finite and the infinite remains a major hurdle for philosophy. The thinking of Hegel has proven decisive for contemporary treatments of this question since it is he who definitively demonstrates the limitations of traditional conceptions of the understanding (*Verstand*), and how classical metaphysics has invariably taken recourse to such intellection in its attempts to grasp and define the existence of God and the relation between Being and beings.

Transcendence is both eradicated and given a new impetus in Hegel's philosophy much in the manner that Luther, arguably the first modern dialectician, both destroys and revitalizes dogmatic ecclesiology. The meaning of transcendence becomes immanently finite and the problem of infinity becomes increasingly downplayed or ignored in numerous variants of post-Hegelian thinking, for example, phenomenology, existentialism, and poststructuralism. But despite these attempts to radically finitize philosophy, the ancient questions of infinity and transcendence are given new impetus in the thinking of Levinas, whose assessment of the violent ontological legacy of the West is inseparable from the tradition of modern dialectical thinking.

Levinas' interpretation of the relation between alterity and infinity serves to assist in the task of locating within Hegel's philosophy those elements that necessitate a rereading of his philosophy in order to address the concerns of contemporary thinking. Intersubjectivity cannot be properly valuated on an ethical level unless the force of this metaphysical demand or command is both theoretically and existentially grasped, that is, realized in the field of concrete social relations as the phenomenon of the interpersonal face to face. This very concretion of philosophy, Hegel will claim, is totally present in speculative dialectical logic. But whether in fact he accomplishes this process of concretion, or whether his thought is limited to the abstraction of pure cognition, remains to be determined; however, it once again brings to light the issue of the status of infinity.

II

Can the concept of infinity be concretely comprehended in the totality of thinking itself, in the unity of the individual and the collective social whole, realized historically as the free political state? If so, then perhaps Hegel is correct in assuming that this infinite is none other than the realization of the concept of God, the "absolute truth" of which "religion" is the final arbiter and testament. This is contingent upon the concept of infinity being adequate to its *ideatum.*

The philosophical understanding of infinity and transcendence are inextricably bound with the domain of religious inquiry in Hegel's thinking. Hegel's Christian-influenced yet pantheistic philosophy is, like Spinoza's, often subject to the charge of atheism, either pejoratively by theologians or metaphysicians, or more positively as a sign of revolutionary overcoming as, for example, in Kojève. Hegel addresses this in his 1827 lectures on the philosophy of religion. What is generally at issue is the status of actuality (*Wirklichkeit*). The charge of atheism often confines one within the prejudices of *Verstand* and finitude since it is not the actuality of things in the empirical world but rather, the actuality of the concept of God or the Absolute, which permeates and subtends all corporeal and non-corporeal entities and yet is not identical with them, that is denoted by *Wirklichkeit.*[3]

Hegel's prefiguring of the contemporary concerns of radical difference and absolute alterity lies in the crucial question of the status of the presence and/or absence of the infinite in the finite horizons of subjective experience. Hegelian thinking is characterized by its insistence that the Absolute is properly conceived as the unity of the subjective and the objective, the sameness of the same and other, the identity of identity and difference, the totality of the finite and the infinite. "The True is the whole"[4] and the whole is the Absolute which, as Spirit, is "the most *sublime* notion."[5] Any philosophical knowing is ultimately predicated upon the fact that "subjectively religion alone is the absolutely true knowledge."[6] Not that a religious predilection is requisite for philosophical exploration, but Hegel qualifies the relation between religion and the movement toward philosophical knowledge as subjective, not objective. That is to say, even though religion aspires to the Infinite, to truth in and for itself, to God, it nevertheless occurs as a subjective, finite thought-configuration.

Hegel claims to surpass all previous forms of thought insofar as it is he who first recognizes that the truth of Spirit is scientific, which is to say philosophical, and is therefore both objectively grounded and grounding. "The course of philosophy leads to the point that the final result of all this is God.... This *One* is the result of philosophy. We make our beginning straightway from this result of philosophy."[7] Yet there is present in consciousness, prior to the development or overlapping (*übergreift*) of consciousness by self-consciousness and absolute knowing, a subjective sense or inkling of the indeterminate Idea (*Idee*) that is indistinguishable from *Trieb*. This primal urge or drive both propels (negation) and compels (desire) consciousness towards recognition of itself as another self-consciousness and so generates the moment of intersubjective awareness and moral and ethical sensibility. This subjective inkling or comportment is the religious apprehension of infinity which is objectively concretized as philosophy through the science of dialectical logic.

III

Is the primordial *Trieb* that empowers the Idea able to be grasped or comprehended by Reason historically externalized as Spirit; or does Hegel gloss over this point in the System precisely because of its mysterious nature? To be sure, there are a number of passages in the Hegelian text that expressly treat the concept of *Trieb*, but they are for the most part confined to delineating the more existential drives or impulses that move consciousness to its various moments of self-awareness. For instance, Hegel's most illuminating remarks on this are found neither in the *Science of Logic* nor the *Phenomenology of Spirit* (the only two books he actually wrote for publication), but in the introduction to the *Philosophy of Right*. In discussing the implicit immediate freedom of the will, Hegel states that

> the specific characteristics of the difference which the self-determining concept sets up within the will appear in the natural will as an immediately existing content, i.e., as the impulses (*die Triebe*), desires and inclinations, whereby the will finds itself determined in the course of nature. The content, together with the specific differences developed within it, arises from the rationality of the will and so is implicitly rational; but, poured out in this way into the mold of immediacy, it still lacks the form of rationality.[8]

The issue is the lack of rationality to be found in non-mediated immediacy. Hegel's whole philosophy professes to be a demonstration that rationality is a continually unfolding, developing process. The heart of rationality is the moment of dialectical mediation and the form of rationality is the concept (*Begriff*), the essence of which is the synthetic, superseding movement of the *Aufhebung*. Hegel must demonstrate the inherent rationality that subtends the movement of *Trieb* if the logic of the dialectic is to truly close upon itself thereby culminating in the genuine truth of absolute knowing; otherwise, his philosophy is nothing more than merely speculative, in the vulgar sense that he rejects. The uniqueness of his philosophy is that this demonstration is effected not as the starting-point for the science of logic, but as its telos.

But what of the differential mystery of *Trieb*, that "moment" of the beginning, of the Idea prior to its unveiling as nature and history, that Hegel's thinking as a whole seeks to eradicate or disclose once and for all?[9] Perhaps part of the mystery, when considered at its most elemental or foundational level, lies in the very definition of *Trieb* itself:

> An impulse [*Trieb*] is simply a uni-directional urge and thus has no measuring-rod in itself, and so this determination of its subordination or sacrifice is the contingent decision of the arbitrary will which, in deciding, may proceed either by using intelligence to calculate which impulse will give most satisfaction, or else in accordance with any other optional consideration.[10]

At the originary stage, *Trieb* is indeterminate and incomprehensible, and yet it is completely focused, "uni-directional," in the essential force of its movement. This primordial drive disseminates as the manifold particularity of impulses or urges in the subjective, finite will which manifests itself as the dialectical struggle for the self-satisfaction of these urges. However, continues Hegel, the "vague demand" for "the *purification* of impulses" necessitates that "the impulses should become the rational system of the will's volition. To grasp them like that, proceeding out of the concept of the will, is the content of the philosophical science of right."[11] Hegel is fully cognizant of the shadowy and ambivalent, though necessary, status of the concept of *Trieb* as the externalized expression of the Idea. But as he is unable to explicate *Trieb* on the originary metaphysical level, he is forced to treat the impulses, inclinations and urges on the more readily determinable level of the *will*, which in the language of the *Philosophy of Right* designates the form or concept (*Begriff*), as opposed to the content, of the Idea.[12] The status of the primal *Trieb* remains in abeyance and perhaps unavoidably so; but it is precisely for this reason it functions as a crucial marker for a postmodern consciousness.

IV

Given the indeterminateness of *Trieb* and its inability to provide an adequate starting point for the system, Hegelian logic is left in the position of demonstrating the truth of *Grund* as both result and beginning. This issue cannot be divorced from the issue of dialectical mediation. If mediation is present from the start within the logic of the Idea, then is unmediated immediacy truly unmediated? To put it another way, is mediation the actual dialectical *other* of immediacy? Is a rationally known absolute origin possible if there is no non-mediated immediacy?

The rationality implicit in the will, and in its drives and instincts, are determined as rational only after the dialectic has run its course and achieves its telos. Thus is *Trieb* inextricably connected with *Grund*. One of the principal concerns regarding Hegel's philosophy centers around the alleged presuppositionless circularity of speculative dialectic. The Idea and its moving force (*Trieb*) must be inherently rational if its truth content is to be demonstrated as such.

Perhaps Hegel's mark of genius is that he understands better than anyone before him the negative self-identical otherness of *Trieb* and the nature or essence of otherness in general.[13] Spirit (*Geist*) is propelled by the labor of the negative, that is, by the internal negation of the radical otherness of *Trieb* which is the primordial conflict or struggle of being with nothingness. *Kenosis*, as the self-emptying of the Idea or Godhead into its opposite (nature and history), is the concrete expression of *Trieb*, and along with *Trieb* constitutes the *Grund* of all life. *Trieb* is the absolute center of the primal urge which unfolds or irrupts as the infinite manifold particularity that is the essence of otherness. As the primal mystery itself, *Trieb* is the original identity which is at the same time the totally other out of which it establishes the fullness of its identity through the process of negative torment or what the mystical philosopher Jacob Böhme, a major source for Hegel's thinking, terms *Qual*.[14] This process of self-realization is the *kenosis* of *Trieb*. The two terms cannot be thought separately. The kenotic movement of *Trieb* is the early philosophical prefiguring of the death of God, what is termed at the very end of the *Phenomenology* the "Golgotha of absolute Spirit," the moment when substance is realized as subject and thus is fully and finally actualized or embodied as concrete sensual history. The otherness that Spirit comprehends as subject is actually its own objectivity; hence the logic of the Idea is circularly enclosed upon itself.

The whole of Hegel's philosophy would be meaningless if the above argument were not granted. Besides the apparent ambiguity or paradox regarding the thesis of implicit originary mediation and the contention that this mediation is *other* than unmediated immediacy, there arises the question of the origin of mediation itself, and with that, the deeper question of the origin of *Trieb*. And if it is the existence of the primal motivating force that is called into question, then so too must the existence of the Idea or Godhead itself (as Hegel understands it) be questioned, since the essence of a thing cannot exist independently of its being, and the essence of the Idea is *Trieb*, the kenotic process of negative, self-identical alterity that is the constitution of *Grund* and *Geist*.

V

It is here that the thinking of Levinas comes to bear on this rereading of Hegel. The force of Levinas' argument is based upon the ancient Judaic and Platonic premises of the ineffability of God and the Good. It is precisely the *non*-conceptual status of infinity that provides the idea (not to be confused with either *Idee* or *Begriff*) of the passive ethical resistance found in the face of the Other. Like Hegel, Levinas too rejects the foundations of traditional forms of metaphysics, but not on the basis of the permanent diremption of the finite and the infinite that characterizes the understanding (*Verstand*).[15] The search for the knowable absolute unitary origin, for the ground of Being, is the hallmark of metaphysics from antiquity through modernity; but Levinas breaks from many of his contemporaries insofar as he holds that radical difference and absolute alterity do not necessarily require the abandonment of the thesis of the primal genesis or origination of being, since created being (totality) is but the trace of the passing of the infinitely other.

Does Hegel's concept of *Trieb* then bear closer resemblance to Levinas' understanding of infinity than would initially appear to be the case? This question will be approached via a brief consideration of Hegel's construal of the concept of infinity and what distinguishes it from earlier conceptions in the history of philosophy, specifically Kant's, before contrasting it with Levinas' interpretation of infinity. At stake is the clarification of the relation between ethics and *Grund.*

Hegel's logic claims superiority over traditional or formal logic in that formal logic does not begin from a critical, presuppositionless standpoint. Formal logic asserts the permanent diremption of the infinite and the finite. But for Hegel, the question of origin is that of the end, and vice-versa:

> The image of the progress to infinity is the *straight line,* at the two points of which alone the infinite is, and always only is where the line—which is determinate being—is not, and which goes *out beyond* to this negation to its determinative being, that is, to the indeterminate; the image of true infinity, bent back upon itself, becomes the *circle,* the line which has reached itself, which is closed and wholly present, without *beginning* and *end.*[16]

If the truth (*Wahrheit*) of Being is indeed a "circle of circles,"[17] then the question of teleology cannot be separated from that of *Grund,* and especially not in Hegelian dialectics. The telos of Spirit is the return via mediation to the beginning.

The infinite of dialectical logic (*Vernunft*) differs from the infinite of formal logic (*Verstand*), which is only a "*finitized* infinite."[18] The understanding (*Verstand*) is confined to an erroneous conception of infinity because it perpetually questions and criticizes the notion of the unity of the infinite and the finite. As such, the understanding continually oscillates between the two determinations of the moments of unity and separation, without reconciliation.

The superseding (*aufheben*) of the infinite as the affirmative negation of the infinite and of the finite as a unitary process constitutes, for Hegel, the genuine infinite. As the negation of the negation (finitude), the infinite is becoming; it is the self-overcoming of limited being. This is the realization of Spirit as freedom, historically actualized as the homogenous political state. The infinite does not stand as completed and superior to finitude as beyond being in the Platonic sense. Being is the infinite becoming of finite being. The infinite is the negation of the finite. The finite and the infinite stand in a relation of qualitative determinate difference to each other while, at the same time, negating and transcending their difference or limitation thus becoming infinite. Infinity is "the indeterminate void, the beyond of the finite."[19] But what is the status of this "beyond" (*das Jenseits*)? Since the infinite is characterized as a circle, then there is no beyond, no radical difference. The finite and the infinite are connected by the very negation that separates and distinguishes them from each other. Each acts as the limitation of the other, but at the same time, each term dissociates itself from the other as its limit, as its non-being, and "as qualitatively separate from it, posits it as *another being* outside it."[20]

Hegel claims to overcome (*aufheben*) the continual oscillation of the finite and the infinite that constitutes for him the spurious or bad infinite. This is precisely the point where Kant's critical philosophy remains fixed when he determines that the transcendental object remains an unknown. Trying to avoid the mere alternation of terms, Hegel claims that the connection between the finite and the infinite is external but essential. Each term needs the other in order to be what it is. The true infinite is a "finite infinite" and an "infinitized finite."[21] Infinity thus reveals itself to consciousness as finitude; it is only the self-transcendence of the finite and as such, it is the affirmative negative. The finite is the infinitely finite. The infinite and the finite are the same, an observation made nearly four hundred years earlier by Cusanus.[22]

Furthermore, the universal substance in Hegel's absolute idealism is realized as subject since "in the negative unity of the Idea (*Idee*) the Infinite overlaps (*übergreift*) and includes the finite, thought overlaps being, subjectivity overlaps objectivity."[23] The infinite return of consciousness to itself mediated by otherness demonstrates the priority that is assigned to the selfsame subject. Subject is determined as the truth of substance and so transcends what is just the object, though the difference between subject and object is purportedly maintained in the unity of the Idea.

Finally, the infinite as posited by *Verstand* is rejected by Hegel precisely on the grounds of dependency:

> The answer to the question: How does the infinite become finite? is this: That there is not an infinite which is first of all infinite and only subsequently has the *need* to become finite, to go forth into finitude; on the contrary, it is on its own account just as much finite as infinite.[24]

This dependent "need to become finite" is *Trieb*, the primal urge or drive that propels the dialectic and constitutes the very power and identity of the Idea. The infinite in itself includes the finite; it is the unity of itself and its other. Creation *ex nihilo* is not only untenable; it is impossible. An otherness that remains intact as otherness is, likewise, an impossibility.

Hegel simultaneously engages in the task of providing a scientific or objective basis for thinking as a whole and preserving a meaningful sense of subjectivity. Levinas too presents his philosophy in the preface to *Totality and Infinity* as a "defense of subjectivity" despite what one might construe as his initially apparent preponderance towards thinking absolute alterity as the constituting factor of subjective being. Here Levinas is within the scope of not modern but postmodern thinking, with its profound hermeneutics of suspicion towards traditional notions of the subject. However, he contends that it is precisely the "idea" of infinity, which again is neither synonymous with *Idee*, *Begriff*, nor *Vorstellung*, that arises in subjective consciousness through the concrete phenomenality of the face to face contact with the Other. The idea of infinity is not posited within the subject from without, from the other; it arises within consciousness and signifies the radical absolute difference that exists between the same and the other. This idea of infinity is the trace of an absolutely heteronomous past, unrecoverable in its totality by consciousness. Levinas agrees with Hegel that being or history is a totality and that infinity is present to consciousness within being; but they part ways over whether infinity transcends this totality and exists independently of being and consciousness.

Is infinity merely another concept among many, albeit the most exalted; or is it the idea in the Levinasian sense that signifies to consciousness the boundaries of its own limitations? Does this not also apply to the Hegelian concept of *Trieb*? If so, what does this entail for a rereading of Hegel's thinking (e.g., the notions of *Moralität* and *Sittlichkeit*), and for a reinterpretation of the ethical intersubjective relation? These are the questions that a rereading of the Hegelian concepts of infinity and *Trieb* entail for the contemporary philosophical consciousness.

Leaving aside the possibility that Hegel's philosophy may indeed be the correct articulation of the movement of consciousness, it is nevertheless a brilliant demonstration of the *imaginative* power of the intellect. Contemporary or postmodern thinking, all too aware of the pitfalls of a deconstructed rational tradition, finds much of its force in the imagination. The problems of philosophy have not changed, only the grounds to address and articulate the questions. Hegel's philosophy remains a primary source for current thinking playing a dual (dialectical?) role as both foil and springboard for the advancement of contemporary assessments of ethical valuation, among other concerns. The necessary yet mysterious function of *Trieb* serves to demonstrate this *differential tension* in his thinking so characteristic of and endemic to the "postmodern" mind.

8

TransGround

The movement of Western metaphysics has been, by and large, an attempt to render the concepts of transcendence and ground accessible to thinking. Beginning with Aristotle and continued by subsequent interpreters of the luminous project inaugurated by Plato, the question of the status of transcendence reaches its apex in the absolute idealism of Hegelian metaphysics which, simultaneously, also signals its conflation or confusion with the concrete immanence of finite historical becoming. And if metaphysical transcendence does not disappear or fully manifest itself as presence in Hegel, then it surely appears to be unresurrectable in the light/darkness of Nietzsche's pronouncement of the death of God. Yet in the wake of Husserl's attempt to establish a transcendental or eidetic phenomenology to ground empirical inquiry, two significant voices rise above the din of an encroaching philosophical and cultural nihilism in defense of the need to revaluate the meaning of transcendence—those of Heidegger and Levinas.[1] Not merely content with reinscribing in yet one more variation "form," "substance," or "presence," both thinkers seek to subvert the modernist project of rendering the invisible expressible to consciousness by focusing on that which has been either systematically rejected, downplayed, or ignored by philosophy as a whole. For Heidegger, especially in the context of his early work, it is the status of nothingness for the determination of the status of metaphysics; and for Levinas, it is the relation between infinity and alterity for the determination of the status of ethical intersubjectivity.

The thematic of the face to face relation is central to the thinking of Levinas and much of his work is in direct response to Heidegger's early philosophy, which is a partial continuation of Hegel's attempt to ground being in and as history (see *EDE* 53–107). The respective positions of Levinas and Heidegger concerning the face to face relation bear on questions of transcendence, the relation between identity and difference, separation and proximity, the ethics of care and responsibility, and finally, in Levinas, the conception of Desire as transcendence. These concerns are rooted in the relation between the primal concepts of nothingness and alterity.

The attention here will focus Levinas' relation to Heidegger's early writings since it is, by Levinas' own admission in a 1981 series of interviews with Philippe Nemo, precisely those themes in Heidegger from the period when *Being and Time* was written that most influenced the development of Levinas' own philosophy. Levinas acknowledges Heidegger's later thinking to be important primarily through his earlier work (*EeI* 33–38/*EI* 37–41). However, Levinas is far less charitable toward Heidegger in his earlier writing (1961). He grants that within Heidegger's "late philosophy" there is "an impossibility for power to maintain itself as monarchy, to ensure its total mastery...[since] the light of comprehension and truth streams into the darkness of incomprehension and non-truth; [and] power, *bound to mystery*, avows its impotence" (*TeI* 308/*TI* 275). Nevertheless, he asks, "What is the import of this admission?" since

> In Heidegger the human being apprehended as power remains, in reality, truth and light. Heidegger hence disposes of no notion to describe the relation with mystery, already implied in the finitude of *Dasein*. If power is at the same time impotence, it is by reference to this power that impotence is described (*TeI* 308/*TI* 276).

Clearly, Levinas is not convinced that Heidegger's own recognition of the failure to ground a fundamental ontology exonerates him from participation in the "ontology of power" that binds his earlier thinking with the course of Western philosophy as a whole. Still, this is a question that has yet to be definitively, if ever that is possible, decided upon. The task here is to stage an engagement between Levinas and Heidegger in a manner that goes beyond Levinas to advance what is positive and negative in their respective offerings with regard to the issue of (ethical) transcendence.

I

Heidegger continues Hegel's quest for a knowable ground of being in his early writing. As late as 1957 he says that "we are attempting to think of Being, as Hegel thought of it, in the same manner, i.e., to think of it historically."[2] Heidegger's endeavor is to find the ground of being in history. Seeking to free himself from the luminous tradition of presence, he sees the question of nothingness as the primary query of contemporary ontology as signifying the need for a new interpretation of transcendence or overcoming. Heidegger's aim is to overcome the dialectic that governs the Hegelian reading of truth and history, namely, the modern relation between substance and subject.[3] He addresses the status of metaphysics with what at first appears to be a very non-metaphysical question: What about nothing?[4] But does Heidegger slip back into the very onto-theological metaphysics he seeks to overcome by turning the nothing (*das Nichts*) into a ground (*Grund*)?

Dasein is placed within the whole of existence amidst a great number of other entities. The thrownness (*Geworfenheit*) into the totality of existence brings subjective being into immediate contact with the realm of metaphysics.[5] Every metaphysical question covers the whole range of metaphysics because it itself is the whole, though the whole of being is easily overlooked by everyday consciousness. Generally, this whole remains in the background and forms the horizon of personal subjective experience.[6]

The disclosure of the totality of being in the moods (*Stimmungen*) of boredom and joy, as the horizon of the world, is the "ground-phenomenon" of Dasein in which the *whole* becomes prominent and manifests itself. Now, despite the fact that one cannot comprehend or experience the totality of being, it is still possible to experience not only things and events, but the nothing as well within the whole. Nothing hides itself in the disclosure of the totality; yet, one is brought "face to face" with nothingness itself in the fundamental mood of *Angst.*[7]

The inability to put one's finger on the source of *Angst* is one of the debilitating features of this state of being. In the mood or feeling of *Angst* there is a movement similar to the Greek notion of nature (φύσις), that is, the swinging back and forth between presence and absence. Yet, while Dasein sinks into a feeling of "indifference," this does not mean that everything disappears; rather, the world is disclosed as finite.[8] Dasein too is revealed as finite in that it is inherently dependent on nothing and cannot of its own volition place itself directly in *Angst* and therefore in the "face" of nothing. In its disclosure, nothing is not detached from being; it is one with totality.[9] It is not nothingness that "oppresses" Dasein; rather, it is the world (*die Welt*) itself (the "most primordial something") that is oppressive as it is the possibility of the ready-to-hand in general.

Herein lies Heidegger's attempt to reinstate the hermeneutic sense of being found in Presocratism. *Angst* is a retreat from something and has its source in nothing. The nature of the nothing is to repel this departure. The oneness of nothingness as it slips away from totality is the essence and activity of nothing which is neither the annihilation of what-is nor something that emerges from negation. The disclosure of nothingness brings Dasein "face to face" with the sheer immediacy of being.

The projection into nothing belongs to the nature of subjectivity and makes it possible to relate to being and to ground the ontological possibility of selfhood and human freedom. Dasein does not project itself of its own will or volition; neither is projection an act of intellection.[10] Subjectivity is a project (*Entwurf*), always already projected and projecting. The projection into nothing reveals the radical finitude of subjective existence. In projection one experiences anxiety in the face of the world which, for Heidegger, is the truly radical other.

It is precisely the projection into nothing, Heidegger maintains, that overcomes the totality of what-is. As being which is always beyond itself in potentiality, subjectivity is transcendent "from the start." The transcendence inherent in subjective being is that of radical freedom which "individualizes Dasein and discloses it as *solus ipse*."[11] The projection into nothing leads one to metaphysics.

Dasein or subjectivity is revealed or disclosed as unique and individual in the relation that it has with death. Death is the ultimate other; but it is not the other's death that constitutes Dasein's horizon. One always dies alone. Since no one can take up another's death, Heidegger claims that this is what discloses the radical solitude of human existence.

But, asks Levinas, is not the anxiety or fear of Being just as primal as the anxiety or fear over death? (*DEE* 20/*EE* 20). The absolutely other is not the impersonal alterity of death. Death does not reveal or disclose subjectivity as *solus ipse* as it does for Heidegger. The meaning of subjective being is founded in the relation with the Other.

In one of Levinas' earliest writings, he opposes to Heidegger's notion of *Angst* the "horror" of the "there is" (*il y a*).[12] Levinas first formulates the theme of the *il y a* while imprisoned during the war. Though rarely mentioned in his later work, it is an always present underlying thematic. The *il y a* is an absence that is present to consciousness as the indeterminateness of being without existents; it is not nothingness or the nihil. Nor does the *il y a* resemble the generosity of Heidegger's notion of *es gibt*, since the *il y a* is impersonal (*EeI* 46/*EI* 48).[13] Rather, it grounds the solitude of separated existence.

The "rumbling" (*bruissement*) that accompanies the anonymous horror of impersonal being (*il y a*) is stopped by the relationship of responsibility that the self has with the Other (*EeI* 51/*EI* 52). For example, when the mother comforts the child in the middle of the night, the lonely terror of the previous moment vanishes. The *il y a* is analogous to the nocturnal. The relation with the Other is one of comfort, not of alienation as it is in Hobbes, Hegel, and Sartre. The filial relation is paradigmatic of the relation between the self and the Other (*TeI* 299–309/*TI* 267–80).

The horror that accompanies the *il y a* is not the *Angst* that Dasein feels in the "face" of the Nothing. "Horror is nowise an anxiety about death" (*DEE* 99/*EE* 61; also see *EDE* 85–89). Death most certainly promotes anxiety, but who feels horror in the wake of one's finitude? Death itself contains a certain banality. Horror signifies the thought of something determinate; it implies experience, or at least the thought of what is possible experientially. The horror that accompanies the *il y a* is produced by the sense that *something* is "out there." *Angst*, on the other hand, denotes a (non) relation with nothing; it subtends the attempt to comprehend nothingness (*DEE* 20/*EE* 19–20). The dialectic of being and nothingness in Hegel and Heidegger continues the traditional metaphysical (ontological) view that evil is merely lack or defect (nothing). Horror is produced in subjective existence by the threat of real evil. Nothingness does not kill; being does.

II

What is the significance of Heidegger's determination of the status of nothing for the phenomenon of intersubjectivity? Heidegger's acceptance of Hegel's proposition that being and nothing are one and the same offers a clue to answering this question. Nothing is not non-being as ontotheology claims; it is integral and necessary to the being of what-is. Nothing is being itself revealed as finitude.[14] The Hegelian concept of the sameness or identity of being and nothing manifests itself in the relation to other existing beings. The relation to alterity in general and to the personal Other in particular reveals itself as a relation of selfsameness. Others are essentially "like me," says Heidegger. Communication and understanding occur through a co-state-of-mind (*Mitbefindlichkeit*).[15] To be is to be alongside others.[16]

But if subjectivity is essentially uniform, what separates Dasein from other entities in the world, both like and different than itself? Heidegger maintains that the they-structure (*das Man*) is a primordial phenomenon belonging to the "positive constitution" of subjectivity. This self of everyday subjective being (*das Man*) is inauthentic being-in-the-world, the dispersion of the identity of the I or self which remains a constant throughout the self's manifold experiences.[17] The difference between inauthentic and authentic being appears to be the difference between social anonymity and radical egoistic solitude, between an object present-at-hand and a subject present-at-hand. To be is to be-alongside-with, but one does not merely exist in a world inhabited by other beings; one exists in relations with others. What does this say about the nature of intersubjectivity, of Dasein's relation (*Mitandersein*) with the Other?[18]

The aim in *Being and Time* is to address the problem of fundamental ontology, the question of the meaning of Being in general, which is to say, the comprehension of the meaning of existence. Since the projection into nothing discloses the totality of existence, the something that becomes intelligible and meaningful is *Sein.*[19] And as Being is being-in and being-with, what becomes graspable by thought is alterity. This alterity includes not only the world but the personal Other.

Herein lies the interface between metaphysics and intersubjectivity. But if to be-in is to be-with, then does the relation of the self to others reveal itself as a relation characterized by comprehension? Heidegger will say that "[b]ecause Dasein's Being is Being-with, its understanding of Being already implies the understanding of Others."[20] However, he will also maintain that the totality of beings cannot be fully comprehended by an act of pure intellect.[21] Levinas also admits this to be the case, but claims that "[i]n Heidegger coexistence is, to be sure, taken as a relationship with the Other irreducible to objective cognition; but in the final analysis, it also rests on the relation with *being in general*, on comprehension, on ontology" (*TeI* 63/*TI* 67). Where does this leave Dasein's relation to the personal Other? What is the relation between the metaphysical projection into nothing which reveals the world, the totality of Being in all its strangeness as other, and Dasein's concrete relation to the personal Other? Are these two relations, one with nothing and the other with something, correlative? It would seem to be the case that if Heidegger wishes to avoid the pitfalls of onto-theology, the very metaphysics he claims to overcome, then Dasein's relations with nothing and with the Other must correlate.

III

The question of alterity is broached by Levinas in what may be construed as a quasi-modernist manner. Joining ranks with those concerned with the rising specter of totalitarianism and the loss of subjective autonomy, he claims that his philosophy, (de)centered around the Other (*l'autrui*), is actually a philosophy of the self. Speaking of *Totality and Infinity*, for instance, Levinas states: "This book then does present itself as a defense of subjectivity, but it will apprehend the subjectivity not at the level of its purely egoist protestation against totality, nor in its anguish before death, but as founded in the idea of infinity" (*TeI* 11/*TI* 26). Of primary concern are the imperialist tendencies of a totalizing conception of subjectivity that has dominated since Aristotle and sees itself as constituting agent of its world and thus of otherness. This rebellion against the objectifying totality of metaphysics is not the same as the Kierkegaardian protest (*TeI* 30/*TI* 40).[22] It is not the individual, the I, who in acknowledging her or his freedom renounces all systems or totalities that impinge upon that radical freedom; it is the Other (*l'autrui*) that refuses such systematization or totalization. The subversive tendencies towards the other (*l'autre*) on the part of the selfsame are contested by the passive ethical resistance of the face of the Other in which there is an infinity of meaning prior to the emergence of signs from it.

The violence of being, of history, is arrested according to Levinas by the manifestation or epiphany of the face of the Other. In fact, goodness is alterity itself. The revelation of the Good as (pre)primordial difference overflows all attempts at encapsulation by thought. In its nudity and defenselessness the face is an appeal for justice and a call to responsibility for the sake of the Other. This obligation towards the Other is the calling into question of the freedom of the selfsame, of rationality's claim to comprehend the other.

The elevation of reason as the supreme criterion of judgment presupposes an already founded truth in which all difference is "weighed in the balances and found wanting."[23] Totality in this sense is the insignification of plurality. Armed with such God-given reason it has been possible to justify any and all endeavors to restore and maintain unity, whether religious, philosophical, or political. This totalitarian thinking that sees itself as the only rational answer to social and political anarchy, is to be rejected on the grounds that it opens wide the gate for the possibility of tyrannical violence. In such an order, the alterity of the individual is absorbed under the illusion or mask of harmony and non-resistance.

For Levinas, the metaphysical relation with the Other, that is, Desire as transcendence, occurs without the benefit of an intermediary. The reciprocity implied in the luminous concept of mediation is replaced by that of the "asymmetry of proximity" (*AE* 246/*OB* 158), a position that maintains the separation of the same and other, of subject and object.[24] The paradox of the notion of proximity lies precisely in that it simultaneously signifies both the concrete personal nature of the face to face *and* the absolute distance or separation that remains between the self and Other. The concept of proximity resembles Merleau-Ponty's notion of *chiasm*, which will be developed in the following chapter. Contrary to the reversibility implied in such a concept, totalization is refused because there is an *irreversibility* in the subject-object, self-Other relation. The two terms do not constitute a tautology, nor do they form a totality. The epistemological separation of the terms is both illusory and real, as Adorno says. It is the same for the metaphysical or ethical relation.

> The same and the other at the same time maintain themselves in relationship and *absolve* themselves of this relation, remain absolutely separated. The idea of infinity requires this separation. It is posited as the ultimate structure of being, as the *production* of its very infinitude. Society accomplishes it *concretely* (*TeI* 104/*TI* 102).

This separation is produced within the self as a psychism, as the *idea* of infinity. The production of the idea of infinity is a direct contestation of the Hegelian rejection of interiority or the inner life.

But does the insistence on absolute separation, the maintenance of which is ethics, result in an ideology that ends in a tyranny of the other? What would prevent such an other from committing the violence of coercion?

The notion of distance or separation functions in a critical capacity for an understanding of freedom and the constitution of subjectivity. One interprets the world only in distancing oneself from it. To be in the world is to adopt a position, to engage in a perspectival relation to it. The primordial and primary stance of subjectivity within the world is one of separation. It is not *Mitandersein* that characterizes our fundamental relation with existence. Such a view ultimately implies comprehension of the other, the primordial locus of ethical violence. Ethics, the welcoming of the Other by the self, is only accomplished through the recognition and maintenance of the radical disjunction of same and other, of subject and object.

IV

The introduction of a neutral third term into the intersubjective relation, whether it be *Geist* or *Sein*, only serves to generalize or thematize the alterity of the Other. It takes away the heterogeneous makeup, or the face of the Other, resulting in a certain dehumanization. Violence, especially murder, is much easier to accomplish when one does not see the face of the afflicted individual. The neutrality of the third term, of thought that becomes the mode of identification by which the other is reduced to a moment of the same, is criticized as a light that illumines not a particular existent but all beings, bringing them into full presence, naked under the lidless eye of Spirit or Being. This notion of being as presence (ontology) is the freedom of the selfsame. Ethics is the questioning of the dogmatic arbitrariness of the same's spontaneous freedom.

The neutrality of mediation constitutes an originary and foundational violence in that it subordinates the ethical before the seat of liberty. In the context of Heidegger's thought, truth is not a relation expressed and made manifest by discourse; truth is a concept already set apart, demanding the coherence or obedience of individual existents.[25] Such truth is impersonal and anonymous; thus is it free from any critique by the individual. As theory, truth *possesses* the other,

> For possession affirms the other, but within a negation of its independence. "I think" comes down to "I can"—to an appropriation of what is an exploitation of reality. Ontology as first philosophy is a philosophy of power. It issues from the State and in the non-violence of the totality without securing itself against the violence from which this non-violence lives, and which appears in the tyranny of the State (*TeI* 37/*TI* 46).

For Heidegger, transcendence, in the sense of going beyond the ensemble of beings in themselves, in its disclosure of the world as radically finite other, is the comprehension of the meaning of being as care (*Sorge*). The activity of comprehension is the activity of understanding or absolute knowing. Heidegger will assert the equiprimordiality of the understanding and state of mind. However, given his ontological privileging of *Sorge*, in the final analysis, he situates understanding over state-of-mind. This seeming incongruency in his thought is really not one at all. The goal of fundamental ontology is the grasping of the meaning of the totality of being through intellection.

Now it is Levinas who first recognizes this prioritizing of understanding over state of mind in his interpretation of *Sorge* as the project of the comprehension (illumination) of being and of the Other. Authentic (*Eigenlich*) existence appears to be, for Heidegger, self or ego-centric despite Heidegger's claim to the contrary: "Neutral Dasein [is not] the egocentric individual, the ontic isolated individual."[26] The they-structure (*das Man*) is inauthentic, which is to say, secondary in importance. The analysis of the metaphysical problem of nothingness reveals this to be the case.[27] The question is whether authentic existence is even involved in a relational mode of being with the Other. Authenticity is radically solitary and non-involved being according to Heidegger insofar as it "orients itself in the modes of concern and interhuman solicitude centrally towards its potentiality for Being, rather than towards the possibility of the 'They.'"[28] The letting-be (*Gelassenheit*) of the Other in his or her own most potentiality for Being is a non-ethical or rather, an a-ethical modality of existence. It posits the primacy of freedom over responsibility, the responsibility that only the appeal of the face can make. The face to face in Heidegger is not primarily a relation with Another; it is an *interaction* with nothingness, with no-thing. The appeal to let the other be reveals itself as an appeal on the part of Dasein for the Other to let Dasein, that is, the self, be.

Despite Heidegger's qualification of the "peculiar neutrality" of Dasein in his 1928 lectures on logic and transcendence as the "primordial positivity and potency of the essence of Dasein," and his insistence that this neutrality refers to the question of *origin* and not to Dasein in its factical concretion as the egocentric individual,[29] Levinas claims that *Gelassenheit*, if seen as a positive and liberating movement, actually reveals itself as a neutralizing mode of interaction with a secretly threatening and oppressing other and so aligns itself with the metaphysics of light (*TeI* 33, 63/*TI* 43, 67–68).[30] In other words, Heidegger's early project of a fundamental ontology remains within the boundaries of the very metaphysics he seeks to displace or overcome insofar as it affirms the primacy of individual freedom over the ethics of the face to face.

Is Heidegger's conception of *Mitandersein* deficient in that it seeks to instantiate a non-ethical mode of interaction with alterity, that is, with the world and other entities? Does alterity have any meaning of its own independent of Dasein's conception of it? Is the move of Hegelian self-consciousness repeated insofar as the other is merely a projection on the part of Dasein of its own self conception of what it itself is like? What does it mean to say that one is able to have a face to face "relationship" with that which does *not* have a face (nothing) and, moreover, is the absence of lack of existence itself?[31]

Levinas will oppose to the *Angst* that one feels when confronted by the nothingness of death the *horreur* produced by the *il y a*. One's relationships are with(in) being. And even

> where the continual play of our relations with the world is interrupted we find neither death nor the "pure ego," but the anonymous state of being. Existence is not

> synonymous with the relationship with a world; it is antecedent to the world. In the situation of an end of a world the primary relationship which binds us to Being becomes palpable. But the word relationship is not appropriate here; it implies terms, substantives. It takes them to be coordinated, but also independent. The relationship with Being is only remotely like that; it is called a relationship only by analogy. For the Being which we become aware of when the world disappears is not a person or a thing, or the sum total of persons or things; it is the fact that one is, the fact that *there is*. (*DEE* 26/*EE* 21)

This is a crucial point of difference between Levinas and Heidegger regarding the face to face, as Heidegger does not limit it to persons. It may be the case that Levinas later invokes this phrase precisely to counter Heidegger's broader usage.[32]

Though Heidegger retracts much of this early position, there are many who still feel that this period of his philosophical activity is his most poignant and fruitful; but the issue of alterity remains in abeyance throughout his work. There is a crucial ambiguity that concerns the status of the they-self (*das Man*). Does this refer to others as such, or just to the mode of anonymity which Dasein, as well as others, can assume? After all, inauthenticity is as much an affair of one's own self as of others. If this is true, then it only serves to reinforce the point that Heidegger lacks a sturdy sense of alterity in his early writing.

V

The correspondence theory of truth is endemic to ontology. Unlike the "meontological" truth of ethics, "which affirms a meaning beyond being, a primary mode of non-being (μή ὄν)," ontology seeks conformity, the dissolution of alterity into the "way of the same" since it reduces its terms to a common denominator (e.g., Reason, Spirit, Being).[33] Remaining within the bounds of this identity is held to be the common good. To step outside the recognized norm is to invite marginalization at best, oppression at worst. This ethic posits the concept of freedom, particularly in its bourgeois manifestation, over that of justice. The freedom of the same is grounded in the history of metaphysics that extends from Parmenides to Heidegger. This epistemological mode is ontology, the comprehension of Being, the depersonalization of beings.

The coexistence of the self with others does not entail having a comprehensive knowledge of them. The self exists in a proximate relation with the Other that allows the self to apprehend, not comprehend, the differences and similarities that exist between them. The claim of being able to comprehend the intentions of the Other or being in general is a theoretical imperialism that subtends all individual and collective violence, on both the physical and mental levels. This is the imperialism of the same which theoretically presents and justifies itself as the ontology of totality. The subjectivity that Levinas sets out to defend is that of the inner life, of interiority—the very notion that has come under such heavy scrutiny by postmodern analysis.

Violence exists primordially for human consciousness in the realm not of the physical, but of the intelligible. Violence is grounded in the conceptualization of

Being as a neutral given that preconditions all thought. This is where Levinas breaks with the phenomenological tradition. The Heideggerian λόγος is rejected by Levinas on the grounds that it is a "verb of no one," says Derrida.[34]

Levinas' opposition to Heidegger's early attempt to formulate a fundamental ontology is based on the argument that to know the existent it is necessary to comprehend the Being of the existent. This position will hold up only if it can be demonstrated that this "truism" represents a truth before judgment, a precondition that sets the tone for all subjective relations. Derrida seeks to defend Heidegger from Levinas' criticism:

> There can be an order of priority only between two existents, two determined beings. Being, since it is *nothing* outside the existent...could in no way *precede* the existent, whether in time, or in dignity, etc. Nothing is more clear, as concerns this, in Heidegger's thought.[35]

And we are informed by Heidegger: "The Being of beings means Being which is beings."[36] So what exactly is the difference between this and Levinas' contention that the absolutely other is the personal Other?

To answer this one should turn to the distinction that Heidegger draws between the *same* and the *identical*, the standard terms in which Hegel expresses the character of selfsameness. Sameness implies mediation, synthesis, and unity; in it all difference appears. Identity, however, homogenizes or levels difference.[37] This is an attempted move away from dialectical thought. The relations between identity and difference in Hegel are reflective thought-arrangements that reveal otherness as an essential moment in selfsame consciousness. Heidegger appears to recover the notion of sameness in the sense articulated by Nietzsche as the eternal recurrence of the *same*. Sameness is not opposed to difference at all; but in line with classical thought, it implies an ontological unity.

VI

Now it may be objected that the retention of the term "transcendence" keeps Levinas within the very ontology that he wishes to displace.[38] The claim that transcendence is non-negative may be construed, as it surely would have been by Hegel, as the mere affirmation of a positive (spurious) infinite. The Other would not be absolutely other if s/he were a positive infinity. Such an individual would be without an identity, without a face. A relation with absolute alterity would require the renunciation of all language, especially of the terms "infinite" and "other," contends Derrida.[39]

Is Levinas' conception of the transcendence of the Other, then, the most violent of approaches? Does ethics only arise out of the deepest violence? Does Levinas merely repeat Hegel with a different twist? According to Derrida, "Levinas is very close to Hegel, much closer than he admits, and at the very moment when he is apparently opposed to Hegel in the most radical fashion."[40] It would seem that Levinas has a difficulty here in going beyond Hegel precisely because of the way in which transcendence is articulated in terms of desire. How is one to understand this as a non-Hegelian notion of transcendence given that it is precisely desire that motivates the interdices of thought towards philosophical knowledge?

For Levinas, the relation between the idea of the face and the concrete face situates one *economically* between the ideal and the empirical, "between a philosophy of transcendence...and a philosophy of immanence" in such a way as to be "uprooted [*arraché*] from history" (*TeI* 44–45/*TI* 52).[41] This is precisely where he truly radicalizes philosophical thought and brings the self-proclaimed sovereignty of the homogeneous concept into proximity, not identification, with the heterological difference that the face signifies. Existentially, or metaphysically, the self is constituted by its relation with the Other. This is a break with the phenomenological tradition out of which Levinas' philosophy grew, and without reference to which it cannot be understood. The relation between subject and object is one of *non-adequation*. The other disrupts the intentionality of consciousness and forces the selfsame to question the capricious spontaneity of personal freedom.

Freedom is absolutely justified in Western thought from Spinoza to Hegel in the identification of will and reason. This is the precise point of Levinas' criticism of totalizing ontologies. This identification is the neutralization of existents under the common concept (e.g., Being, totality, Spirit). The I or subject posited as a-theistic and created by Levinas, thus constituting "the condition for language" since "speaking implies a possibility of breaking off and beginning" (*TeI* 87/*TI* 88), enables subjectivity to escape the arbitrary neutrality of freedom.

The meaning of individual existence is derived from the totality of being, from the plane of history. Signification or meaning arises from the face of the Other and calls upon the selfsame, the ego, to engage in communication, in the face to face of the speech-act, and to take responsibility for the possible tyranny of the self's freedom. Responsibility, commitment[42] on the part of the self for the other person, even to the point of substitution (*AE* 156–205/*OB* 99–103; *LR* 88–125) for Another, is the locus of ethical signification.

But responsibility for the Other is not to be construed as pity, a notion forcefully commented upon by Nietzsche. Responsibility is an awesome undertaking, unending in its obligation according to Levinas. At times it takes the harsh form of justice, both on the personal and communal levels. The Other does not make the self weak; rather, one becomes stronger or better through an active reaching out towards the Other. As with Nietzsche, Levinas' invocation of responsibility neither assumes the form of traditional Christian charity nor resembles the guilt of original sin (*AE* 193/*OB* 121).

Levinas substitutes the notion of responsibility for the Heideggerian notion of care (*Sorge)* and extends the thematic of responsibility as a post-metaphysical thought. But to what extent is Levinas' conception of peace and responsibility different from the peace that letting-be implies?

Responsibility implies both the notions of *Gelassenheit* and *Sorge*, but Levinas distances himself from these concepts insofar as they remain locked within the traditional ontological project of comprehension, of determining the meaning of being for consciousness in a totalizing modality. Letting-be is actually a non-ethical approach or comportment towards other beings. Responsibility, fundamentally pretheoretical, signals a reversal of the traditional, conceptually based hierarchical bifurcation of theory and practice. Responsibility is the precognitive disposition towards the Other, solicited by the appeal of the face. Heideggerian care, in letting the other be as its basic mode of relating intersubjectively, *suspends* responsibility and keeps Dasein within its own subjective domain, being primarily interested in the preservation of its own freedom; whereas for Levinas, ethical responsibility takes the form of a ὑπόστασις, a movement outside of the selfsame for the Other's sake. The ek-stasis of ethical responsibility, though, is contingent upon a "dis-inter-estedness" on the part of the self. Says Levinas,

> When I talk of ethics as a "dis-inter-estedness," I do not mean that it is indifference; I simply mean that it is a form of vigilant passivity to the call of the other, which precedes our interest in being, our *inter-est*, as a being-in-the-world attached to property and appropriating what is other than itself to itself.[43]

Dis-inter-est is opposed to the self-interest of care and letting-be; whereas Heideggerian *Sorge*, insofar as it is tied to *Mitsein*, seems to necessitate a certain reciprocity which the Levinasian sense of ethical obligation repudiates. This only serves, however, to accentuate what is a formidable, if not the major problem for Levinas, namely, how to reconcile the asymmetry of the ethical relation with the reciprocity requisite for legal and political praxis, especially in a democratic framework.

One always falls short of one's infinite ethical obligation; the self is never able to do enough for the Other as subjective interests are continually in conflict. That is the nature of ethics for Levinas and the reason he claims that peace is an eschatology. He cites Dostoievski from *The Brothers Karamozov* in support of this position: "We are always guilty before the other and none more than I" (*TO* 108; *CPP* 168; *EeI* 105, 108/*EI* 98, 101). Guilt is not be construed here in the Pauline or Augustinian sense of original sin.[44] Guilt for Levinas takes the form of responsibility for the Other to the point of substitution.[45] Freedom always carries with it a certain weight, that of responsibility.

Levinas does not provide his readers with the schema for a normative theory of ethics or morality. His concern is with the determination of what Derrida terms an "ethics of ethics [*l'éthicité de l'éthique*],"[46] of determining in a philosophical context the non or rather, pretheoretical ground of ethics. Since violence is first conceptual, the ontological structures that foster it must be put into question. Surely this is not an ahistorical endeavor. The absolute separation of infinity and totality is not the denial of relation between the terms. The concept of proximity allows one to be with and yet to be separate in one's existence. The maintenance of this distance is praxis and the overcoming of violence. Transcendence is praxis; theory is not praxis.

Regarding the relation of praxis to transcendence, a theme to which Sartre has greatly contributed to, praxis is perhaps best understood in the Aristotelian sense, that is, as the relation between politics and ethics. Historical being is condemned as much to politics as it is to freedom. Hegel realizes this and Levinas does not contest him on this point. But they part ways in that, for Levinas, the ethical is prior to and "better" than the political. In Hegel's philosophy, the ethical moment is always communal; it is *Sittlichkeit* and not *Moralität*, and serves the interests and aims of the universal political State. Insofar as Desire (*désir*) expresses the ethical superiority of the Other over the selfsame and challenges the self-proclaimed sovereignty of the State, and as Desire is transcendence, transcendence and praxis are conjoined. The non-classical metaphysical notion of transcendence proffered by Levinas thereby interprets the One as a social multiplicity and not as a transcendent entity outside of history.

Transcendence as praxis is precisely deconceptualization in the sense that ethics or metaphysics is the priority of action over theory. It is not the self that constitutes the meaning of the Other's existence; rather, it is precisely the opposite: subjectivity is constituted in and through its relation with alterity. One is not aware of his or her individuality until one enters into a relationship with Another and so calls the subjectivity of freedom itself into question.

Transcendence is not conceptual, nor is it suprasensible; it is prior to thought in the lived experience of the face to face. A direct relation with the absolutely other is an impossibility; one only enters into relation with the concrete Other, the other person who speaks and petitions, who beseeches us to take responsibility not only for ourselves but for them as well via the trace of the Infinite present in the face. Traditional notions of transcendence are rooted to conceptuality and intelligibility; but transcendence as Desire finds its being, its locus, in action, in the non-theoretical ethical interaction. This interaction does not necessarily take the form of exchange. What is amazing and troubling to many about Levinas is precisely the claim that there is a non-reciprocity to the ethical relation based on the fundamental asymmetry of the self and Other. The self and Other do not form a totality; the ethical obligation to be good, to be just, is not contingent upon the Other's mutual reciprocation. If it were, ethics would merely be all that it ever has been in the tradition, a subset of ontology, a pragmatics, a utilitarianism. This is why ethics is the first philosophy.

VII

Now, if Levinasian desire is essentially the maintenance of the separation of self and other, then what distinguishes it from Hegelian desire? This is, to some extent, the heart of Levinas' critique. Hegelian desire culminates in the act of forgiveness in which the Other is allowed to go free as different, as distinct, as separate. Is there an actual and radical distinction between Levinasian desire as the maintenance of the alterity of the other and Hegelian desire which realizes itself precisely in the action of forgiveness in which the Other is established as other? Is it merely the teleology of the dialectic to which Levinas refers in which the difference of the other is superseded by the notion of citizenry in the State?

Levinas' distinction between *désir* and *besoin* in *Totality and Infinity* is operative in the sense that Hegelian desire (*Begierde*) is actually need insofar as it seeks to fulfill or satiate itself in a total way. Hegelian desire implies a sense of lack, a separation that must be overcome or bridged in the self-other, subject-object relation. This occurs in the intersubjective relation in the moment of reconciliation, the moment of mutual and self-forgiveness after the initial clash or conflict for recognition takes place.

Desire is a movement towards the Other that does not strive to bring the Other into any comprehension on the part of the selfsame consciousness. The Other is desired precisely because the Other is other and not for any ulterior motive. The Other will always remain outside of the self's conception of her or him. This non-negative movement, and Levinas explicitly designates the movement of desire as such, and even as prior to any affirmative proposition or determination, is also the moment of truth, the very instantiation of the ethical relation. Desire does not originate from the selfsame; it originates from the Other. The Other calls upon the self to respond to the face; and the face, in turn, calls one's subjective freedom, one's domesticity, one's at-homeness, into question. The movement of metaphysical Desire that is solicited by the Other is a movement that commences with the I. Alterity is only possible beginning from one's realization of one's separateness from the Other. Desire, therefore, is non-teleological in the sense that it does not attempt to draw the Other within the totalizing domain of my consciousness. Desire is a reaching out towards the Other in a way that more than just lets the Other be. Desire calls upon the self to insure that the Other is not subsumed under some rubric of totality, consciousness, universal citizenry in the homogeneous State, or of any institutional form, whether social or religious, that would purport to be a source of the self's own unique identity.

Hegelian desire is a negativity in that it is an overcoming of the difference that alterity signifies. Thus does Levinas characterize *Begierde* as *besoin.* The Hegelian concept of desire falls under the same critique reserved for the Heideggerian notion of *Sein* and the project of fundamental ontology in general—as a will towards comprehension, towards leaving nothing outside or exterior to the totality of conscious being or thought.

As this relates to transcendence, metaphysical Desire, the desire for the absolutely other, for the Good, is transcendence in the very sense that Plato understands it. One does not desire the Good as object; the guardians and rulers in the Platonic republic relinquish the negative desire in the face of which the Good takes flight. The Other signifies the goodness of desire in a concrete sense, the desire to let the different be different. Desire is the allowance and maintenance of individual and cultural integrity and diversity without reducing the marginal, the exterior, to the apparatus of economic, cultural, political, social, or ecclesiastical machinery. Transcendence, as the movement of Desire, is the celebration of difference and radical separation. Transcendence is profoundly ethical for Levinas; that is its meaning. Ethical transcendence is praxis; the unity of the political and the ethical. More precisely, the eschatological vision of ethics is the eventual dissolution of the political which is ultimately unable, contra Hegel, to usher in the age of peace. And Desire as transcendence does not assume the form of ego transcendence as it does, for instance, in Husserl and Sartre.

Dialectical metaphysics does not allow for an ethical critique of politics in the same manner that it does not allow for a religious critique of philosophical theology; and no thinker has shown as forcefully as Hegel that theology and philosophy are essentially the same project: the subordination of (ethical) transcendence to the concept thought. Ethical transcendence (Desire) is the refusal of the ontotheological viewpoint that radical exteriority is subject to totality. In this sense, transcendence *is* infinity, that is, the impossibility of encompassing or totalizing alterity. The non-theological nature of transcendence is genuine a-theism. This is opposed to, say, Kojève, who maintains that Hegel's alleged atheism, for example, is a result of not positing a beyond the totality of existence as Plato did. But for Levinas, a-theism is neither the affirmation of the purely immanent nor pejorative in meaning.

The opposition of religion and politics is meant to serve as a relational modality that does not reduce the self and the Other to moments in a collective totality. Democratic politics rests on the primacy of reciprocal recognition (equality). It attempts to ensure happiness by reconciling the personal freedom of the I with the freedom of the Other; but "the distance that separates happiness from desire separates politics from religion" (*TeI* 58/*TI* 64). Desire is not the fulfillment or satisfaction of the ego. Happiness is not commensurate with Hegelian desire (*Begierde*) but with need. Again, the status of infinity is the crucial point to bear in mind. Since the absolutely other is meaningful only in the face of Another person, infinity remains irreducible to selfsame consciousness.

9

DiaGround

The radicalizing of transcendence as immanence in the concretion of the interfacial relationship brings contemporary philosophical analysis to that modality of being that expresses signification and meaning, that is, to language. In his last major work, *Otherwise Than Being or Beyond Essence*, Levinas opens this question in an enigmatic way. Levinas' thinking is primarily situated within the phenomenological context of his time. Consequently, there is a strong correspondence between his thinking and that of Maurice Merleau-Ponty on the conception of intersubjectivity and language, particularly with regard to the notion of *paradox*. Merleau-Ponty is engaged with the very dialectic that subtends the course of the present work, that of the visible and the invisible, and by extension, of the same and the other. In his later writing, he posits the concept of intertwining or *chiasm*, and the reversibility implied in such a concept, as the ontological clue to understanding the relation between subjectivity and alterity. Now, Levinas' hermeneutic of ethics is contingent on the claim that there is a fundamental *irreversibility* in the intersubjective (metaphysical) relationship. This essential nonreciprocity is pronounced in Levinas' later writing as the difference between the ethical saying (*le dire*) and the ontological said (*le dit*). The asymmetry of the metaphysical relation is further denoted in the temporal distinction between diachrony and synchrony. Both Levinas and Merleau-Ponty seek to move away from the positivity of idealism and transcendental forms of phenomenology. Merleau-Ponty seeks to accomplish this in his theory of the incarnational constitution of language. This has ramifications for Levinas' theory of language upon which it is the task of this chapter to elaborate.

The paradoxical predicament which both thinkers find themselves in, through the employment of traditional metaphysical and ontological language to indicate that which is exterior to or beyond the totality, gives rise to Jacques Derrida's critique of the project of establishing (in Levinas' case at least) an ethical metaphysics that avoids the violence of the predicative structure of ontological language. Derrida's seminal essay "Violence and Metaphysics," the first major commentary on Levinas, stands as a *tour de force* in its own right. An examination of Derrida's argument will be followed by an analysis of the relation between language, totality and the face to face relationship. Gilles Deleuze and Félix Guattari's analysis of faciality will also be taken up in relation to Levinas.

I

The self does not invent language; it finds itself already situated within language, taking language as its own in response to the Other. Language involves interlocutors; mere thought (διάνοια) does not constitute the essence of language. But even the disclosure of the illusory nature of the ego by Nietzsche, and later by Freud, which revolutionizes thinking, does not preclude the possibility of being in a relationship. Language institutes the metaphysical (ethical) relation, though such a relation is prior to any affirmative or negative proposition that can be said about it. The ethical self is desirous of the Other, not for the sake of possession or dominance, but to formulate a *dialogical* relation. If negative or affirmative propositions about the absolutely other were situated *before* the institution of language, the Other would already be reduced to a preconceived category, that is, brought down to the level of the same, thereby constituting the originary violence towards the Other.

The absolute separation between the self and Other is ethically maintained in the face to face relation that is the essence of speech, of discourse. According to Merleau-Ponty, to be in the world is to already be imbued with meaning, with an "incarnate logic." He appears to be very close to Hegel in this regard; but this is a "logic in contingency,"[1] a language of which there are two types: institutional language and creative language, that is, language that creates itself in its expressive acts. The language (*le langage parlé*) of institutions (e.g., cultural, political, economic, ecclesiastical) is the "sedimented" language of the prejudiced reader. Moreover, truth is but "another name for sedimentation."[2] Speech (*la parole*) takes sedimented language and through a transformative operation creates *new* significations.

The paradox of language is that it exists only through speaking individuals or subjects, and yet it is not something produced by them. Like language, the speech-act is "that paradoxical operation through which, by using words of a given sense, and already available meanings, we try to join up with an intention which necessarily outstrips, modifies, and itself, in the last analysis, determines the meanings of the words which translate it."[3] Language is "completely accidental and completely rational;"[4] it "leads us to the things themselves to the precise extent that it *is* signification before *having* a signification."[5]

Moving away from an algorithmic conception of universal signs, the project of much positivist analytic philosophy, a language that "manipulates," Merleau-Ponty seeks to ground language neither in a reflective *cogito*, the constituting consciousness of *Geist*, nor in a transcendental ego, but rather, in the *perceptual* contact with the world. In his last lecture course, he traces a historical thread between the Cartesian attempt to conflate objectivity and subjectivity and the later philosophies of Hegel and Husserl, which tend to valorize identity and subjectivity to the point of eclipsing the difference that is inherent in the categories of the object and the other.[6] Supportive of Hegel's early "existentialism" and critical of his later writings (*Science of Logic* and the *Encyclopaedia*), Merleau-Ponty maintains that the philosophy of the past century and the task of this century is to reread and expand the insights of Hegel's "attempt to explore the irrational and integrate it into an expanded reason."[7] He sees much of Husserl's phenomenology as essentially an extension of Hegel's project. But due to his early demise, Merleau-Ponty never completes his projected ontology which includes an attempt to overcome or transcend, in an immanent sense, the "bad" Hegelian dialectic, transforming it into a non-synthesizing "good" dialectic in a manner that, reminiscent of Adorno's negative dialectic, leaves existence non-closed in terms of either metaphysical or epistemological extension:

> The only good dialectic is the hyperdialectic [*hyperdialectique*]. The bad dialectic is that which does not wish to lose its soul in order to save it, which wishes to be dialectical immediately, becomes autonomous, and ends up at cynicism, at formalism, for having eluded its own double meaning. What we call hyperdialectic is a thought that on the contrary is capable of reaching truth because it envisages without restricting the plurality of the relationships and what has been called ambiguity.[8]

Merleau-Ponty's non-synthesizing dialectic bypasses the overpositivity of speculative idealism by excluding from consideration the power of the negative that moves the Hegelian dialectic. The key to this is found in the notion of chiasm which is not only a "co-functioning" intersubjective exchange but an exchange between the self and the world unified in the commonality of a primordial "flesh."[9]

Merleau-Ponty's emphasis on the corporeal, perceptual constitution of subjectivity and intersubjectivity moves him into close proximity with Levinas insofar as the linguistic phenomenon is rooted or grounded in the concrete relation of interfaciality. The speaking subject (*le sujet parlant*) embodies language, enters into language, through the historical event of speech. Language is more than mere mental or verbal signs. It is movement or expression which, simultaneously, "is never absolutely expression [since] what is expressed is never completely expressed."[10] Were language otherwise, it would turn itself into that which can be fully comprehended, that is, a concept, a sedimented truth. Expression is necessarily tied to the body, either as speech or as physical gesture; it presents itself to perception. Levinas understands the infinity produced in the relationship with alterity, the point of ethical signification, as first revealed or expressed in the face. But as well, part of the question could be to determine what is *not* expressed in expression, as Merleau-Ponty attempts to do in *The Visible and the Invisible.* For Levinas, this would be correlative with the absolutely heteronomous past of the other.

For one who strives for originality, who is not content merely to repeat what has already been done, new significations must be created. In a passage that resonates deeply with Nietzsche,[11] Merleau-Ponty says that such an individual "wants to fulfill language and destroy it at the same time, to fulfill it *by destroying it* or to destroy it *by fulfilling it.*"[12] Again, the paradox of language. Meaning is not inherent in the verbal chain itself; it is the "total *movement* of speech."[13] Meaning is anything but static; it is dynamic, forceful. "Language is a battering ram [*perce-muraille*]" (*EDE* 236/*CPP* 125). Whether interpreted in terms of

Gadamerian play, active-reactive forces of Nietzschean will to power, or Marxian praxis, meaning is always hyperstatic and never able to be fully grasped.

Language does not conform to a prereflective objective text; it is understood only through the interaction of signs which, if taken singly, signify nothing. Meaning is to be found within the whole, not in parts of the whole.[14] Language only becomes meaningful in the immanence of the gesture, in speech.

The reason language presents itself so well, says Merleau-Ponty, is that it is "much more like a sort of being" and, as such, does not exist solely for itself.[15] Language thus has an ontological bearing. The power of language exists totally in the present, though in the "milieu of the exterior holy."[16] Without the Other that one confronts in the world, there would be no communicative aspect to language; one would be as God, in dialogue, actually monologue, with oneself in the silence of memory. Perhaps the interrelation between a subjectivity and the world it inhabits is better understood as "an inextricable tangle."[17] Language is something that is learned; it is not innate. One is born into language. Language is not a natural but rather, a cultural phenomenon. Synchronically viewed, language is the fundamental aspect of the intersubjective phenomenon; it is the essence of intersubjectivity. It belongs to everyone and to no one.

Language is not something transcendent; it is the very *act* of transcendence that expresses itself incarnately bringing "rationality…down to earth," to the perceived world.[18] This "original incarnation of thought," says Levinas, "which cannot be expressed in terms of objectification…is prior, in Merleau-Ponty's view, to the taking up of any theoretical or practical position. An *Urdoxa*: a synthesis prior to all syntheses" (*HS* 147/*OS* 97; also, *AE* 63/*OB* 36). Language is never a one-way operation, a matter of the pure "I know" which never leaves the realm of cognition. Neither is language identical with the mere "I can" of the motor subject. One exists not only as a biological organism but as a speaking subject, and only as such is one capable of an active transcendence of the world. The transcendence that language is capable of through the speech-act is the way in which the speaking subject mediates the lived experience. Language is transcendence precisely because it alone is capable of bridging the *distance* that exists between the self and the Other that is perceived.

Now while Levinas repeatedly acknowledges the importance of Merleau-Ponty's "fundamental historicity" (*AE* 76, 113, 250, 259/*OB* 45, 70, 160, 167; *HH* 32/*CPP* 84–85), and situates much of his own thinking in relation to it, he nevertheless cautions that

> to take incarnation as a primary fact of language, without indicating the ontological structure it accomplishes, would be to assimilate language to activity, to that prolongation of thought in corporeality, the *I think* in the *I can*, which has indeed served as a prototype for the lived body (*corps propre*) or incarnate thought, which dominates one part of contemporary philosophy. (*TeI* 224/*TI* 205)

Levinas' interpretation rests on the radical separation of thought and sensibility, of linguistic expression and bodily action. The relation between the invisible trace of meaning and the corporeality in which it fundamentally resides and reveals itself is "the irreducible paradox of intelligibility: the other in the same, the trope of this for-the-other in its antecedent reflexion" (*AE* 113/*OB* 70).

II

The paradox of language is pronounced in the enigmatic diachronic difference between the *saying* and the *said*, the terms Levinas employs to indicate how the ethical signifies within the ontological order of language.[19] Saying refers to subjectivity's "exposure" to the Other where the demand of responsibility and obligation is impressed upon the self. This "pre-original saying" (*AE* 17ff/*OB* 5ff) is expressed as the an-archic trace of the Infinite within the face, whereas the said is the thematized result of the saying. The said is language which makes propositional statements or declarations about the truth and falsity of an event or thing. To exist is to necessarily enter into the domain of the said via a reduction of the said to the saying outside the logos. But because the *logos is ambiguous*, the verb "to be" fixes itself synchronically and thereby assumes historical identification, that is, situates itself as a noun. Synchrony is the artificial synthetic sense of time that allows memory to recuperate the past and predict, or at least project into the future. Diachrony, on the other hand, bears close resemblance to Berson's notion of duration (*la durée*); it is non-simultaneous temporality that refuses the effort of consciousness to totalize the succession of instants. The absolutely heteronomous past of the ethical saying—an-archy—is the insertion of the primordial diachrony into the synchronic order of the ontological said. This results in an *interruption* (*AE* 262–26/*OB* 169–71) of essence or being preventing the closure of the said.

Levinas refers to the verb "to be" as a "synchronizable diachrony" (*AE* 73/*OB* 42). Here he is both close to and far way from Merleau-Ponty's fundamental historicity, which represents an "impossible synchronization of the unassemblable, which the diachrony of proximity has already escaped" (*AE* 76/*OB* 45). This is the paradox and the enigma of the ethical relationship that testifies to the radical exteriority associated with the absolutely other prior to the incarnational constitution of the world of meaning for subjectivity. The ethical saying, though antecedent to ontology, which is to say to history, is diachronically present in the corporeal proximity of the face to face relationship. This is precisely where Merleau-Ponty's phenomenological analysis of the synchronicity of language yields fruit for Levinas.

The presence of the saying in the said, the other in the same—the paradox of intelligibility—is none other than a radical recasting of the traditional metaphysical problem of the infinite in the finite. Levinas repudiates the notion that there is a knowable ground to adjudicate the truth of this dilemma. "The ethical is the field outlined by the paradox of an Infinite in relationship with the finite without being belied in this relationship" (*AE* 232/*OB* 148). But Levinas is not the first to distinguish between the saying and the said of language, especially in the context of the relation between the infinite and the finite. Hegel also makes this distinction.

> In *saying* what the infinite is, namely the negation of the *finite*, the latter is itself included in what is *said*; it cannot be dispensed with for the definition or the determination of the infinite. One only needs to *be aware of what one is saying* in order to find the determination of the finite in the infinite.[20]

The infinite and finite to which Hegel is referring are the terms as they present themselves in their *immediate* determination, which is to say, in their *alternating* determination. This is the point of contact with Hegelian thinking which Merleau-Ponty incorporates into the notion of chiasm, although with the very important *corporeal* twist that he assigns it. Now even though Levinas rejects the Hegelian concept of infinity precisely on the grounds that it is *merely* a concept, there is a correspondence or affinity at play between their respective understandings of the saying and the said. For both, the terms are co-dependent in their meaning for subjective being. For Hegel, it is a question of being aware, that is, of being *conscious* of what one says in order to comprehend the subtending unity or totality of the infinite and the finite. For Levinas, the ethical signifyingness of the saying only takes on meaning in its entering into the ontological order of the said (*AE* 76/*OB* 44). A *betrayal* of the Infinite is thus *necessary* for the revelation of the ethical imperative expressed in the face. *This is the enigmatic paradox.* But the crucial difference here is that conceptuality, the order of the said, cannot function as the *ground* for grasping ethical responsibility, that is, justice. The ethical signification of the saying is expressed in the alternation or "spiralling movement" (*un movement en vrille*) between the saying and the said (*AE* 76/*OB* 44).[21] The saying cannot stand apart from the said absolutely; its "ground" is the very ontological order that it calls into question as a "play of the same." Neverthess, antecedent to speech, to words in the order of the said, saying signifies in the distinct relationship of proximity.

The problem facing the philosopher is the maintenance of the integrity of the saying and the otherwise than being that it signifies after its invariable and necessary collapse into the said. "How is the saying, in its primordial enigma, said?" (*AE* 23/*OB* 10). This is not a mere matter of hermeneutics: "saying is not a game [*le dire n'est pas un jeu*]" (*AE* 17/*OB* 5). Levinas' answer, which governs the entirety of his work, is *responsibility*. And if it is true that "all speaking is an enigma" (*EDE* 212/*CPP* 69), then so is the force or power of ethics which is, paradoxically, the very renunciation of power, of "my ability for power [*mon pouvoir de pouvoir*]" (*TeI* 215/*TI* 198). It is the passivity of the exposure that discloses the uniqueness of subjectivity as "one-in-responsibility" (*AE* 94/*OB* 56). Speech, that is, the saying in the said, is "the passivity in passivity…to which the ego is reduced in proximity" (*AE* 148/*OB* 92).

At this point one might be prone to construe Levinas' notion of passivity as a refusal to participate in an *active* way with the world and the Other, but nothing could be further from the case. Passivity does not denote withdrawal or complacency on the part of subjectivity; it is not the retreat into liturgy or a sequestered life as a means of reconnecting with the Absolute. Passivity is exposure to the point of being commanded by the Other to take up not only self-responsibility for one's own freedom, but sacrifice to the point of substitution of one-for-the-other. Saying is this incessant command of obligation conveyed (*traduit*) as the betrayal (*trahison*) of the said. The paradox of the saying in the said is that even though it appears to be activity (i.e., responsibility), saying is actually a prolongation of this radical passivity (*AE* 239/*OB* 148). Saying is not a *Sollen* imposed on a subject. The responsibility impressed by the saying is a *reversal* of the interest of the same (*AE* 26/*OB* 12), the *dis*-inter-est converted by philosophy through an abuse of language into the "pretensions" of a "new said" (*AE* 200/*OB* 126).

III

Both Merleau-Ponty and Levinas seek to decenter the *cogito* and overcome or transcend the epistemological dualism of subject-object and the internal-external bifurcation, and with a new epistemology, one ever aware of its paradoxical "ground." Though his early efforts are essentially concerned with the role of the subject, Merleau-Ponty's later writings move towards a notion of the chiasmatic or intertwining relationship between the self and Other. Branching off Heidegger, he teaches that to be in the world implies a primordial chiasm of the world and self. Levinas notes Merleau-Ponty's "not surprising" later evolution towards Heidegger's thought as well; both share the contemporary inclination towards the dismantling of traditional subject-object structures. Still, Levinas harbors a profound suspicion that "perhaps at the source of all these philosophies, we find the Hegelian vision of a subjectivity that comprehends itself as an inevitable moment of the becoming by which being leaves its darkness the vision of a subject aroused by the logic of being" (*HH* 29/*CPP* 82). Nevertheless, Merleau-Ponty's incorporation of Heidegger's notion of being-in-the-world is developed to explicate the intertwining, not so much of the ontic-ontological difference, but rather, of the intimate relation between perception and the world, through the locus of the body. The chiasm is an ambiguous concept; and "this initial *paradox* cannot but produce others."[22]

In order for there to be a genuine encounter with the Other, consciousness, or language, has to be primarily conceived of as perceptual consciousness, not as the constituting consciousness of a pure being-for-itself. "Language does not take place *in front of* a correlation from which the I would derive its identity and the Other his alterity.... Speech is not instituted in a homogeneous or abstract medium, but in a world where it is necessary to aid and to give" (*TeI* 238/*TI* 216). The Other is not present as pure mind; the other person is present as a phenomenal body with a "sort of locality," says Merleau-Ponty. Perceptual consciousness pushes the traditional epistemological antinomies aside and opens up the *space* for the lived face to face relation.

The other person is a subjectivity, a haunting, wandering double of the self insofar as both the Other and the self inhabit bodies:

> Myself and the other are like two *nearly* concentric circles which can be distinguished only by a slight and mysterious slippage. This alliance is perhaps what will enable us to understand the relation to the other that is inconceivable if I try to approach him directly, like a sheer cliff.[23]

Being is synonymous with its thought and therefore self-identical; but it is also differential flux. Thus is it possible to speak of the logos of the world and of the anonymous one that speaks. There is neither an epistemological nor an ontological center; the subject is an object and the object a subject. Only thereby are understanding and meaning possible. The self and the Other are inextricably intertwined in a chiasmatic relationship and share a common generality. Inspired by the words and work of the artist Paul Klee, Merleau-Ponty's reflections on language may best be summed up as follows: "To the extent that what I say has meaning, I am a different 'other' for myself when I am speaking; and to the extent that I understand, I no longer know who is speaking and who is listening."[24] Nevertheless, the Other is not just another self, an alter-ego, though the self and the Other are both totalities in the world, bound together through the mutually shared linguistic experience. Language is the bridge between the self and the Other and in this sense serves as a mediator of sorts, though not in the absolute manner in which Hegel construes mediation.

The intersubjective reciprocity requisite for the working of social and political relations is not synonymous with metaphysical symmetry. The asymmetry of intersubjectivity, according to Levinas, is bound with the irreversibility of that relation. But the chiasmatic self-Other relation is a reciprocal and reversible event for Merleau-Ponty:[25] "The mystery of the other is nothing but the mystery of myself."[26] Levinas, too, refers to the relationship with alterity as a "relationship with a Mystery" (*TA* 63/*TO* 75), but the essence of the mystery is that it is a relationship, a discourse, between *unequals*.[27] It is at this point that Levinas moves away from Merleau-Ponty's analysis. In a passage that invokes Hegel's imagery of the dialectic of lordship and bondage, albeit with a different twist, Levinas states:

> The "communication" of ideas, the reciprocity of dialogue, already hide the profound essence of language. It resides in the irreversibility of the relation between me and the other, in the mastery of the Master coinciding with his position as other and exterior. For language can be spoken only if the interlocutor is the commencement of his discourse, if, consequently, he remains beyond the system, if he is not on the same plane as myself. The interlocutor is not a Thou (*Toi*), he is a You (*Vous*); he reveals himself in his lordship. Thus exteriority coincides with a mastery. My freedom is thus challenged by a Master who can invest it. Truth, the sovereign exercise of freedom, becomes henceforth possible. (*TeI* 104/*TI* 101)

The "mystery" of intersubjectivity is not found within subjectivity but in the Other. The irreversibility of the self-Other relation grounds ethics and *transcends* the chiasm between subjectivity and the world. The absolutely other is transhistorical. Language is founded upon neither a mediated dialectic nor a chiasmatic reversibility.

Now Levinas agrees with Merleau-Ponty, whom he says shows "among others, but better than others," that disincarnate thought constituting the world of speech is a "myth" (*TeI* 225/*TI* 205), that the principal modality of existence in the world is that of embodiment. But they differ on several crucial points. Whereas Merleau-Ponty maintains that "the other is never present face to face,"[28] Levinas holds that "meaning is the face of the Other, and all recourse to words takes place already within the primordial face to face of language" (*TeI* 227/*TI* 206). In addition, Levinas is insistent that meaning or signification arises within the irreversible relation between the same and the other anterior to the concrete lived experience. The presentation of meaning in the face constitutes the primordial essence of language, not the corporeal relation that discloses it intersubjectively and encapsulates it within a thought. Only the unique idea of infinity can express this primordial ethical signification to consciousness, not the totality or relationship expressed in the notion of the chiasm. But despite their differences, both are in agreement that being cannot be approached directly (*intentione recta*) but only laterally, through immersion in the world (cf. *HH* 36/*CPP* 88).

IV

Language and reason are limited in laying hold of the ethical relation. All language is a violence, an abuse or betrayal of the saying, when it attempts to name or lay hold of the ineffable Absolute. The metaphysical (ethical) relation institutes the very possibility of discourse as it is prior to any negative or affirmative propositions that can be made about it. Language does not arise from the I as though from a source. Speech is always response, solicited from the Other; it "proceeds from absolute difference [*la différence absolue*]...inconceivable in terms of formal logic, [which] is established only by language" (*TeI* 212/*TI* 194–95). Even though speech is commensurate with the I, it is nevertheless evoked. Speech is *revelation*, which is why Levinas adamantly maintains that the absolutely other is an epiphanic ἔσχατον. Disclosure is an inadequate term as it implies the bringing forth of what is universally hidden to thought. Revelation, on the other hand, is always surprise, non-thematizable and non-totalizable. The evidences of reason are of no avail confronted with the "opinionated" postures of subjective divination.

Levinas' proto-deconstruction of ontology and the apocalyptic thinking that subtends it, unlike Derrida's revelation of the double play of reason, turns to the philosophically distrusted stance of *opinion* under which he groups ethics and eschatology (*TeI* 6–7/*TI* 22). The primacy of Being before beings, of ontology before metaphysics, of freedom before ethics: these terms must be readdressed or reversed if a non-allergic relation with the Other is to occur, if the self is to renounce its claim to gather all difference under the sway of its consciousness. Opinion marks the point of departure of philosophy from non-philosophy, an exodus that is traced back to the *Platonist* interpretation of the so-called divided line where the intelligible realm is supposedly separated from the apparent one. Now unlike Levinas, Gadamer remains faithful to the tradition and affirms the ancient distrust of opinion:

> Plato shows in an unforgettable way where the difficulty lies in knowing what one does not know. It is in the power of opinion against which it is so hard to obtain an admission of ignorance. It is opinion that suppresses questions. Opinion has a curious tendency to propagate itself. It would always like to be the general opinion, just as

> the word that the Greeks have for opinion, δόξα, also means the decision made by the majority in the council assembly.[29]

Levinas, however, affirms opinion for the very reason that Gadamer rejects it, that is, on the grounds that it preserves the freedom of the question. Derrida opens his essay on Levinas (1964) with the very topic of preserving this liberty. Opinion puts both the question and the answer to the test. Rather than suppressing questions, opinion oftentimes asks the unanswerable, embarrassing, or the politically inexpedient questions, e.g., questioning the authority of the State. Plato rejects δόξα precisely because it does not allow itself to be rendered either fully visible or intelligible. Opinion can obviously never serve as the point of mediation as the concept does for Hegel. The encounter with the Other, if it is to be ethical, must occur without the intervention of an intermediary or neutral third term. This is accomplished via proximity.

In rejecting the truth claims of both idealism and empiricism, Levinas situates his philosophy *between* transcendence and immanence; and it is precisely at this level, claims Derrida, that Levinas' thinking makes one "tremble":

> Within this experience of the other the logic of non-contradiction...is contested in its root. This root would be not only the root of our language, but the root of all Western philosophy, particularly phenomenology and ontology.[30]

The face is the experience of the Other to which Derrida refers. The face to face does not collapse or conflate the infinite and the finite into the simulated order of a totality. The epiphany of the face is the breaking forth of the Infinite into the finite order of history. "The other can also not appear without renouncing his radical alterity, without coming into an order. The breaks in the order reenter the order whose weave lasts unendingly, a weave these breaks manifest, and which is a totality" (*EDE* 206/*CPP* 64). The renunciation of alterity is the continual kenotic movement of the Infinite which humbles itself in its revelation as the trace of itself. And "what is this original trace, this primordial desolation? It is the nakedness of a face that faces, expressing itself, interrupting order" (*EDE* 208/*CPP* 65). In the face the Infinite is revealed in all its glory *and* defenselessness. The ethical power or resistance that is conveyed through the face is paradoxically the absolute renunciation of power in the political (broadly construed) sense of domination of the Other: pure, absolute *passivity*, "the way opposed to the imperialism of consciousness open upon the world" (*AE* 148/*OB* 92).

But does Levinas constitute a violence towards the very alterity he seeks to preserve in that he places the signification of otherness beyond history and therefore *de*-existentializes the suffering and oppression of the Other? Does the opposition of ethics and history, of metaphysics and ontology, of infinity and totality, negate (a term that Levinas reluctantly, if ever, uses in an affirmative sense) ethical praxis itself? That is to say, is Levinas' criticism of violence too abstract to have any concrete meaning? Is there a distinction between the totalizing activity of consciousness and the concrete totality of the world? This would be the point of difference between ethical metaphysics and critical social theory.

There appears to be an internal contradiction between the affirmation of ethical transcendence and the refusal of historical mediation. The Other is not only refractory to categorization by thought; the Other is also "flesh," to borrow Merleau-Ponty's term. Does the denial of mediation as a path to the "royal road of ethics"[31] render the problems of injustice, suffering, and murder meaningless?

Derrida provides a provocative and, in some ways, most damning criticism of ethical metaphysics, when he points out that positing a *pure non*-violence is a contradictory position that inevitably winds up in violence.

> Pure violence, a relationship between beings without faces, is not yet violence, is pure nonviolence. And inversely: pure nonviolence, the nonrelation of the same to the other (in the sense understood by Levinas) is pure violence. Only a face can arrest violence, but can do so, in the first place, only because a face can provoke it.[32]

Does Levinas actually think that pure violence and non-violence are possible real ities? Though his discourse is a discourse against the ontological (the said) foundations of violence, Levinas understands that a certain violence is necessary, the violence that accompanies the saying in its *provisional* reduction into the said. "The surprising saying which is a responsibility for another is…an interruption of essence, a disinterestedness imposed with a good violence" (*AE* 75/*OB* 43). But despite this surprising acknowledgment of a *bonne violence*,

> The true problem for us Westerners is not so much to refuse violence as to question ourselves about a struggle against violence which, without blanching in non-resistance to evil, could avoid the institution of violence out of this very struggle. Does not war perpetuate that which it is called to make disappear, and consecrate war and its virile virtues in good conscience? (*AE* 272/*OB* 177)

History is an *economy* of violence (and peace) and no one seems to understand that better than Hegel. Being without violence would no longer be history; therefore, it would be nothing outside the existent. Language, the medium of history, is violent on the very basis of *predication* itself. If the relation between subject and object is truly one of *non*-adequation, then the language employed to describe this relation is, by nature of its entanglement in the economy that is being, essentially selfsame, also inadequate. The reality of the metaphysical relation (ethics) and the metaphysical language used to describe it are of necessity non-correlative in any absolutely determinable sense. Heidegger locates the problem of ontotheology in the reification of the verb "to be" as a noun. Would a non-violent language be one *without* the verb "to be"? If that were the case, there would no longer be language and history as we know them. Derrida's skepticism toward Levinas' notion of non-mediated proximity leads him to conclude that this contradictory position without historical reconciliation compromises Levinas' thought and leads him to a true alley of despair.[33] But perhaps this only reinforces Levinas' conviction that the meaning of ethics or metaphysics is the lived concrete exchange of the face to face in the necessarily violent arena of the totality of historical being.

V

Levinas' conception of the absolutely other as the Other is also challenged by Derrida on the grounds that it results in the destruction or denial of the Other's ego-quality. Derrida argues that Levinas' understanding of the Other as *alter non-ego* abstracts the concrete egoness of the Other's subjectivity to the point of rendering the Other unreal or illusory. And what of the role the self plays in alienation or negation? The separation of self and other is for Levinas already present before there is any conception of the self by the self-reflecting I or ego. This pre-originary separation conditions or determines, in a decidedly non- or rather, pre-cognitive way, the ethical boundaries of the intersubjective relation. While this can be said to be a transhistorical moment, it is nevertheless *not* opposed to history as the present work has attempted to demonstrate throughout.

Certainly the claim of the ethical primacy of the Other seems to imply mediation insofar as the self and the Other are both egos, but Levinas will insist on the *asymmetrical* character of the self-Other relation. "The other is not only an alter-ego; the Other is what I myself am not" (*TA* 75/*TO* 83; *DEE* 162/*EE* 95). There is something irreducibly different about the Other that resists conceptualization of him or her as just another person.

This paradoxical tension leads to the criticism that the notion of radical exteriority is either nothingness or an impossibility. Derrida reasons that there can be no absolutely other in the sense proposed by Levinas.[34] The Other can only be properly conceived as alter-ego since the Other conceived as alter *non*-ego would collapse the alterity of the other and so constitute violence towards the Other. To conceive of such a radically other would mean to conceive of alterity as absolutely not the selfsame (non-ego). The absolutely other would thus be divorced from any relation with the ego. And the treatment of the other as stranger or as alter non-ego would be the deprivation and destruction of the Other's equality as an ego. The Other must be recognized, as Hegel claims, as both other and the same to avoid this position. Mutual recognition is therefore an "economy" of the "transcendental symmetry of two empirical asymmetries."[35]

The whole position of an ethical metaphysics as proposed by Levinas rests on the contention that the asymmetry of the ethical relation is *also* transcendental since violence becomes necessary and unavoidable the moment thought becomes speech. Derrida's principal concern is with preserving the ego-quality of the Other without which the Other could not function as "origin of the world" and therefore as the locus of ethical signification.[36] In effect, the proposal of an ethical metaphysics stands accused by Derrida of perpetrating the very violence that it seeks to avoid.

Derrida argues that the renunciation of the primacy of the concept, that is, of the transcendental horizons of language and meaning (a priori), leads Levinas to the truth claims of empiricism, the "*dream* of a purely *heterological* thought." Levinas is the most audacious and profound of such thinkers since by taking this project (the radicalization of the theme of infinity) to its end, he totally renews empiricism, and inverses it by revealing it to itself as metaphysics.[37] However, even though the complicity between empiricism and metaphysics is quite old,

Derrida could be countered here on the grounds that the idea of infinity, though elicited from the empirical face, is nevertheless produced internally as an *idea*, as a psychism. And it is precisely this idea which shakes the very ground of the Logos, father of concepts, as Derrida is well aware, leading "to a dislocation of our identity, and perhaps of identity in general...but toward an *exhalation*, toward a prophetic speech already emitted not only nearer to the source than Plato or the Presocratics, but inside the Greek origin, close to the other of the Greek."[38]

In his 1973 response to Derrida, Levinas turns the table, so to speak. The paradox that confronts Levinas throughout his work also resonates deeply within Derrida, namely, the necessity of having to employ the language of European metaphysics to deconstruct philosophy. Levinas suggests that Derrida's own skeptical discourse remains logocentric despite his efforts to deconstruct the language of the history of the metaphysics of presence, the same charge levied by Derrida "against" Levinas nearly ten years earlier:

> What remains constructed after deconstruction is, certainly, the stern architecture of the deconstructing discourse which employs the present tense of the verb "to be" in predicative propositions.... One might be tempted to infer an argument from this use of logocentric language against that very language, in order to dispute the produced deconstruction: a path much followed by the refutation of skepticism, but where, although at first crushed and trampled underfoot, skepticism got back up on its feet to come back as the legitimate child of philosophy. A path, perhaps, that Derrida himself has not always disdained from following in his polemic. But, in following this path, one would risk missing one side of the signification which this very inconsequence bears. *One would risk missing the incompressible nonsimultaneity of the Said and the Saying, the dislocation of their correlation.*[39]

Certainly Derrida's skepticism is well warranted and even healthy for philosophy. As the "legitimate child" of philosophy, skepticism helps keep its "parent" cognizant of its actions. Indeed, Levinas will refer to the oscillating differential tension between skepticism and philosophy as the very "enigma of philosophy."[40] Besides, skepticism is not the enemy of thinking. "Western philosophy and the State, which have issued out of proximity, nonetheless refute it in discourse absorbed in the said and in being, in ontology: the history of Western philosophy has not been the refutation of skepticism as much as the refutation of transcendence" (*AE* 262/*OB* 169).

VI

The absolutely other is present in history, in being, through the epiphany of the face, but its alterity is held intact in that what appears is but the *trace* of an essentially heterogeneous absence, a past that was never present. The enigmatic claim that the Other is alter non-ego is paradoxically the claim that the Other is simultaneously both ego and, not non-ego, but that which is *other than* ego. Levinas does not stipulate that the Other be construed as non-ego; if that were the case, then there would be no possibility of relation, of speech, of language. Nor is the

Other merely an alter-ego, as in Hegel, since that too would reduce alterity to a selfsame concept, that of totality.

The radicality of Levinas' position is that the Other is both ego and that which is other than the concept of ego. "Subjectivity is the other in the same" (*AE* 46/*OB* 25). The I exists in proximate relation with the Other. The absolute relational unity expressed in mediation is an impossibility; mediation implies terms joined together in a conceptual totality. Proximity denotes the breach of selfsame conceptualization by and through the simultaneous presence and absence of the Other. As a *historical* entity, the Other is present to consciousness via the face; but as the trace of the transhistorical Infinite, of the absolutely other, the Other conveys the invisible passivity of ethical obligation and establishes, prior to any discourse, the relationship between the self and the Other. The originary signification, the meaning of all meaning, is the appeal of the face of the Other not to do violence to it. The first word is an *imperative*[41]—the prohibition against murder (TeI 217/TI 199). Meaning, which is to say language, is not the unfolding of an idea within a consciousness essentially hermetic.

Egoity only arises out of being in relation with the Other. Were the I a totally isolated or solipsistic entity, there would be no sense of selfhood, of personal identity. Freud's Wolf-Man is a classic example of this as his identity is inexorably bound with his chiasmatic intertwining with the pack.[42] Hegel delineates the formal structure of this in the dialectic of lordship and bondage; but he differs from Levinas in that he affirms the equiprimordiality of totality, substance, and subject. These terms are selfsame in the end, which is also to say, selfsame in the beginning. This realization is expressed in the transition from natural to philosophical consciousness in the *Phenomenology* and in the *Logic* where the famous comparison between infinity and circularity is drawn.

In a sense, both the Other and the self function as egos. And since the self-ego is a construct continually in the process of development, it would seem that it is both same and other. Hegel aptly demonstrates that this process is dialectical. The self is not a constant but an identity; it consists in identifying itself through the multifarious events it encounters. Here Levinas and Hegel are in agreement. The self does come upon a world of plurality which it finds alien and indifferent towards it. But Levinas will not follow "Hegelian phenomenology, where self-consciousness is the distinguishing of what is not distinct" as a genuine affirmation of the radical distinctness of alterity apart from the same since "the difference is not a difference; the I, as other, is not an 'other'" (*TeI* 25–26/*TI* 36–37). The world may indeed *appear* as radically other, as Heidegger asserts, and internal self-reflection may also reveal a *certain* alterity, but the I merges with this inward other and becomes "a play of the same." Self-negation merely becomes self-affirmation; "the negation of the I by the self is precisely one of the modes of the identification of the I" (*TeI* 25/*TI* 37).

This play of the same is correlative with Nietzsche's interpretation of the ego. The individual is a composite of a multiplicity of forces (wills) unified as subject or ego by the will to power. Self-reflection discovers the ego to be but a becoming of the play of forces, an infinity of wills, an internal chaos. The I is revealed as illusory, as a grammatical fiction.[43] Real and yet not real, both concrete and phantastic, the I assumes an identity but is not a constant in itself. Subject is both subject and object; self is both same and other. Again, the issue Levinas confronts is how to maintain the metaphysical asymmetry of the ethical relation while holding on to the reciprocity requisite for the legal working of justice.

The I identifies itself as the same not as a tautology, but as one who sojourns in the world seeking a position, to be at-home (*chez soi*) (*TeI* 21f/*TI* 33f).[44] This site provides the selfsame with the means by which it can retreat from the hostile heterogeneity of the world where it finds itself not as an I, but as an other. At home, the self (*soi*) feels protected, surrounded by that which is familiar, which it inhabits.[45] The need (*besoin*) for possession is the way of the same, the "concreteness of egoism." Continuing this line of thinking, Levinas anticipates Derrida's very concern and objection: "But how can the same, produced as egoism, enter into this relationship with an other without immediately divesting it of its alterity?" (*TeI* 27/*TI* 38). Repudiating the metaphysical relation (Desire) as representation, on the grounds on transcendentalism, Levinas responds to his own question, hearkening back to the themes with which the present study commenced:

> The other with which the metaphysician is in relationship and *which he recognizes as other* is not simply in another locality; this other recalls Plato's Ideas which, according to Aristotle's formula, are not in a site. The *sway* (*pouvoir*) of the I will not cross the distance marked by the alterity of the other (*TeI* 28/*TI* 38).

The Other is beyond the confines of the world in that it signals the irruption of the absolutely other, whose transcendence the face signifies before all language and thought, is history. Religion, the access to this "divine" alterity, occurs not through prayer or liturgy, but through responsibility for the Other motivated by Desire. This is not to say that the Other mediates between the self and God. There is no sense of mediation in *ethical* intersubjectivity, though there is in all democratic political and legal relations. In this tension or difference between the lack of ethical mediation and the necessity of other forms of mediation lies the creative, transformative power of becoming, of ἁρμονία in the Platonic sense of the term.

The Other is foreign to the I; the Other disrupts the at homeness of the selfsame. Over the stranger the I has no power. A relation with the Other can occur only through the medium of language which commences out of the initiative of the I, that is, through Desire (*désir*), "a paradoxical structure without doubt, but one which is no more so than the presence of the Infinite in a finite act (*EeI* 97/*EI* 92). In order to initiate and maintain a relation with the Other, it is imperative that the I reach out to the Desired, the Other, through speech; "*thought consists in speaking*" (*TeI* 30/*TI* 40). Διάνοια does not disclose a relation with another person. It is an act of violence to synthesize the same (*le Même*) and the other (*l'Autre*) into a logical unity expressed through theoretical reflection. "The metaphysical other is other [*L'Autre métaphysique est autre*] with an alterity that is not formal, is not the simple reverse of identity, and is not formed out of resistance to the same, but is prior [*antérieure*] to every initiative, to all imperialism of the same" (*TeI* 28/*TI* 38–39). If the relation between the selfsame and the Other is to be one of goodness, then the radical alterity of the Other must be kept at a respectful distance, in which case it must deny the overarching self-imposed sovereignty of θεωρία.

Language does not operate from a base of reason of which it is merely the reflection; it presupposes a plurality of interlocutors. Language makes universality possible. The speech of the Other is a *revelation* and resists the schema of the subject-object correlation. There is no transcendental ego; the I is incapable of such aloofness. It is impossible to abstract that which is already abstract (the I-ego).

Then how is it possible to maintain a relation with an Other so other if such an other were totally divorced from any relation with an ego? "It is in order that alterity be produced *in being* that a thought is needed and an I is needed" (*TeI* 29/*TI* 39). The I is necessarily produced only insofar as a pole of identity is needed so that the opposite pole of alterity can be expressed. The self is a theoretical fiction; and to reduce the metaphysical terms of exteriority and interiority (other and same) to a cognitive level is to commit the violence of the same.

The Other remains refractory to any conceptual categories that the self may form to define or situate the Other within precisely because the other person defies conception of herself as object for consciousness. The self's conception of the Other is founded on the inability to come to terms with alterity in any absolute and totalizable conceptual manner. The idea of infinity overflows the form of its theoretical structure. To totally think the infinite would be to think the other infinitely, an obvious impossibility, Hegel notwithstanding, for finite being. Only the infinite deity of scholasticism (including the Cartesian conception) or the Hegelian *Geist* is capable of comprehending infinity, a being whose essence is to continually self-reflect. It is this infinite conceptual turning upon itself that Hegel identifies with the Idea. But for Levinas, infinity presents itself as ethically meaningful for exactly the opposite reason: that consciousness is unable to think or rather, hold onto the idea of infinity. The very inability of thought to come to terms with radical alterity, difference, conveys a sense of radical, subjective, and finite solitude.

There is certainly a paradox at play here; but paradox is not construed as an impasse so much by Levinas as by the overly rationalistic tradition of classic metaphysics and epistemology. Indeed, Levinas' conception of ethical responsibility bears an affinity to the Kantian notion of duty (*Pflicht*) as being antinomical with the limited scope of *Vernunft*, of "pure" reason. Be that as it may, paradox actually seems to function for Levinas as the means by which one is able to overcome the need or desire, in the Hegelian sense of *Begierde*, to reconcile the contradictory dyadic pairing of linguistic terms in every dialectical relation. There is not so much a sense of paradox in Hegel's thought as there is mere logical contradiction prior to reconciliation in the moment of the *Aufhebung*. The decidedly non-philosophical, irrational moment of ethical self-displacement and substitution is "religion." Paradox, as Kierkegaard notes, belongs to the very (non) essence of the religious phenomenon. Conversely, Hegel's conception of religion, a tripartite structure composed of the natural, artistic, and revealed, is but a contradictory moment in the movement of Spirit that is finally superseded (*aufgehoben*) by and as absolute knowing. The ethical in Hegel takes the form of communality, of

Sittlichkeit, of participation in the State-machine. It is not the apex of subjectivity, of the individual, as much as it is a renunciation and relinquishment of the private life. The State is, for Hegel, the supreme good; for Levinas, it appears to assume the form of an evil necessary for the acquisition of a provisional goodness which is expressed as law, as adjudication.

VII

Metaphysics is and has always been haunted by the need to recover a knowable origin from which one can derive meaning. But even though the genesis of being is forever unrecoverable in its totality for consciousness, the *meaning* of this immemorial past is not lost on consciousness. The an-archic past, rather than being dismissed as meaningless or a-signifying, is revealed as the non-grounding ground of ethical signification (the saying) itself. The signification that presents itself to thought as the idea of infinity is not something that the Other conveys to the self; rather, infinity is produced within the consciousness of the selfsame as the inability to contain the *idea* of infinity within thought itself. However, Levinas is undaunted by this inability. "The paradox of an Infinity admitting a being outside of itself which it does not encompass, and accomplishing its very infinitude by virtue of this proximity of a separated being—in a word, the paradox of creation—thenceforth loses something of its audacity" (*TeI* 106/*TI* 103).

Though he never explicitly indicates it as such, Levinas proposes a distinction that will be crucial in assessing his relation to, say, the speculative dialectics proposed by Hegel, namely, the difference between the "idea" and the "concept." He says that Kant was the first to separate thought from knowing by distinguishing between ideas and concepts, *Vernunft* and *Verstand*, thereby discovering "in the practical usage of pure reason a plot which is not reducible to a reference to being" (*CPP* 175–76). This difference also parallels the ancient insight first articulated by Plato as the difference between εἶδος and ἰδέα. Hegel equates the concept of infinity not only with the concept of the finite, but also with the key operative concept of totality. The reciprocity that Hegel claims exists between these terms is predicated on their mutual conceptual status. The Idea in Hegel is the totality of conceptual arrangements. In the final analysis, in the teleology of *Geist*, the Idea is synonymous with the concept (*Begriff*); any distinction is purely formal.

Still, one does not have a personal relation with a thought or concept on the same order that one has with a face that responds and moreover calls one's subjective freedom into question. Infinity, present in the face, simultaneously signifies a heteronomous past that cannot be retrieved. Subjectivity or being is the trace of the passing of an infinite alterity that is unrecoverable in its totality by thought. Again, the question returns to the status of *Grund*. Is this concept present to consciousness in the fullness of its actuality; or is it fundamentally absent, present to thought only as the trace?

The face to face is a personal relationship; yet Levinas maintains that something else is implied in the face to face, namely, the *idea* of the Infinite which appears in the face, perhaps even as the face. Meaning or signification is manifest in the face prior to signs emerging from it. With that goes the corollary item that the face to face brings with it the infinite distance or separation that will always remain between the same and the other. Desire is also construed as the mode of relation with the infinitely other and coinciding with this line of thought is an interpretation of the past of the subject as absolutely heteronomous. Here is introduced a second language with regard to the Other. The first is through the language of the infinite; the second is through the language of an absolutely heteronomous past, or alternatively, to refer back to Merleau-Ponty, through a past that was never present. Yet the face is something that we always experience exclusively in the present, as a presence. In addition, there is the idea of death, so crucial for Heidegger, that must be reckoned with, that is, the notion that the past is non-recoverable or unrecollectable in some indestructible sense.

How does Levinas put together these various themes: the notion that the face to face is somehow personal, that it is a form of iconactivity, a way of being in some form of non-mediated relationships, since the notion of mediated relationship is replaced with proximity? Is proximity a self-imposed separation or exteriority? How does one reconcile proximity with the apparently countervaling ideas of infinity and absolute heterogeneity that are placed at the very heart of this relationship that Levinas calls personal? How does one bring together these two strands, one a personal strand out of which come ethics and metaphysics and the other the connection between infinity and absolute heterogeneity?[46]

It would appear, first of all, that proximity is not a self-imposed separation; rather, proximity seems to suggest an already given ontological mode of being with the Other that is founded on the absolute metaphysical separation that the idea of infinity implies. Levinas asserts that the absolutely other is the personal Other in an effort to bring metaphysics out of the conceptual power in which it has traditionally found itself and thereby redesignate metaphysics as the actual lived interpersonal relation. He characterizes traditional forms of metaphysics as ontology, as the will towards the comprehension of Being. But this bespeaks a problem that Levinas faces in his project: he never renounces the terminology of *Totality and Infinity* though he does abandon the language of ontology in his later writing, perhaps attempting to minimize the confusion that often occurs in the use of terms such as "transcendence" and "metaphysics."[47]

Furthermore, the paradoxical use of spatial terminology to express the (de)conception of the other as simultaneously temporally present and supratemporally absent is an active, though admittedly imperfect, and necessarily so, way of expressing the limitation of rational thought. Reason, language, consciousness, and thus proximity and faciality, are not originary; they are created, revealed. In this regard, Levinas is aligned with Nietzsche. The mystery and surprise of the continuing proliferation of these totalities is the wonder of the relation of being with that which is otherwise than it.

Language is always inadequate to the task of fully describing or elucidating, and thus assigning value and meaning, to the relation with the other. "This value is, by an abuse of language, named. It is named God" (*HH* 78/*CPP* 136). Within this thesis lies the heart of Levinas' critique of classical metaphysics as an ontology of totality. Levinas' position is not so much contradictory as it is enigmatic or paradoxical insofar as it is not a positing of the infinite over and against the finite totality of being as history; rather, infinity is to be found, he says, within history, within the totality. The actual paradox is that the infinite *overflows* the totality of history and of thought and that the meaning of this surplus or plentitude is ethical. The responsibility of the I for the Other, obligation to the point of substitution, of giving bread out of one's own mouth, of sacrificial death if need be, is the rupture of subjectivity, while at the same time the commencement of it.

VIII

An important question for Levinas is whether his own discourse still reclaims concepts from the tradition in order to set forth his position. For example, the very idea of the personal lived experience appears, if not to totalize, then to grasp, if not comprehend, infinity for the sake of a discourse in and through that which totally exceeds conceptuality by the fact that the idea of infinity is continually sliding back into the flaws of conceptual thought. For instance, the idea of a person seems inevitably to be united with the concept that there is not any person except as one person at one time. What are the ways in which the very conditions of discourse will always draw back into the realm of the concept that which in principle exceeds the concept as idea?

Levinas' whole project can only succeed with a precise way of understanding totalization. There is to be a paradox in that totalization, the epitome of identity and selfsameness, itself has a pure form of identity. That is, the self delivers itself on numerous occasions to various modes of totalization. But if that is the case, how does one distinguish between the plurality or multiplicity of ways of totalizing and the forms of multiplicity that Levinas construes as liberating from the ontology of the One? What are the ways in which plurality and multiplicity, namely, the face to face relations, keep getting coopted by the unities of things like persons—since it is often the case that, conversely, those things which ought to remain under the headings of "the One," "system," and "totality" keep on proliferating themselves and leaning towards a plurality that is suspiciously similar to what is supposed to be true of the face to face? What exactly is the status of totalization in Levinas' conception of the history of philosophy?

A central concern is whether there is a *continued proliferation* of totalities of various systems that inevitably fall into a totalizing thematization of the face to face relation. Levinas does not deny the thesis that being or history is a totality and in addition that totalities (e.g., languages, subjectivity, systems of thought and governance) are continually coming-to-be. The totality of the history of being is broken up, ruptured, by the epiphanic presencing of the Other in and through the face to face relation.

What prevents an absolute totalization from occurring in the intersubjective relation and in the noetic reflexivity of thinking for Levinas is the introduction of *illeity*, the third party, the moment when the ethical obligation in the form of justice is made manifest. The third person is generally an invisible third, the gnawing realization of the poor, widowed, orphaned, oppressed, the destitute, the stranger—in other words, among those beings that are, for whatever reason, excluded or unable to participate in the discourse of society, be it popular, philosophical or legal. Substitution, the most extreme and pronounced form of the unending responsibility for the Other, requires taking up the preservation of the liberty of their existence, in a sense that extends beyond the Heideggerian notion of *Gelassenheit*, before the care or attentiveness of our own subjective freedom. This is the maintenance of the separation of self and Other that already exists prior to the thematization by consciousness of intersubjectivity, without founding peace or reconciliation on the notion of the legislating State. It is perhaps this absolutely obligatory subjective aspect of Levinas' conception of ethics that is most resisted by his readers and by the modern philosophical tradition with its emphasis on sovereign subjectivity.

Deleuze and Guattari offer an interesting perspective with regard to this problem. They maintain that the quantification of the multiple by the social assemblage delimits a field that *neutralizes* the significance of the face;[48] whereas for Levinas, the meaning of the ethical is present in the nudity of the face which conveys to consciousness the absolute separation between the self and the Other, a separation that is produced as a psychism, as the idea of infinity. The face is the *trace* of the passing of an absolutely heteronomous past, a prehuman "*signification without a context*" (*TeI* 8/*TI* 23). The face is not the mask of the individual; it is the locus of the alterity which is the social multiplicity. Similarly, Deleuze and Guattari declare that "faces are not basically individual" as they essentially denote "redundancies of significance or frequency." That is to say, "the face constructs the wall that the signifier needs in order to bounce off of."[49] The face is a phenomenal surface for both thinkers, simultaneously transmitting the signification of the absolutely other (Levinas) or "something absolutely inhuman."[50] The face *overcodes* the bodily head; the question is the meaning of this codification.

Now, Levinas' philosophy is exclusively preoccupied with the meaning of the *human* face to face relation, the loci of all ethical interactions,[51] in which transcendence and phenomenality meet producing in their wake the ethical signification. Peace is contingent upon the recognition of the significance of the face of the Other. But this is precisely where Levinas and Deleuze/Guattari part in their analyses on faciality. According to the latter, if there is any human destiny at all, it is to "escape the face" in order to get "on the road to the asignifying and asubjective."[52] Of course, it is the traditional conceptions of subjectivity and the significations identified with it which Deleuze and Guattari wish to break free from, as does Levinas. The territorialization of classically defined subjectivity, from its place in the πόλις to the present State-economic assemblage, is what both thinkers desire to overcome. All three realize that it is often within these parameters that violence most acutely manifests itself, primarily on the horrific large-scale level of war.

However, whereas Levinas remains steadfastly anthropocentric in his analysis of the face, Deleuze and Guattari correlate the face with the *landscape*, "which is not just a milieu, but a deterritorialized world." It represents an "*absolute* deterritorialization" as it is no longer merely relative to the head but to the strata of signification and subjectification.[53] Deterritorialization is inseparable from the question of reterritorialization. This is not to suggest a return to a certain primitiveness, as Rousseau suggests, nor to older, more originary territorial sites.

Drawing on Nietzsche's analysis of active and reactive forces in the will to power, territorialization is the ever-shifting, fluid interplay of deterritorialization and reterritorialization. Facialization is always in the process of being reterritorialized just as the landscape or "wildscape"[54] is continually undergoing transformation by either the forces of nature or those of plasticity. The meaning of the face is determined and redetermined by the ground in which it is present—be it the wilderness, the suburbs, or the city streets.

So even if it is the case that the face to face relation is continually corrupted on account that it is a relation within being and not exterior to it, there is always a possible surprise assessed beyond the reconceptualizations of the Other which have recently taken place in thinking. But how does Levinas reconcile the antinomy between the absolutely other as the trace of an irrecoverable heteronomous past and a future fecundity? All of this is temporal terminology, and yet the medium in which the moment of fecundity will occur is deeply saturated in the language of *spatiality*, e.g., exteriority, separation, illeity, the face to face, the *il y a*, proximity. How can it be that hope is given on the one hand, in the slenderest and most distant projective terms, and on the other, experientially in the most concrete and ordinary manner, namely, in the face to face relation?

In the Levinasian construal of the face, the infinite is made completely accessible through this fertile and deconstructed idea of the interspatial. Levinas does not make available the fullness of time in any *Augenblick* which could be in this presence; it is always in some future sense. What is left is a moment that is not a moment, or a moment that is perpetually deferred and rejected from the one and only moment, namely, the space that it takes to encounter it wherein the self could hope to find hope. Or does this paradox subtract that very element of hope?

There is no explicit theory of hope outlined in Levinas as there is, for example, in Marcel's philosophy.[55] Derrida notes that Levinas writes of an "eschatology without hope for the self or without liberation in my time."[56] Hope appears to be *implied* in Levinas' considerations on messianic eschatology, but Levinas also deconstructs certain theories of hope, particularly apocalyptic, as they are subtended by traditional metaphysical formulations based on unity and permanence.

Levinas does not present his philosophy as any sort of rational or methodological way of breaking free of the totality. In a sense, he agrees with Hobbes, Nietzsche and Hegel that the totality (being) is violence, war, πόλεμος, and that it presents itself as such to thought. This is why he will ultimately reject the claims of philosophy that purport to found peace on the notions of totality, identity, unity, and sameness in an attempt to reconcile the "allergy" that exists between same and the other. Rather, Levinas takes recourse to the non-philosophical notion of eschatology, the idea that if peace should occur it will not do so through the synthesis or homogenization of the self-other relation in the form, for example, of the Hegelian notion of the State. The non-violent rupture of the totality will be a moment of surprise, occurring in a futurity that one cannot foretell or portend.

10

HyperGround

The death of God, arguably the most profound contemporary philosophical-theological revelation, has left (post)modernity in the clutches of nihilism, struggling to find a *terra firma* on which to continue its enterprise. While Hegel may have been the first to articulate philosophically the demise of the deity, Nietzsche stands out as the primary voice in the wilderness of this cataclysmic event. This chapter considers Nietzsche's refusal to continue the long defunct project of transfiguring the divine into the ontological order of the said. His repudiation of any attempt to establish *any* metaphysical *ground* is considered by way of his thoughts on the ontologico-metaphysical primacy of *chaos.* This is taken up with the intention of advancing Levinas' conception of the pre-original, an-archic alterity revealed in the face of the Other. The paradoxical "structure" of intelligible reality signals an irreversible hypermovement beyond the dialectical framework which has, ironically, proven to be both so useful and so violent. The work concludes by engaging the eschatological and apocalyptic visions of the future in Hegel, Nietzsche, and Levinas, and their relation to the (trans)historical effort to engender a new non-totalizing, non-violent conception of subjectivity and intersubjectivity.

I

The task confronting contemporary thinking is the formulation of *new non*-foundationalist conceptions of ground and Godhead. The challenge is the determination of the Absolute *either* as one that allows for the possibility of a genuine once and for all beginning that would be synonymous with the promise and fullness of knowledge, grace, and salvation, *or* as the absolutely other that conditions knowledge and ethical signification on the very basis of its ineffable transcendence and radical alterity. Clearly, Levinas rejects the former option as one which invariably slides into the imperialism of the same, thereby deconstructing the very unified peace it strives to achieve.

As suggested earlier, Hegel's text contains the possibility of undermining his own attempt to form a rational notion of ground. This is the concept of *Trieb*, the originary urge or drive that makes the system originate in the first place. But given the ambiguous, enigmatic and mysterious nature of *Trieb*, several questions come to the fore: Is the primal energy (*Urgrund*) of becoming dialectically recoverable by thinking as *Grund*? Or is the *Urgrund* the abyss (*Abgrund*) about which *nothing* determinate can be said? And if so, then is the *Abgrund* charged with a prepositivity of meaning in the manner that the pre-original saying is for Levinas?

No one has demonstrated better than Hegel that the concept of *Grund* is the product of an imaginative consciousness endowed with the creative power of synthetic articulation. Nietzsche will expose and dissimulate this ground as chaos, as *Abgrund*, thereby signaling the groundlessness of consciousness. But does the "beautiful chaos of existence"[1] shroud the abyss, or is it identical with it? Is the *Abgrund* the collapse of consciousness upon itself, the nihilistic "postmodern condition"? Is it the pre-origination of consciousness (will to power), or even the horrific state of anonymous existence in general (*il y a*)? These are the questions that contemporary interpreters face in addessing the ambiguity of the hyperbatic hyperbolicity of the Nietzschean text.

There is something appealing about maintaining the *mystery* of an incomprehensible Absolute, especially when considering the equally dangerous alternative of using knowledge in a negatively powerful sense, e.g., as a device or means of oppression. But the *coincidentia oppositorum* need not be contingent upon the cognition of consciousness, whether apprehended in the manner of Nicolas of Cusa's mathematically defined universe, or comprehended in Hegelian logic, or realized in the most modern radical theology. Merleau-Ponty's concept of the chiasm serves as the existential and phenomenological concretion of the abstractly conceived *coincidentia oppositorum*. But is it possible to retain the new epistemology implied in such a formulation without losing or doing violence to the irreversible asymmetry that "grounds" an ethical metaphysics?

Why should one opt for a radical and infinite exteriority as opposed to what seems to be the fullness of sensuality and historical concretion in dialectical thinking? In short, though the dangers of mystery are many and readily apparent as history has too often demonstrated (one grasps here why Hegel asserts the human access to the divine consciousness as the fullness of salvific grace and redemption), in a world tottering daily on the brink of a capitalist, technologically induced nihilism, and where the concerns of the few far outweigh the needs of the many, it seems that human consciousness needs *humbling* more that exaltation.[2] On the metaphysical level, perhaps this is best accomplished by grasping the Infinite through its *idea* and not its concept (the tool of instrumental rationality), as uniquely and concretely universal in the trace *without* collapsing it into the immanence of the finite world of becoming.

Is there a difference to be made between the Nothing and the Abyss and therefore between the nothingness or emptiness which seems to be simultaneous with the dialectical understanding of the eternal beginning of the infinite Godhead? Certainly for Hegel, even if the death of God is not truly and actually possible, it is philosophically grasped for the first time in Western thinking. But exactly *what* God dies, asks Levinas?

> The loss of unity has been proclaimed—and consecrated through a contrary movement—by the celebrated paradox, become a commonplace, of the death of God.

> The crisis of sense is thus experienced by our contemporaries as a crisis of monotheism.... The status of his transcendence, despite the immanence of his revelation—a transcendence new with respect to the unbridgeable transcendence of the Aristotelian god—*the status of this transcendence of the supernatural was never set forth.* (*HH* 38/*CPP* 89; italics added)

The death of God, the loss of a *particular* selfsame vision of exalted subjectivity, is not denied by Levinas; but neither does his thinking revolve around it, lost in the nihilistic quagmire of an irretrievable loss of meaning.[3] Levinas' work centers around the task of reestablishing the transcendence of the Infinite, and the ethical saying that gives it form as the face, the revelatory locus of continual surprise and creative power, simultaneously tempered and freed in the demand of ethical obligation. Each and every moment in the spatio-temporal continuum is the possibility of a *new* commencement or beginning.[4]

The efforts of Levinas, Adorno, Merleau-Ponty, and Derrida, among others, allow the advancement of the great ongoing dialectic of Western metaphysics—that between visibility and invisibility—to proceed (the "end of philosophy" is not the end of dialectic) with one important difference. The dialectic continually turns back towards corporeal, incarnate being, actually (un)grounding itself, paradoxically, in the phenomenal ground of the world. Reason (*Grund*) proceeds from an already situated existence, from a space-place. Hegel is correct in this respect. Cognitively, ground is a result, though immediately present in the world apprehended by the natural consciousness. But the Hegelian account of ground remains tied to the domain of conceptuality, of thought in and for itself. The great advance of Merleau-Ponty's notion of hyperdialectic, apart from its moving beyond of older conceptions of positive dialectic, lies in its continually bending back towards the world. This hyperdialectic incorporates the revolutionary insights of twentieth-century physics, leading to what Levinas refers to as the "curvature of intersubjective space."

> The truth of being is not the *image* of being, the *idea* of its nature; it is the being situated in a subjective field which *deforms* vision, but precisely thus allows exteriority to state itself, entirely command and authority: entirely superiority. This curvature of the intersubjective space inflects distance into elevation; it does not falsify being, but makes its truth first possible.... This surplus of truth over being and over its idea, which we suggest by the metaphor of the 'curvature of intersubjective space,' signifies the divine intention of all truth. This 'curvature of space' is, perhaps, the very presence of God. (*TeI* 324/*TI* 293)

The hyperdialectical trajectory is not hyper because it turns in upon itself; the positive dialectic of idealism accomplishes as much. Hyperdialectic is the movement beyond the ideal, beyond the domain of the concept, carrying rationality along with it only as the effect or trace of incarnate being. Levinas designates this hyperactivity as the curvature of space because it is the very movement of the said's reduction to the saying. The paradoxical presence or expression of the saying in the said is the moment when the ethical interrupts or disturbs the order of the ontological, the commencement of the moment when God, or infinity, is *produced* in relationship. The *desired* effect or end is, paradoxically, the very beginning of God, eternally *re*produced.

The question of the end is, as Hegel realizes, the question of origination. But if the origin is a *pre*-original saying, immemorially and irretrievably past, then does not that indicate, perhaps more than anything else, that the end or ἔσχηατον is likewise hidden? If this is indeed the case, and granting the thesis of the irreversible forward movement of time, then is not the Hegelian vision of an apocalyptic culmination of history merely the projection of a nihilistic will seeking to finally and irrevocably overcome itself?

While the imagination can surely conceive of an absolute origin, imagination and knowledge are not the same. This is one of the great insights of Plato's *Republic.* Again, the question surrounding the status of origination is whether it is eternal, and graspable as such, or if it is determinate in the Hegelian sense. Surely, if cognition is unable to lay hold of an eternal beginning, then it is also equally the case for a once-and-for-all beginning. But it is also the case that "if we cannot think a unique and absolute beginning, *or purely think it*, we nevertheless cannot think apart from it."[5]

II

No one has disrupted the course of classical through modern thinking and set the mark for postmodernity as profoundly as has Nietzsche, who maintains that the quest for a knowable, rational ground is a veritable chase after a will o' the wisp. In the Nietzschean framework one finds the basis for reconceiving, or actually, *revaluating* the meaning of being. Traditionally, philosophy has tended to define truth as the adequation of the object perceived (phenomenon) with the object known (noumenon), and to equate God, the "'thing in itself,' the *horrendum pudendum* of the metaphysicians,"[6] with the hidden. However, this way of thinking does not acknowledge the fundamental hermeneutical sway of the ontological; rather, it negates interpretation by positing being as subject to logical principles of conformity. But as David Allison succinctly states, "Nietzsche knows no noumenon."[7] The phenomenal world with all its shifting appearances is the only "true" world.

Likewise, Levinas refuses to situate being, the thing itself, present "in its word," as the hidden form behind phenomena:

> To posit the thing in itself as hidden would be to suppose that it is with respect to the phenomenon what the phenomenon is to the appearance. The truth of disclosure is at most the truth of the phenomenon hidden under the appearances; the truth of the thing in itself is not disclosed. The thing in itself expresses itself. (*TeI* 198/*TI* 181)

The face is the expression of the thing in itself signifying the primacy of the ethical relationship which "does not function in proximity as a sign of the hidden God who would impose the neighbor on me. It is a trace of itself, a trace of an abandon, where the equivocation is never dissipated" (*AE* 150/*OB* 94). Faces are the presence of multiplicity or plurality in the world, the One prior to singularity that makes the phenomenal event of singularity possible. The meaning of being presents itself as open to a multiplicity of interpretations, resisting all efforts at dogmatization or canonization. Being is infinite becoming and thus essentially and necessarily hermeneutical; it gives itself over to innumerable readings and valuations. Endeavors to construct the meaning of being in a purely coherent, rational manner are themselves interpretations. They are exercises in deconstruction since such actions nullify themselves by ending all *other* interpretations and the possibility for future hermeneutical activity. Plural in "essence," existence is also ambiguous. Being does not present or conceal itself in a logical mode; "true" being is not confined to the intellect or soul. Being is hermeneutical because it is phenomenal.

The notion of being that reifies truth as the Truth and equates the thought of existence at its highest level (God) with this truth is, to use the words of Levinas, an ontology of totality. Existence loses its essentially ambiguous character in the *light* of the philosophies of identity. But if being is fundamentally ambiguous and teleologically indeterminate, then is it essentially *chaotic*?

Chaos is a key concept for the understanding of Nietzsche's ontology. According to him, the "most terrible reality" for the Greeks was disguised by an ever changing veil in order to hide the great *horror metaphysicus*.[8] This veil or mask is the phenomena of the world which hides the chaotic composition of being. Chaos cannot appear as anything but being masked. To look behind the mask or veil is to invite madness; it is to see that Truth is the great myth and ruse of the West, that it is a lie. Nietzsche's writing is an encouragement to peek behind the Veil of Isis.[9] The path to *self-overcoming* necessitates this.[10]

The hyperborean[11] strength needed for self-overcoming rises from the affirmation of the chaotic composition of being expressed in the pathos of the eternal recurrence. To affirm the "beautiful chaos of existence" is to realize the limitless limitedness of human freedom, a liberty continually conjoined with the possible advent of madness. After all, "human existence cannot be understood without reference to madness, nor could we be human without carrying madness within as the limit of our freedom."[12] The will that affirms chaos displaces itself outside the neatly ordered boundaries of society. Such *individuals* have often been deemed irrecuperably mad or at times evil by their peers because they threaten the tranquility that "civilized" society offers to the majority, to the herd.[13]

Interpretation is but the donning and/or exposing of a mask or veil. The mask conceals no hidden transcendent truth or reality. Western philosophy, with its supreme insistence that existence is rational and knowable, often seeks to deal with the ambiguous nature of phenomena by attempting to separate the being and the appearance of the phenomena. But in so doing, philosophy falls prey to phenomena because "phenomena cheat," says Jean Granier: "the phenomenon masks what it manifests, *without enabling us to dissociate dissimulation from manifestation*."[14] Chaos is the continual non-teleological movement of exposure and dissimulation, disclosure and concealment. Truth is "only" appearance since appearance (phenomena) is the *only* reality. Anything that opposes itself to appearance is therefore illusory.

Chaotic being is groundless; it is abyss (*Abgrund*). Chaos is not differentiated substance or substrate; it lacks all structure, telos, or meaning.[15] Chaos is not essence; it is force(s). Simultaneously grounding and *un*grounding, it is the foundation that has no foundation. But from within the depths of this abyss lie the creative and destructive forces of life. It is because being is chaos that there is the possibility for hermeneutical activity.

Is chaos the *Abgrund* of the saying of which the said is the field on which the "game" of hermeneutics is played? One cannot speak of the whole of this radical plurality of interpretations since it is infinite; but as *in*-finite the multiplicity becomes accessible, ensuring the possibility of constant creations, of continual "divine" action within the world. All interpretation is a creation, a molding of the primordial clay, a transformation of chaos, a purpose to life, a release from boredom. Chaotic being is existence that is *interesting*.

In general, Western thought has been an attempt to *name* the ultimate ground, the transcendental signified, God. But interpreting chaotic being as ground does a violence to existence in general; it *neutralizes* Being as a concept, rendering it susceptible to manipulation and domination by Reason. Nietzsche rebels against the notion of forming a ground to substantiate meaning. In fact, he doubts

> whether a philosopher could *possibly* have "ultimate and real" opinions, whether behind every one of his caves there is not, must not be, another deeper cave—a more comprehensive, stranger, richer world beyond the surface, an abysmally deep ground [*ein Abgrund hinter jedem Grunde*], under every attempt to furnish "grounds" [*Begründung*]...every philosophy also *conceals* a philosophy; every opinion is also a hideout, every word also a mask.[16]

In understanding being as essentially chaotic, as infinitely differentiated, Nietzsche's conception of existence can be characterized as non-metaphysical or "transmetaphysical."[17] The metaphysical quest for a knowable ground of existence is abandoned. There is *no* final or ultimate mask to uncover. The paradoxical groundless ground of chaos is the flux of shifting veiled appearances, of faces expressing the endless uniqueness of singularity, which is not to say identity since "no one is identical with himself. Beings do not have identity; faces are masks" (*CPP* 34). But Levinas also says that the face "is not a form concealing, but thereby indicating, a ground, a phenomenon that hides, but thereby betrays, a thing itself. Otherwise, a face would be one with a mask, but a mask presupposes a face" (*HH* 58/*CPP* 102). Is he saying two different things regarding the relation between the face and mask? If faces are indeed masks, then it is only because the face is the epiphanic appearance of the absolutely other as the Other. But the face signifies more than the saying that is present within and through it. This overflowing of signification is the continual production of the uniqueness of singularity, of subjectivity, of the paradox of the other in the same. The mask presupposes the face as subjectivity presupposes its constituting relationship with alterity. The face is the thing in itself, the *altared ground* of God.

Chaotic being must necessarily manifest itself as phenomena in order to be interpreted. Chaos is force itself and thus always in tension with other forces. The production of meanings, identities, consciousnesses, values, indeed of life itself, Nietzsche will—through his own abuse of language—designate as *will to power.* Nature and phenomena, manifestations of will to power, are inextricably linked together as the *same.* Sameness here does not imply identity; rather, it is closer in meaning to the ancient and later enlightenment concept of *harmonia,* as creative, dynamic tension. The difference acted out in the antagonistic relation between the forces of nature and phenomena is the space for hermeneutic play. Only the will to power brings what is concealed to light, that is, gives meaning to the chaotic composition of being.

The nihilism that necessarily follows (or accompanies?) chaotic being is countered by the will to power, that is to say, by the continual creation of meaning, of interpretation, of donning veils, of dancing in the macabre masquerade ball of life and death. The Veil of Isis, that dangerously beautiful and ever so thin drape, in its infinite folds hides its part and thus its secret. Perhaps the will to power is the will to lift the veil—and then to laugh.

III

The question of the meaning of Being is ultimately the question of *valuation.* But if the transcendental source of valuation is exposed as illusion, as deceit, as trickster, what then? "The desert is growing" warns Zarathustra, "God is dead!" And as the madman cries out, it is *we* who have killed him.[18] The demise of God, the loss of any transcendental source of meaning, has been construed as the self-annihilation of the deity by various radical theologians (e.g., Altizer), but it is generally agreed that if it is not the result of the loss of faith, then it at least signifies the loss of faith in any transcendental referent. And if it is not the loss of faith, then it is the abuse of such a notion, e.g., faith in the utopian hope of technology or the State, bringing us to the brink of nuclear meltdowns and totalitarian politics. Nietzsche recognizes (prophesies?) the *rhizomatic*[19] trajectory of metaphysics in the present century:

> What were we doing when we unchained this earth from its sun? Away from all suns? Are we not plunging continually? Backward, sideward, forward, in all directions? Is there any up or down? Are we not straying as through an infinite nothing?[20]

The "greatest event of the age," the death of God, still largely unrecognized, leaves humanity on the throes of *nihilism.*[21] The question now: whither meaning?

In naming the world or becoming as will to power and the movement of time as eternal recurrence, Nietzsche repudiates the teleology implied in the notion of ground, that is, in a reason capable of reaching to the depths of the past while simultaneously extending into a knowable horizon of futurity. The becoming or flux of existence is chaos which denies rational totalization by consciousness. The nihilism that characterizes the condition of modernity is the very nihilism that subtends the history of metaphysics and ontology, a nihilism that has continually undermined every system of valuation, resulting in the irreversible consequence of the death of God.

But can one *know* an absolute beginninglessness? Is chaos congruous with the knowability of an absolutely necessary beginning? Levinas has built his entire philosophy on the premise that one can have an "idea" of a pre-original infinity. Since the Infinite is not in itself or καθ'αὐτό, is it then merely a synonym for chaos? To put it another way, is chaos infinite in its spatial and non-spatial composition? Perhaps Levinas shies away from any positive articulation of chaos because it denotes the *absence* of the saying, of the ethical force itself. But then, perhaps Levinas and Nietzsche are actually quite close in their formulations of the pre-original Infinite and chaos insofar as both conceptions not only defy conception, but function as the *Urgrund* of valuative meaning, revealed respectively as the trace and the hierarchical ordering of will to power.

Nietzsche speaks of the absolute break with and the subsequent dissolution of metaphysics, signaling the advent of a new infinite horizon. Like Levinas, he sees the construction of an *absolute* metaphysical genealogy as an impossibility.[22] There is an affinity between Nietzsche and Levinas in that both posit a rejection of classic and Hegelian conceptions of ground while simultaneously acknowledging the totality as both conceptual and historical, or to employ Heidegger's terms, as both ontological and ontic. In addition, both thinkers proclaim the need for a revamped conception of infinity. For Nietzsche, this "new 'infinite'" is found *within the world* and is a moment of both liberation and trepidation, "inasmuch as we cannot reject the possibility that *it may include an infinite number of interpretations.* Once more we are seized by a great shudder; but who would feel immediately inclined to deify again after the old manner this monster of an unknown world?"[23] This apprehension is also shared by Levinas who, in his own way, rethinks infinity so as to avoid a return to the sterile conception of the transcendent deity of Platonist-Aristotelian metaphysics. The task bequeathed to contemporary and postmodern thinking is still none other than that of classical philosophies: to determine the nature of the relation between the finite and the infinite. The death of God is not the end of this ancient question. And while both Nietzsche and Levinas reject the thesis that the world is infinite in the sense of being "eternally novel,"[24] the idea of infinity is not abandoned to the mausoleum of obsolete metaphysical concepts. According to Nietzsche, infinity signifies the horizon of hermeneutical possibility; for Levinas, infinity signifies the absolute difference of alterity and the idea of the ethical in the face. The relation between them centers around the question of determining the ethical significance of will to power and the epiphany of ethical sensibility.

Nietzsche affirms the notion of the totality of existence as an infinite becoming but without any teleological orientation. The constitution of subjectivity, itself a becoming or process, does not rest upon the Idea's reflection of itself as Spirit, as it does with Hegel.[25] Subjectivity, a force in the infinite chaotic play of forces, is an "issuing forth" of the will to power. The rejection of Hegelian philosophy requires a new metaphysical base upon which to (not) predicate the ethical relation.

In Levinas one finds no less paradoxical and radical a position, namely, that subjectivity is constituted by alterity. The totality does not ground conscious existence and the world in general. Subjectivity is "founded in the idea of infinity" which is "produced in the relation of the same with the other" (*TeI* 11/*TI* 26). In his philosophy one finds the basis for the possibility of thinking the will to power, generally construed as an amoral or immoral thought, ethically. The premise of an ethical metaphysics is contingent upon a prior deconstruction of previous metaphysical and ontological forms. Nietzsche is among the first great destroyers of such myths in the West. And though radically different in many respects, both are united in their conviction that the advancement of subjectivity depends upon a transvaluation of values, a radical prioritizing of the plural over the singular with the expressed intention of preserving and advancing subjectivity. Levinas' interpretation of the metaphysical One as ethical social multiplicity, as a non-totalizing thought, contra Hegel, is offered here as the decisive insight of twentieth century philosophy.

IV

The notions of chaos and *amor fati* bring into play the element of *chance* "which the wisest providence could not think up a more beautiful music than."[26] But does the necessity of the contingency embodied in chaos preclude the spontaneity or chance occurrence of events within the world? Modern physics is illuminating on this point and surely the recent chaos theory lends support for the thesis of a radical order subtending the chaotic composition of phenomenality. Altizer, for instance, postulates a "chaos that is the very order of the cosmos" and locates a connection between the absolute event of genesis and the chaos which is the absolute necessity of God.[27]

Now, if one assumes that the death of God is the moment of an irreversible beginning (a Hegelian proposition), one may be somewhat justified in positing the notions of an absolute good and evil. But does this speak of an inherent affinity with dialectical thinking on Nietzsche's part, or of the complete sundering of any relation with it? Nietzsche's principal texts on ethics or morality lack the evidence to support the thesis that Nietzsche understood "good" and "evil" in an absolutely dichotomous (not dualistic) fashion, or that his notion of beyond (*Jenseits*) carries with it any of the Hegelian sense of the *Aufhebung*. To think "beyond good and evil" is a rejection of such absolute concepts as abstract, speculative and, ultimately, illusory. Nietzsche makes it clear that he does not include the historically determinate and relative opposition of "good" and "bad" in this beyond.[28]

Levinas' essay "Humanism and An-Archy" contains his most "Nietzschean" response. The idea of the pre-original is the prevailing thought throughout and is connected to the notions of the archaeology (genealogy) of reason and the relation between good and evil. Levinas indicates that his philosophy does not affirm the equiprimordiality of Good and Evil, the theodic thought that governs the Hegelian text and leads to Nietzsche's early atheist declaration.[29] The asymmetry of the metaphysical relation is also present in the relation between good and evil. Ironically, the very asymmetry of ethical responsibility for the Other without return to the selfsame lies at the base of the "insurmountable ambiguity of evil:"

> Thus there is, in the midst of the submission to the Good, the seduction of irrespon-

> sibility, the probability of egoism in the subject responsible for his responsibility, that is, the very birth of the ego in the obeying will. This temptation to separate oneself from the Good is the very incarnation of the subject or his presence in being.... Evil shows itself to be sin, that is a responsibility, despite itself, for the refusal of responsibilities. It is neither alongside of nor in front of the Good, but in the second place, beneath, lower than, the Good. The being that perseveres in being, egoism or Evil, thus outlines the dimension of baseness itself, and the birth of hierarchy. Here begins the axiological polarity. (*HH* 81/*CPP* 137–38)

In opting for the hierarchy of good over evil, Levinas is not reverting to the Augustinian position of evil as lack or absence of the Good. The reality of evil is not questioned, only its supposed equiprimordiality with goodness. Certainly Levinas and Nietzsche part ways at this point. Yet Nietzsche's conception of chaos and fate undermines any notion of the *absolute* dichotomy of good and evil. Nietzsche is a truly modern thinker of totality and, in this sense, he shares the company of Spinoza, Hegel, and Whitehead. The primary point of difference between Nietzsche and Levinas regards the status of the *beyond.* And yet, this is the very moment that a surprising and disturbing alliance between them can be formed.

Like Nietzsche, Levinas attempts to rescue the issue of ethical valuation in a *trans*valuative manner, that is, *beyond* the societal grounds of morality. What obscures this endeavor from many readers is that Levinas effects this revaluation not by positing something new, but by recovering something ancient and radical, namely, the Platonic apprehension of transcendence. The force of this position is the realization by consciousness of the trace of an absolutely heteronomous past, signified by the idea of infinity. Nietzsche, as is well known, rejects the Platonic model of the Good for the very reason that Levinas affirms it—because it is *beyond* being. Nevertheless, the present work postulates a potential correlation between Levinas' understanding of radical alterity and Nietzsche's thought of the will to power. The question rests on the status of the *overflowing* of the totality of finite existence.

The will that wills the selective ethic of the eternal recurrence is a will that wills the ethical joyously, and not merely as submission to responsibility. Such a will is a heightened sense of strength, able to affirm that which is more terrible than the power of the negative (i.e., chaos, chance, fate), that which is *unknown* and *other*, with no assurances whatsoever. In affirming the eternal recurrence, the will affirms total freedom and independence within absolute necessity (of being tied to a finite chaotic universe). Now if Levinas is correct, this sense of freedom is necessarily bound to the ethical relation, but in a secondary modality. Ethics precedes freedom; ethics is the acknowledgement of the primacy of the Other. The affirmation of the eternal recurrence liberates the will from *ressentiment* and the tyranny of time and affirms the creative freedom of the will constituted by that which is other than it. Freedom is crowned by the Good: "Existence is not in reality condemned to freedom, but is *invested* as freedom. Freedom is not bare. To philosophize is to trace freedom back to what lies before it, to disclose the investiture that liberates freedom from the arbitrary" (*TeI* 83/*TI* 84). The eternal recurrence is infinity within the totality. Michel Haar refers to the eternal recurrence as a "bursted totality, a shattered totality."[30] In other words, the infinity within the totality of the eternal recurrence cannot be contained—it overflows. This radical exteriority is will to power where the power, never satiated (like Desire), orients and signifies to will and force prior to definition or determination.

As a doctrine concerned with the relation of being and time, the eternal recurrence also impacts views on history.[31] Nietzsche's polemic is against the dominant interpretation of history during his time—the Hegelian interpretation. The eternal recurrence is diametrically opposed to any theory of the movement of history articulated as rational and teleological; rather, it is the articulation of a movement beyond such a totalizing conception of being. The eternal recurrence takes on the form of a "religion" for Nietzsche, much in the manner of the universal religion of ethics in Levinas' sense. Indeed, Nietzsche refers to the eternal recurrence as a "prophecy,"[32] as a "divine" mode of thinking; it is the "religion" of pure possibility, that which will enable humanity to rise far above its present state, to attain the level of the *Übermensch*. The eternal recurrence is the non-apocalyptic eschatological "religion" of the will to power.

V

What are the elements or aspects of existence capable of producing the will requisite for determining "a subjectivity born from the eschatological vision?" (*TeI* 11/*TI* 25). According to Nietzsche, it is the elemental force of will to power which is the essence and the act of affirmation itself. Deleuze interprets Nietzsche differently from others in that he focuses, in part, on critical distinctions between force and will, force and power, and the interplay of forces and will to power.[33] To briefly summarize Deleuze's reading: Nietzsche distinguishes between active and reactive qualities of force and between the affirmative and negative qualities of will to power. Active/affirmation and reactive/negation are linked together but are not identical in meaning. Affirmation is actuated active force, that is, force becoming-active; conversely, negation is force becoming-reactive. Will to power can be either the affirmative Yes-saying to life (Dionysian) or the No-saying of nihilism.

Furthermore, though active force, when separated from what it can do by reactive force, becomes reactive itself, the contrapositive is not the case. Reactive force does not become active by reaching the limit of what it can do; were that so, it would require a completely different sense of becoming along with a new sensibility and a new sense of affectation. It would require a will that is *not yet* present, a will that is wholly *other* than the reactive will which now characterizes consciousness; in other words, an eschatological will. Such a will would be in total command of itself and its world; it would be will to power actualized.

Deleuze's enigmatic interpretation reads in Nietzsche's text that the will to power is *added to* the concepts of force and forces.[34] Construed thus, will to power is a radical exteriority interiorized within the being upon whom the will to power is affecting. It is important to ascertain here the significance of the word *zur* (towards) in *Wille zur Macht*. The dynamism of will to power is implied by the term *zur*, not by *Macht*. Will is the intersection in which the play of forces that comprise life occurs. A force, but not the essence of force, will orders the flux (forces) of becoming. Force and will are inextricably, though not synonymously, linked together. Together they comprise the totality of becoming. So what is *power* then? That which force is always reaching out towards, in search of more. Power is *beyond* the totality of forces and wills as the *other* of will, which is to say, outside the domain of comprehension by selfsame consciousness.

Will to power cannot be defined solely as force or will, or even as the interplay of forces and wills. Will to power is the becoming-active of force, but it "still needs to be *completed*: an *inner* will must be *ascribed* to it, which [Nietzsche] designate[s] as 'will to power.'"[35] How does one reconcile the need to "complete" the will to power with the non-teleological movement of will to power? Deleuze describes this complementary relation between force and "inner will" in terms of a *synthesis*. As the genealogical (differential and genetic) element of force, will to power reveals its nature as "the principle of the synthesis of forces."[36] This is not synthesis in the Hegelian sense; rather, it bears closer resemblance to Kant's use of the term.[37] The synthesis of force and will in will to power finds its expression in the eternal recurrence which, when affirmed, is the becoming of active force.[38]

As the force of interpretation itself, will to power is linked with language. Consciousness arises out of the need to communicate, which requires adherence to the accepted grammatical and syntactical framework of society (failure to do so would result in incoherence). But since consciousness cannot absolve itself of its relation to the self or ego, it falls under the critique of the ego as a grammatical fiction.[39] The dualism between thought and object, the adequation of which has traditionally been defined as truth, reveals itself in the relation between subject and predicate. This notion of truth, however, is no longer tenable in the Nietzschean framework since there is no substantiality to the "I" as origin. Descartes interprets the "I" of the *cogito* to be the subject of "think," but for Nietzsche, just the opposite is the case.[40] Thoughts do not emerge or originate from the self; rather, they *come to the self*. The self is just another thought. "We are a plurality that has imagined itself a unity."[41] The I does not think thoughts; it receives them. We do not possess language; language possesses us. There are strong parallels to be drawn here with Levinas' conception of the pre-original saying and the ontological said where the saying arises not from within the said, but is revealed from without, from the face of the Other, to subjectivity. Being is the trace of the infinitely other; or, put differently, the product of the will to power.

The fundamentally relational character of force is inseparably tied to chance in Nietzsche's philosophy. Will to power, as the determining factor in the relation of forces, implies chance which, as flux and spontaneity, constitutes the movement of chaos and the "essence of force."[42] What was once the most terrible thought for the Greek mind is affirmed via the will to power. To seek the dissolution or annihilation of reactive force would be to invite nihilism, that "most uncanny of guests."[43]

Will to power is the metaphorical heading for the dynamic chaotic interplay of forces and wills in the process of continually becoming. Will to power is chaotic unity, not unified chaos. Chaos (difference) precedes unity as existence precedes essence.

As the originary "differential and genetic" abyss (*Abgrund*) of active and reactive forces, will to power is the originary copula or separation manifest in becoming as "gradations of divergence."[44] As *Abgrund*, it resists all determination as ground or founding principle. Chaos is ordered, regulated, and molded by will to power which denies any firm categorization, any conceptualization of itself as a unitary, knowable substance. Only metaphorically designated, will to power is other than or beyond the inadequacy of conceptual thinking by a subjectivity essentially reactive. Will to power is the creative organizing force of existence and meaning without being organizable itself for thought. The concepts of oneness, totality, meaning or purpose are not applicable to it; they are constructs, "issuings forth."

Will to power is, paradoxically, not only originary difference but also originary sameness. Sameness is not synonymous with identity. The same that recurs in the eternal recurrence is the chaos of difference itself, a difference that is both infinitely repetitive *and* variable *without* collapsing into the modern atheistically disguised theological proposal of the world as an eternal novelty. The abyssal "structure" of will to power is a bypassing of traditional metaphysical notions of ground, origin, and identity. Will to power is anti-metaphysics insofar as it contests traditionally conceived binary-based logic by inverting the relation between unity and multiplicity. This ontological reversal of the thesis of self-identical primordiality is a "breach of the totality" (*TeI* 8/*TI* 23).

Not an essence (οὐσία; ὑποκείμενον; *essentia*) and prior to any *Grund*, will to power subtends and permeates all being thereby making interpretation possible. The proper question is not who interprets, but rather, *what* interprets?[45] The power to interpret, to create meaning, is the affirmation of difference and alterity. Will to power denies rendering of itself in terms of absoluteness or finality since as the force of originary difference it insures that there are no knowable unconditionals, to use Kant's term. The undecidability of absolute origination leaves one faced with the recognition that the only absolute knowledge is the realization that there is none. Levinas' whole philosophy can be characterized as an attempt to deduce a certain (ethical) meaning from this seeming meaninglessness.

VI

The concept of eschatology is opposed in the present study to the concept of apocalypse which dominates classic metaphysics or ontotheology. Literally, the ἔσχατον signifies that which lies at the extreme; it denotes a sense of the limit or end of time and history. Αποκάλλυμα, on the other hand, refers to the revelation, disclosure, uncovering, or unveiling of the truth about a thing. Both terms convey a sense of *terminus*, of teleology, and moreover, are often conflated in their meaning. Now, it is possible to speak of an apocalyptic eschatology, that is, of a revealed *truth* at the end of things, generally construed as the end of history. But Levinas avoids the joining of these similar yet distinct terms for perhaps this very reason:

> To tell the truth, ever since eschatology has opposed peace to war the evidence of war has been maintained in an essentially hypocritical civilization, that is, attached both to the True and the Good, henceforth antagonistic. It is perhaps time to see in hypocrisy not only a base contingent defect of humanity, but the underlying rending of a world attached to both the philosophers and the prophets. (*TeI* 9/*TI* 24)

Eschatology is not to be construed here as the "end of history" as promulgated by Hegel and commented on by Heidegger. Eschatology is the moment of prophetic messianic revelation. It does not designate a revealed continuum of time or purpose, open to the scrutiny of rationalization, of philosophical evidences. Rather, eschatology points to a *rupture* of linear futurity, of the totality of historical being. Instituting a relationship with a radical exteriority, eschatology leaves open the possibility of radical surprise, a "breach" of totality, precisely because it is the primordial orientation of subjectivity to the other (*l'autre*), of being to that which is wholly otherwise than being or essence. This *surprise* may take the form of a cosmic event, the breaking in of the Infinite into the spatio-temporal horizon of worldly existence, what in scriptural Hebrew is termed *qadosh*; or it may indicate the more mundane, though no less radical and important, revelation of the Other through speech or discourse.

What is it possible to say regarding the eschatological moment capable of breaking open history? Does the overcoming of traditional metaphysics, of onto-(theo)logy, signal the end of history? What is the relation between history and eschatology? What is the relation between history and apocalypse? Is there an actual difference between history, eschatology, and apocalypse? And with regard to the most extreme ethical abuse—war—where does that leave thinking?

Heidegger states that "Being itself is inherently eschatological,"[46] but Levinas claims that "history is not an eschatology" since it is a relation beyond the totality (*TeI* 270/*TI* 241). The universal State seems precluded by Levinas as an eschatological possibility. Eschatology, which promises messianic *peace* as a way of existing, is opposed to the political being of ontology. Distrusted because it is based on opinion and not on the evidences of reason, the importance of eschatology for Levinas is that it establishes a primordial relation with being, that is, the saying in the said. However, according to Derrida, it is precisely this discourse that eclipses the promise of messianic peace: "eschato*logy* is not possible, except through violence. This infinite passage through violence is called history."[47] But Levinas is well aware of the violent economy of the totality. Besides, "it is not at all certain that at the beginning there was war. Before war, there were altars" (*EDE* 234/*CPP* 124). Peace may occur (for a while) after war or conflict, but it never is able to restore that which has been undone. That is why *something else* is needed: a revaluation of the idea of *infinity* whereby transcendence, as the primordial relation with being, can be *re*established.

And if Nietzsche is that thinker who has impressed most upon modernity the need to reconceive infinity, then Levinas has most ardently taken up that task. Despite their profound differences, they are united in their mutual eschatological orientations. That is to say, both retain the element of surprise, of radical transformative potential, as essential to the realization of the future. Eschatology is not synonymous with apocalypse, characteristic of Hegelian dialectics.[48] Even though both notions are goal oriented, only apocalyptic thinking is truly teleological in that it posits a finality that is able to be comprehended as such. Eschatology, on the other hand, makes no determinative proposition regarding the nature of the end or completion of time or history, or even whether it will of necessity occur.

In spite of his ardent disavowal of teleological thinking, Nietzsche's most goal-oriented yet enigmatic thought is that of the *Übermensch*; yet this thought never attains much more than the status of a speculative yearning. Similarly, the ἔσχατον in Levinas, equivalent to messianic peace, is left open to interpretation. It is a hope without guarantee, and therefore constitutes a certain test of willing just as the eternal recurrence does for Nietzsche.[49]

While it is certainly the case in Nietzsche that the present is instrumental in deciding the shape of futurity, it is not so clear in Levinas. Is the ἔσχατον a moment within the horizon of the totality of history, or is it to be construed more in the sense of the rupturing of history by the unexpected breaking in of a radical alterity exterior to the totality? Levinas' philosophy seeks to situate itself between transcendence and empiricism, a position that Derrida says makes one tremble. The infinite, as eschatological possibility, is present or manifest within history, in the face of the Other, even though history itself is not an eschatology which is a "relationship with *a surplus always exterior to the totality*" (*TeI* 7/*TI* 22).[50] The "objectivism of war" is opposed by the vision of eschatological peace which engenders a new subjectivity.

Both eschatology and apocalypse concern the end of historical being. But this is not to say that the eschatological is completely divorced from history. If the absolutely other is indeed the Other, as Levinas claims, then the eschatological moment or messiah is as likely to appear from *within* history as it is by an imposition from without. The Other, transcendent of history, carries within it the seeds for new possibility, for peace. In whatever form this peace arrives, it will not be of the ontological order that rests on the allergy between the same and the other. It will be in the guise of a *transformed* history, in which case, it will no longer be, in a sense, "history."

The key to Nietzsche's insights on future individual and collective configuration is the fragmentary teachings on the *Übermensch*. Nietzsche will call (audaciously perhaps) the eschatological moment the *Übermensch* much in the manner that dogmatic Christian theology names Christ the realized ἔσχατον. Such a being will recreate history anew, perhaps even establishing in his or her wake the age of messianic peace. But what form will this individual or individuals assume? According to Nietzsche, that is to be decided only at the moment he (or she) is manifest by this epiphanic will itself, and not by the many (οἶ πόλλοι). This moment is beyond the scope of philosophy or theory; yet philosophy is not exonerated from any participation in the preparation of the *Übermensch*. Nietzsche's typology of human existence indicates that the foundations for the future must be laid in the present, as fecundity and as a reconceived pedagogical purpose, not the general education of the masses for insertion into the labor machine (this will continue as a secondary aim), but towards the advancement of the *future* embodiment of affirmative will to power. Levinas echoes this position: "There is a vulgarity and a baseness in an action that is conceived only for the immediate, that is, in the last analysis, for our life. And there is a very great nobility in the energy liberated from the hold of the present...no doubt, the summit of nobility" (*HH* 44/*CPP* 93). For better or worse, perhaps only the language of prophetic religion is apropos for grasping this eschatological (not apocalyptic) dimension of thinking.

VII

What is the relation between the prophetic, eschatology, and fecundity? The theme of prophecy is introduced in conjunction with the concept of eschatology in the preface to *Totality and Infinity* in an effort to broach the text's opening question of whether or not morality "dupes" us. These non-thematizable themes accompany a discussion on violence and the ontological structures of thought that promote if not engender it. The reader is left with the impression that this decidedly non-philosophical (though not opposed to it) notion of prophetic eschatology, counterposed to the war-fostering ontology (*TeI* 6–11/*TI* 22–25), is to be a recurrent theme throughout the work. However, Levinas does not pick up again on this theme, though it conditions the remaining text in its very absence.[51]

Prophecy is a modality of eschatological expression because prophecy transcends the alleged panopticism of Reason which posits and attempts to comprehend the whole of being and so *judge* the totality. Prophecy accompanies revelation whereby the self is called to responsibility for the spontaneous capriciousness of its own freedom and for the freedom of the Other. Ethical signification is revealed in the vulnerable face of the Other as the call to respond, as does the prophet Isaiah, to the Invisible, to *Adonai*—"Here I am."

> The judgment of history is set forth in the visible.... The invisible must manifest itself if history is to lose its right to the last word, necessarily unjust for subjectivity, inevitably cruel. But the manifestation of the invisible cannot mean the passage of the invisible to the status of the visible; it does not lead back to evidence. It is produced in the goodness reserved to subjectivity, which thus is subject not simply to the truth of judgment, but to the source of this truth. *The truth of the invisible is ontologically produced by the subjectivity which states it.* (*TeI* 272/*TI* 243; italics added)

But what form will this subjectivity assume? Though its origin may be transhistorical, exterior to the totality, its epiphany is certainly historical. Merleau-Ponty phrases it well: "It is because I am a totality that I am capable of giving birth to another and of seeing myself limited by him."[52] Levinas speculates on this vision of a subjectivity that "breaks with essence" and grasps the "truth" of the relation between goodness and judgment. While there have been numerous glimmers or moments of such transcendence in the history of ideas, as the present work has attempted to demonstrate, "the Nietzschean man was above all such a moment" (*AE* 21/*OB* 8), "shaking the world's passage to the overman...by the violence of an unheard word...by the non-saying of dance and laughter" (*HH* 94–95/*CPP* 147). But Levinas is troubled by the seeming nihilism of Nietzsche's language and by the tragic, near madness of such a model of (post?) subjectivity. Though Nietzsche's "laughter which refuses language" may indeed be the very affirmation needed to overcome the self and the nihilism of history, the philosopher (and one presumes even the mad ones) "must return to language to convey, even if in betraying them, the pure and the unutterable" (*HH* 95/*CPP* 148). But even then, "negativity, still correlative with being, will not be enough to signify the *other than being*." (*AE* 22/*OB* 9).

Opposing the apocalyptic veil of Hegelian philosophy that *necessitates* the occurrence of strife and war, both Nietzsche and Levinas propound an eschatological position which they maintain is the only possible avenue for peace. Nietzsche alludes to this as the *trans*historical moment of the *Übermensch*, the "lightning" (*Blitzes*)[53] who will wage wars for the sake of knowledge[54] and not dominion over others, who will be revealed as the truly affirmative embodiment of subjectivity. But can one truly consider the *Übermensch* a subjectivity, if the notion of subjectivity is a product of the very modernism to which Nietzsche, in some readings at least, signals an end, at least discursively? There is a strong affinity between Nietzsche and Levinas, despite their obvious and numerous differences, on the importance of the eschatological future. In Levinas' philosophy, this futurity takes the form of fecundity. Likewise, Nietzsche stipulates that culture's primary aim should not be the present of our own private selfhood, but the fecundity requisite for the production of the new higher will, of a future (non?) subjectivity, that of the *Übermensch*.

One cannot philosophize about eschatology which resists all attempts at comprehension; but it *is* a principal task of philosophical thinking to determine that which is capable of being transformative and transformed within being. That capability Nietzsche names the will to power. The individuals who not only understand but harness that capability are the "children of the future [*Kinder der Zukunft*]."[55] It is precisely in the interpretation of future possibility as fecundity that Nietzsche and Levinas converge most in their thinking. The question is whether this future subjectivity is a product of what is presently termed "history," or whether it is transhistorical in its genesis. But if the latter is the case, then is it possible to philosophize about its form at all?

Hegel's thinking poignantly exemplifies for Levinas the Western penchant for a totalizing ontology based on the sovereignty of rationality and freedom. Hegelian dialectics is apocalyptic in tone and trajectory, as opposed to the suprarational dimension of Levinasian eschatology. There is also a line of comparison to be drawn between Levinas and Nietzsche through the fertile category of the fecund. Nietzsche's future progenitors of the *Übermensch*, and Levinas' construal of the transcendence of the I in fecundity in which "my child is a stranger (Isaiah 49), but a stranger who is not only mine, for he *is* me" (*TeI* 299/*TI* 267), serve as distinct and yet interrelated examples of prophetic witness to the eschatological possibility of radical exteriority. What is endemic to both Levinasian and Nietzschean notions of prophetic eschatology (and what is Zarathustra if not a prophet?) is the response to a command issued from alterity, a command to the self to command and obey itself without the promise of reciprocity.[56]

The distinction between eschatology and apocalypse lies at the very heart of the present work.[57] Hegel conflates the meanings of the terms, and while he does not claim to predict the future, only the necessary structure that is time itself, he still posits a certain (political) telos as history. Apocalyptic thought rests on some measure of determination regarding the status of the end. It claims to fortell or divine the shape of the future. Eschatology, on the other hand, remains at the level of surprise. It is the domain of the absolutely other that stands outside all theoretical analysis and synthesis. Its form is that of no form—chaos: the possibility of all possibilities. One can never count on the ἔσχατον as one can on the apocalypse; one must work for eschatological peace. Levinas is explicit on this point, which serves as one of his concluding observations in *Totality and Infinity*:

> The unity of plurality is peace, and not the coherence of the elements that constitute plurality.... Peace must be my peace, in a relation that starts from an I and goes to the other, in desire and goodness, where the I both maintains itself and exists without egoism. (*TeI* 342/*TI* 306)

The possibility of an eschatological peace rests on the *affirmation* of the radical spontaneity of chance, of surprise, which, again paradoxically, is not commensurate with any operative notion of metaphysical or epistemological necessity. There is a strong affinity between the notions of peace, surprise, and risk. Subjectivity lives on the edge of nihilism, on the dangerous path of the possibility of no meaning. But only upon that precipice does one most fully affirm in the freest sense.

Eschatology nowise represents in Levinas the gripping fear and hope of nihilist religious dogma, that of the destruction of the present world and the recreation of the cosmological order, that is, the synthesis of time and eternity. His own religious background runs too deep for that. No one understands time as well as the wandering Jew. But the relation between Jerusalem and Athens is ancient and, as with any such historical relation, there inevitably occurs an osmosis of ideas. Levinas' philosophy calls into question the entire Greek logocentric enterprise. Derrida summarizes the "debate" thus:

> And does the strange dialogue between the Jew and the Greek, peace itself, have the form of the absolute, speculative logic of Hegel, the living logic which *reconciles* formal tautology and empirical heterology after having thought prophetic discourse in the preface to the *Phenomenology of Spirit*? Or, on the contrary, does this peace have the form of infinite separation and of the unthinkable, unsayable transcendence of the other?[58]

Though it would appear from Derrida's perspective that the choice is an either/or situation, Levinas does not advocate the radical divorce of Greek and Jewish thinking because "both the hierarchy taught by Athens and the *abstract* and slightly *anarchical* ethical individualism taught by Jerusalem are simultaneously necessary in order to suppress violence" (*TH* 103). The question then comes down to this: What is the possible relation between the *eschaton* (a fundamentally Greek concept) and (a non-Greek) history? A *new* (non-philosophical) language?

Is that possible? Certainly, philosophical language determines the λόγος of being in all its present-day manifestations, as Levinas knows all too well. Perhaps that is why he ultimately abandons the language of ontology and quizzically turns to the paradoxical and enigmatic language of the saying and the said.

> The enigma of a God speaking in man and of man not counting on any god?... The enigma of the Infinite, whose saying in me, a responsibility where no one assists me, becomes a contestation of the Infinite.... The enigma separates the Infinite from all phenomenality, from appearing, thematization and essence. (*AE* 240/*OB* 154)

The enigmatic "ground" of the ethical relationship, of meaning itself, is, paradoxically, the absence of all grounds. Discourse with the Other is discourse with God. It is the phenomenon of continual revelation itself. The language of prophetic eschatology breaks with the λόγος precisely because it speaks a different language (a μή-λόγος?).[59] Its tongue is that of the *absolutely other* and its (proper?) "name" is responsibility, the call to respond—ethically.

The task ahead for thinking, for action, is the *embodiment* of the saying in the said, of the continual production of divinity. There is no absolute assurance; but there is also no final limit on the horizon of possibility. "Peace then is under my responsibility. I am a hostage, for I am alone to wage it, running a fine risk, dangerously" (*AE* 259/*OB* 166).

Notes

Chapter 1: BackGround

1 Levinas characterizes traditional forms of metaphysics as "ontology." Even though he does not retain the term "metaphysics" in his later work, it will continue to be used in reference to his philosophy. Depending upon the context, it will be distinguished from classic or traditional metaphysics.

2 The convention in translating *l'autrui*/*l'Autrui* (the personal other/s) as "Other" with a capitalized "O" and *autre*/*Autre* (otherness in general; alterity) as "other" will be followed. At times *autrui*/*Autrui* will be translated as "Another."

3 Emmanuel Levinas, *Le temps et l'autre* (Paris: Presses Universitaires de France, 1947; 1983), p. 20 (henceforth cited as *TA*); *Time and the Other*, trans. R. Cohen (Pittsburgh: Duquesne University Press, 1987), p. 42 (henceforth cited as *TO*).

4 Emmanuel Levinas, *Totalité et Infini: Essai sur l'extériorité.* Le livre de poche edition (La Haye: Martinus Nijhoff, 1971), p. 340 (henceforth cited as *TeI*); *Totality and Infinity: An Essay on Exteriority*, trans. A. Lingis (Pittsburgh: Duquesne University Press, 1969), p. 304 (henceforth cited as *TI*). Also see Emmanuel Levinas, "Ethics as First Philosophy," trans. S. Hand and M. Temple, in *The Levinas Reader*, ed. S. Hand (Oxford: Basil Blackwell, 1989), p. 75–87 (henceforth cited as *LR*).

5 See Hanna Arendt, *The Origins of Totalitarianism* (New York: Harcourt Brace Jovanovich, 1973) for what is perhaps the finest exposition of this question to date.

6 Also called Cusanus, Nicolas is the first to call into question the heterogeneous concept of space espoused by substance metaphysics. Though the concept of spatial homogeneity is initially articulated in Euclidean geometry, it is Cusanus who first proffers the mechanistic view of nature and challenges the atomism of the Greeks. Cusanus' variant of Neoplatonism deconstructs, in a manner of speaking, the Aristotelian and scholastic metaphysics of spatiality and objectively knowable essences. In so doing, the dialectic between object and subject begins its tilt toward the subject and so prepares the way for the concept of the autonomy of the individual existent. Cusanus' philosophy also contains the seeds of democracy. The "flattening" of the hierarchical medieval universe signals the beginning of the end of feudalism. All entities are viewed as being in equal proximity to the Absolute. Immanence reflects or mirrors the transcendent; all beings are in equal relation to one another. With the desubstantiation of the divine right of monarchical rule and the subsequent de-emphasis on the collective, organizational, or institutional aspects of existence, individuality and relationality emerge as central concerns. He also prefigures Levinas' use of the term "absolute proximity," maintaining that the universe

has no circumference and that only God can be described in terms of a positive infinity, not the universe. God is and is not the center of the cosmos as well as being and not being the circumference of the cosmos.

7 Enrique Dussel, *Philosophy of Liberation* (Maryknoll: Orbis, 1985), p. 25.

8 Ibid.

9 Michel de Certeau, "The Politics of Silence: The Long March of the Indians," *Heterologies: Discourse on the Other*, trans. B. Massumi (Minneapolis: University of Minnesota Press, 1986), pp. 226–27.

10 G. W. F. Hegel, *Phänomenologie des Geistes* (Hamburg: Felix Meiner, 1952); *Phenomenology of Spirit*, trans. A. V. Miller (Oxford: Oxford University Press, 1977), § 90.

11 On this topic see Mark C. Taylor, *Erring: A Postmodern A/Theology* (Chicago: University of Chicago Press, 1983), esp. pp. 34–51.

It can be argued that the proclamation of the death of God also signifies a critique of the validity of another particular modality of discourse, that of the patriarchy. Nietzsche's views of "woman" and women are ambivalent and often hyperbolic, and the issue of misogyny in his thinking is far from resolved. Still, does the enigmatic question that opens the preface to *Beyond Good and Evil* ("Suppose truth is a woman—how's that [*Wie*]?") undermine the privileged status of *truth* in the West? Surely Nietzsche is not making a sweeping characterization of *women* in general here. The metaphorical concept of "woman" here is revealed as an essentially male construct, given meaning and reified in its signification over centuries of oppressive definition. As such it is meaning or valuation that has been assigned from without, that is, from a distance. Patriarchal culture has tended to see the art of woman as "seduction." Yet "truth" is not an object, nor is "woman," no matter how high the pedestal on which one places them. Woman resists objectification just as truth resists dogmatization. This is the essence of the passive power of "woman": like truth, she escapes comprehension and totalization because she is not a *determinable* entity, i.e., a logical category. The male created notion of "woman" is a fiction, a notion devoid of power. Nietzsche's enigmatic statement turns this conception of truth against patriarchal metaphysics. There is a play here on two conceptions of the metaphor of "woman": One, the male created image of "woman" for women; and two, the inverted image that is linked with the notion of truth. It is the same metaphor, only now revealed in a double perspective. Nietzsche is critical of "woman" precisely because of what the metaphor signifies, because he knows her to be mere illusion; moreover, he knows the origin of the sham. In this metaphorical economy, "woman" (truth) represents the supreme frustration for "man" (reason). Man desires woman precisely because he cannot have her completely and yet, for this very reason, fears her. (Recall Marcel Duchamp's *The Bride Stripped Bare by Her Bachelors, Even*). Woman is thus denegrated, marginalized, oppressed precisely because her truth is eternally elusive, because she resists Truth in the absolute sense desired by (male) logic. Woman is thus distance, representing the terror of existence for man. In the eternal noumenal order of patriarchal truth, there is nothing left to do but dominate her temporal phenomenal truth, to define her existence only in relation to male existence. Opposed to masculine reason, she is the irrational, which is to say, the *chaotic*.

Derrida comments on the themes of distance and seduction as they relate to the "question of woman" in Nietzsche in *Spurs*, trans. B. Harlow (Chicago: University of Chicago Press, 1979). For an opposing view see Gayatri C. Spivak, "Displacement and the Discourse of Women," *Displacement: Derrida and After*, ed. M. Krupnick (Bloomington: Indiana University Press, 1983), pp. 169–95. Also see Kelly Oliver, *Womanizing Nietzsche: Philosophy's Relation to the Feminine* (New York and London: Routledge, 1995). On metaphor in Nietzsche's thinking see in *The New Nietzsche*, ed. D. Allison (Cambridge, MA: MIT Press, 1985): Eric Blondel, "Nietzsche: Life as Metaphor," trans. M. Macrae, pp. 150–75; and Sarah Kofman, "Metaphor, Symbol, Metamorphosis," trans. D. Allison, pp. 201–14.

12 The reason for embracing the idea of creation "is the fact that intelligibility precedes me. It is just the contrary of the notion of *Geworfenheit.* This is not a theological thesis; we reach the idea of creation out of the experience of a face" which is the expression in being of the trace of the Infinite. Emmanuel Levinas, "Liberté et commandement," *Revue de Métaphysique et de Morale* 58, no. 3 (1953): 240; "Freedom and Command," in *Collected Philosophical Papers*, trans. A. Lingis (The Hague: Martinus Nijhoff, 1987), p. 22; reference deleted (henceforth cited as *CPP*).

The notion of the trace is pivotal for Levinas and recurs throughout his writings. For a sustained discussion see Emmanuel Levinas, "La trace de l'autre," in *En découvrant l'existence avec Husserl et Heidegger* (Paris: J. Vrin, 1949; 1967; 1974; 1988), pp. 187–202 (henceforth cited as *EDE*); "The Trace of the Other," trans. A. Lingis, in *Deconstruction in Context: Literature and Philosophy*, ed. M. Taylor (Chicago: University of Chicago Press, 1986), pp. 345–59. Also see Emmanuel Levinas, "La signification et la sens," in *Humanisme de l'autre homme* (Montpellier: Fata Morgana, 1972), pp. 57–63 (henceforth cited as *HH*)/*CPP* 102–7.

For secondary sources see Robert Bernasconi, "The Trace of Levinas in Derrida," *Derrida and Difference,* ed. D. Wood and R. Bernasconi (Coventry: Parousia Press, 1985), pp. 17–44; and Edward S. Casey, "Levinas on Memory and the Trace," in *The Collegium Phaenomenologicum*, ed. J. Sallis, G. Moneta, J. Taminiaux (Dordrecht: Kluwer, 1989), pp. 241–55.

The notion of trace also figures prominently in Derrida's work. When I asked M. Derrida during a visit to Stony Brook in April 1989 about his relation to Levinas' employment of *la trace* he replied that there is essentially no difference between his use of the term and Levinas' except for the tone of the language employed to describe it: Levinas' terminology, he said, conveyed too many religious overtones, as compared to his own efforts to present it in a more historical manner.

13 Hegel, *Phenomenology of Spirit*, § 17f. Levinas too wants to preserve the interiority of subjective existence, though in a radically different manner from the tradition. The closure of European metaphysics, the aftermath of the death of God, is also the closure of the inner life. The "inward world" denounced and contested by Heidegger and supported by the sciences, the so-called end of subjectivity, ends "either in the triumph of mathematical intelligibility, repressing the subject, the person, his uniqueness and election, into ideology, or else in the enrootedness of man in being, of which he would be the messenger and poet" (*HH* 90/*CPP* 144).

14 Levinas discusses the relation between scripture and philosophy in *Éthique et infini* (Paris: Librairie Arthème Fayard et Radio-France, 1982), pp. 15–20 (henceforth cited as *EeI*); *Ethics and Infinity*, trans. R. Cohen (Pittsburgh: Duquesne University Press,

1985), pp. 21–25 (henceforth cited as *EI*).

15 Kojève, for one, would decidedly disagree with this interpretation. Philosophy and theology, he argues, are mutually exclusive terms. Kojève reconceives the relation between eternity and time in his innovative interpretation of Hegel's *Phenomenology.* The end or completion of history is the telos of Spirit. Time is not synonymous with history; eternity is time. Plato is the first theologian precisely because he posits a *beyond.* Hegel, on the other hand, the philosopher par excellence, is necessarily an atheist. Philosophy proper is *anthropo*logical as opposed to *theo*logical. There is no distinction between theology and religion. See Alexandre Kojève, *Introduction to the Reading of Hegel*, trans. J. Nichols and A. Bloom (New York: Basic Books, 1969), esp. pp. 71–74ff.

16 Emmanuel Levinas, *Autrement qu'être ou au-delà de l'essence.* Livre de poche edition (La Haye: Martinus Nijhoff, 1974), pp. 17–18 (henceforth cited as *AE*); *Otherwise than Being or Beyond Essence*, trans. A. Lingis (The Hague: Martinus Nijhoff, 1981), p. 6 (henceforth cited as *OB*). Also see *EeI* 92–93/*EI* 88; *LR* 183.

Levinas gives his reasons for separating religion from theology: "Theology would be possible only as the contestation of the purely religious, and confirms it only by its failures or its struggles" (*OB* 196 n. 19) and because "theological language destroys the religious situation of transcendence. The infinite 'presents' itself anarchically, but thematization loses the anarchy which alone can accredit it. Language about God rings false or becomes a myth, that is, can never be taken literally" (*OB* 197 n. 25). Also, "rational theology, fundamentally ontological, strives to take account of transcendence in the domain of being by expressing it with adverbs of height applied to the verb being; God is said to exist eminently or par excellence" (*CPP* 154).

17 Thomas Altizer has been instrumental in the formulation of these important considerations for this work.

18 Emmanuel Levinas, "Judaism and Kenosis," *In the Time of the Nations*, trans. M. B. Smith (Bloomington: Indiana University Press, 1994), p. 114 (henceforth cited as *TN*).

19 G. W. F. Hegel, *The Philosophy of History*, trans. J. Sibree (Cambridge, MA: Harvard University Press, 1956), p. 15.

20 Clyde Lee Miller was most helpful in posing a number of these questions.

Chapter 2: UnderGround

1 Fr. 53, Hippolytus *Ref.* IX, 9, 4: "War is the father and ruler of all, and some he reveals as gods, others as mortals; some he creates slaves, others free." In G. S. Kirk and J. E. Raven, *The Presocratic Philosophers* (Cambridge: Cambridge University Press, 1957), p. 195.

2 Aristotle, *Nicomachean Ethics* 1096a10–30, 1096b1–27; *Metaphysics* 986a22–26.

3 Augustine's most innovative and far-reaching philosophic formulation is the near equation of the concepts of the Good, Being, and God. Though he borrows from Plotinus the position that true reality is invisible and not corporeal substance, he does not follow him in asserting the radical separateness of the One. In Augustine one finds the first full expression of the philosophy of totality that has dominated the history of Western thought and is a key determining factor in the subsequent assessment of the nature of violence and ethics. In an early treatise, *On the Free*

Choice of the Will (trans. A. S. Benjamin and L. H. Hackstaff [New York: Macmillan Publishers, 1964]), evil, the cause of violence, is interpreted as the neglect of eternal things, as a "turning away" (*aversio*) from the immutable goodness of God towards changeable goods. Though the free choice of the will is numbered as one of the great goods, nevertheless, it is through the will that evil is introduced into the order of the world; the will is only an "intermediate good." Through its proper use, the will is an indispensable aid in coming to know the truth and goodness of God; but in itself, the will does not come to this truth. Only through the proper alignment of the will (*volitio*) with reason (*ratio*) and understanding (*intellectio*) does one attain truth. This is possible insofar as the human soul, being rational, participates (μέθεξις) in the wisdom of the divine λόγος. Participation is not the equation of divine and human reason; and the Universal or Logos reason, as articulated by the Enlightenment mind, is not necessarily the reason of the mind of God. But it is through such reason that we have access to the immutable truth and wisdom of the Creator (*ens realissimum*). The question of philosophy henceforth becomes that of the status of reason. The violence of evil or sin appears when the will rejects the truth that is given to the intellect by the light of reason (*lumen naturalis*). The idea that God is responsible for evil is thus a logical impossibility. As goodness itself, God admits of no imperfection. There are no stages of perfection, only varying degrees of corruption. Evil implies lack, where the Good or Being (i.e., God) is not. Evil is relegated to the status of non-being. All being, by virtue of its very creation, is essentially good. Moral evil, the result of the Fall, signals the separation of will and understanding (a theme present in philosophy up through Descartes) whose harmony reflects the perfect goodness of God. But since perfect knowledge is a possibility for Augustine, error (the root of evil) can be blamed on neither a limited capacity of the understanding nor the will exceeding the understanding in making judgments (as is the case with Descartes). This position remains relatively unchanged in Augustine's thinking, as he makes clear in his later *Retractations* (Washington: Catholic University of America Press, 1968).

4 Friedrich Nietzsche, *Götzen-Dämmerung*, in *Werke in Drei Bänden*, herausgegeben von Karl Schlechta (München: Carl Hanser Verlag, 1955), 2: 963ff; *Twilight of the Idols*, trans. and ed. W. Kaufmann, in *The Portable Nietzsche* (New York: The Viking Press, 1954), pp. 485–86ff.

5 On the overcoming of and subsequent return by contemporary thinking to Platonist metaphysics Levinas says: "Platonism is overcome with the very means which the universal thought issued from Plato supplied. It is overcome by this so much disparaged Western civilization, which was able to understand the particular cultures, which never understood themselves...[but] to catch sight, in meaning, of a situation that precedes culture...is to return to Platonism in a new way. It is also to find oneself able to judge civilizations on the basis of ethics." Levinas includes Husserl in this late return to Platonism and states that "we are not obliged to follow him" since "we think that we have found the straightforwardness of meaning by another method" (*HH* 55–56/*CPP* 101). For Levinas' views on contemporary anti-Platonism see *HH* 30–33/*CPP* 83–86.

The theme of the end, or put in more current terms, of the closure of metaphysics continues to be a central theme in Continental philosophy. John Sallis' study,

Delimitations: Phenomenology and the End of Metaphysics (Bloomington: Indiana University Press, 1986), is particularly relevant here for its reading of the role of imagination in the determination of metaphysics and the ambiguity that lies at the heart of the Greek origins of metaphysics.

6 One of the most pronounced attempts this century to delineate Plato's importance for modern thinking based on a reading of the *Timaeus* is that of Whitehead, who proposes a third metaphysical nexus apart from conceptual or empirical causal chains. Modern physics (e.g., quantum theory) testifies to the truth of Platonic cosmology (Alfred North Whitehead, *Process and Reality* [New York: Free Press, 1978], p. 95). The challenge is to recover a cosmological alternative to either an eternal material universe of the present order, or a universe created and teleologically ordered by the fiat of a transcendent deity. The Platonic hypothesis of the receptacle tends to join or fuse together the doctrines of Imposition and Immanence (Alfred North Whitehead, *Adventures of Ideas* [New York: Macmillan, 1933], p. 121). Whitehead's use of the term "fusion" parallels a Hegelian conception of being thought in terms of totality. Whitehead's appropriation of the *Timaeus* as the primary referent or model for cosmology and his refusal to acknowledge the claim in the *Republic* regarding the transcendence of the Good, subordinates metaphysics to cosmology, or rather, conflates the two. This is the mark of "process" philosophy. In many ways, this move is desirable as metaphysics but only has meaning in the lived actual experience or occasion. But the reduction of metaphysics to a mere moment or event in the cosmological scheme of things reduces, in the end, difference to identity, infinity to totality, otherness to sameness. Here Whitehead's thought parallels that of Hegel. The precise point of difference between Plato's and Whitehead's metaphysical cosmologies regards the status of the invisible or the infinite. Plato regards both the receptacle and the Good as beyond comprehension. As the "nurse of all generation," the "mother of all created and visible things," and the "receiving vessel," the receptacle is assigned a predemiurgic priority. But Whitehead, employing the Platonic model insofar as it makes a distinction between Creativity (receptacle) and God (demiurge), does not acknowledge the Good as transcendent in the sense of beyond being; Being is the only fact. There is no nihil, no beyond, no absolutely other in Whitehead's philosophy. Still, process philosophy merely repeats Platonic thought insofar as "in the *Timaeus* the origin of the present cosmic epoch is traced back to an aboriginal disorder, chaotic to our ideals" (*Process and Reality*, p. 95). Whitehead seems to suggest here that the receptacle functions as an originary chaos or difference, though he explicitly rejects such a position. But despite the numerous advances that he makes in speculative metaphysics, Whitehead remains a Platonist insofar as he interprets the forms as suprasensible archetypal ideas. These are the "eternal objects" which it is the task of God to order. The idea of the Good is thus interpreted by him, in line with Aristotle, as the highest of the forms of being and not as beyond being (infinity). It is precisely this interpretation that this study calls into question.

7 Martin Heidegger, *Platons Lehre von der Wahrheit* (Bern: Francke Verlag, 1947), p. 37; "Plato's Doctrine of Truth," trans. J. Barlow, in *Philosophy in the Twentieth Century*, ed. W. Barrett and H. D. Aitken (New York: Random House, 1962), p. 263.

8 Ibid.

9 The reasons for refusing to translate ἀλήθεια as "truth" are given in Martin

Heidegger, *Sein und Zeit* (Tübingen: Max Niemeyer Verlag, 1967), p. 219; *Being and Time*, trans. J. Macquarrie and E. Robinson (New York: Harper & Row, 1962), p. 262. Also in Martin Heidegger, "Das Ende der Philosophie und die Aufgabe des Denkens," in *Zur Sache des Denkens* (Tübingen: Max Niemeyer Verlag, 1969), pp. 76–77; "The End of Philosophy and the Task of Thinking," trans. J. Stambaugh, in *Basic Writings*, ed. D. F. Krell (New York: Harper & Row, 1977), pp. 388–89.

10 Martin Heidegger, *Einfürung in die Metaphysik* (Tübingen: Max Niemeyer Verlag, 1966), 148; *Introduction to Metaphysics*, trans. R. Manheim (New Haven: Yale University Press, 1959), p. 194.

11 Heidegger, *Platons Lehre von der Wahrheit*, pp. 41–43/"Plato's Doctrine of Truth," pp. 265–66. Also see, *Zur Sache des Denkens*, p. 78/*Basic Writings*, p. 390.

12 Heidegger, *Platons Lehre von der Wahrheit*, p. 23/"Plato's Doctrine of Truth," p. 256.

13 Ibid., p. 30/p. 259.

14 Ibid., p. 42/p. 265.

15 Ibid., p. 35/p. 262.

16 Paul Friedländer, *Plato: An Introduction* (Vol. 1 of three volumes), 2nd ed., trans. H. Meyerhoff (Princeton: Princeton University Press, 1969), p. 229.

17 Sallis, *Delimitations*, pp. 170–85, esp. pp. 176–80.

18 Ibid., pp. 178–83.

19 Heidegger, *Einfürung in die Metaphysik*, p. 11/*Introduction to Metaphysics*, p. 14.

20 Ibid., p. 139/p. 182.

21 Heidegger, *Einfürung in die Metaphysik*, p. 46, 137–38/*Introduction to Metaphysics*, p. 60, 180–81. Also, *Platons Lehre von der Wahrheit*, pp. 34–42/"Plato's Doctrine of Truth," pp. 261–65.

22 Heidegger says: "The word ἰδέα means that which is seen in the visible, the aspect it offers. What is offered is the appearance, εἶδος, of what confronts us" (*Einfürung in die Metaphysik*, p. 137/*Introduction to Metaphysics*, p. 180).

23 Sallis, *Delimitations*, p. 6.

24 Ibid., p. 7.

25 Plato, *Republic*, 517b.

26 Ibid., 509d–510a.

Chapter 3: HelioGround

1 Plato, *Republic*, 505a.

2 Ibid.

3 Ibid., 509b.

4 The receptacle is "an invisible and formless being which receives all things and in some mysterious way partakes of the intelligible" (Plato, *Timaeus*, 51b).

5 Plotinus, *Enneads*, 1: 6, 1–9.

6 Hans-Georg Gadamer, *The Idea of the Good in Platonic-Aristotelian Philosophy*, trans. P. C. Smith (New Haven: Yale University Press, 1986), pp. 126–58. Also see Hans-Georg Gadamer, *The Relevance of the Beautiful and Other Essays*, trans. N. Walker, ed. R. Bernasconi (Cambridge: Cambridge University Press, 1986).

7 Martin Heidegger, "Brief über den 'Humanismus,'" *Platons Lehre von der Wahrheit. Mit einem Brief über den "Humanismus,"* p. 53; "Letter on Humanism," trans. F. A. Capuzzi and J. G. Gray, in *Basic Writings*, p. 193.

8 Hans-Georg Gadamer, *Wahrheit und Methode* (Tübingen: J. C. B. Mohr [Paul Siebeck], 1972), p. 450; *Truth and Method*, trans. J. Weinsheimer and D. G. Marshall, 2nd rev. ed. (New York: Continuum, 1993), p. 474.

9 Gadamer, *Wahrheit und Methode*, p. 441/*Truth and Method*, pp. 465–66.

10 Ibid., p. 450f/p. 474f.

11 Ibid., p. 111f/p. 117f.

12 Ibid., p. 423f/p. 447f.

13 See Plotinus, *Enneads*, 5: 5, 4–6; 6: 9, 2–6. Plotinus rigidly adheres to the doctrine of the Good beyond being while discarding the inconsistencies of Plato's metaphysics, and in so doing establishes a hierarchical order of being while insisting upon the radical alterity of the One. Like Plato, he considers philosophy and religion (not theology) to be mutually interdependent. All existence for Plotinus is ultimately either mind or thought, thus paving the way for the Hegelian concept of *Geist*. The two terms presuppose and necessitate the existence of the other. Plotinus' philosophy, again like Plato's, while clearly pantheistic, is nevertheless non-theistic. The Divine Intelligence and the One do not form a totality. It is the conflation of these two terms which serve as the Godhead for classic natural theology. The notion of absolute separation that is so fundamental for Levinas is first hinted at by Plato. This theme finds fuller expression in Plotinus, who draws on Aristotle's understanding of the metaphysical relation between form and matter and potentiality and actuality and on his position regarding intellectual cognition, and then adds these formulations to the essentials of Plato's thought. This enables Plotinus to explain the relation or "interpenetration" of subject and object, of self and other, albeit in the spiritual realm which is being. But what distinguishes him most from his contemporaries is his refusal to conflate the Good and the Unmoved Mover into a single entity consituting the apex of a hierarchical totality of being. Like the Platonic Good, the Plotinian conception of the One engenders being. The One is not the totality of being nor is it the Being of beings. It is not possible to speak of the One in any positive or negative sense since "it is the measure and not the measured," says Plotinus. The Plotinian One is "wholly otherwise than being," to use Levinas' phrase; but being unique, the One is not itself multiplicity, which is an essential characteristic of being. Beyond all differentiation and plurality, it is the absolute *source* of the multiplicitous. The One neither denies nor negates the plural; rather, its transcendence signifies separation, radical alterity, absolute difference. Though Plotinus links the One of the *Parmenides* with the Good of the *Republic*, he expressly distinguishes between the two terms. In one sense, the Good and the One are the same; but in another sense they are different since, as Plotinus says, "The One cannot aim at any good or desire anything, it is superior to the Good; [and yet], it is the Good, not for itself, but for other things to the extent to which they can share in it." There is an essential *paradox* within the One/Good itself. As the cause of goodness, the One is not the Good, though it is the Good for all being(s). This distinction, irrational to consciousness, signifies the inability, first recognized by Plato, of rational thought to totally grasp the nature of the Absolute. In the Plotinian conception of the universe, which is not the negation of corporeal existence, the hierarchy of being is subtended by the ineffable One. It is crowned by the divine Spirit or Intelligence which takes the totality of the Forms of being for its object as well as the One itself. The hypothesis of an all-knowing Spirit

is clearly a derivation of the Platonic demiurge. The One, by implication, is analogous to the Platonic notion of the receptacle and thus to chaos insofar as it resists all determinate definition.

According to Levinas, goodness is "not an attribute that would multiply the One, for if it were to multiply, if the One could be distinguished from the Goodness that sustains it, the One could take up a position with regard to its goodness, know itself to be good, and thus lose its goodness" (*AE* 96/*OB* 57). On the trace and the One in Plotinus see *EDE* 189–90, 201; *HH* 62/*CPP* 105–106. On the relation between the One, the Good and God in Plato see "Enigme et phénomène," *EDE* 204/*CPP* 62.

14 Gadamer, *Wahrheit und Methode*, p. 459/*Truth and Method*, p. 484; also, *The Idea of the Good*, pp. 86–87.

15 For example: identity/difference, truth/error, totality/infinity, one/many, white/black, intelligible/sensible, light/darkness, good/evil, subject/object, presence/absence, heaven/hell, salvation/damnation, sky/earth, self/other, reason/emotion, mind/body, God/human, etc.

16 Gadamer, *Wahrheit und Methode*, p. 453/*Truth and Method*, p. 478. Nietzsche would decidedly disagree with Gadamer at this point: "For a philosopher to say 'the good and the beautiful are one' is infamy; if he goes on to add, 'also the true,' one ought to thrash him. Truth is ugly. We possess *art* lest *we perish of the truth*" (*The Will to Power*, § 822). On the distinction between beauty and the beautiful in Plotinus (which Gadamer does not comment upon) in relation to the Good, see J. M. Rist, *Plotinus: The Road to Reality* (Cambridge: Cambridge University Press, 1967), pp. 53–65.

17 Gadamer says that "in the *Sophist*, just as in the *Timaeus*, cosmological concepts like motion and rest are fused in a curious way with the concepts of reflection, difference and selfsameness. This fusion is the basis of Hegel's claim that dialectic makes the entirety of ideas thinkable.... [the] thesis rests on the assumption of unity here" (Hans-Georg Gadamer, *Hegel's Dialectic*, trans. P. C. Smith [New Haven: Yale University Press, 1976], p. 80).

18 Gadamer, *Wahrheit und Methode*, p. 456/*Truth and Method*, p. 481.

19 Gadamer, *The Idea of the Good*, pp. 88, 100f.

20 Gadamer, *Wahrheit und Methode*, p. 459/*Truth and Method*, p. 484.

21 Gadamer, *The Idea of the Good*, esp. pp. 9–10, 16–20, 113.

22 According to McFague, "historicity...appears to mean not cultural, sociological, or economic determinism to Gadamer, for he does not see that some texts, whether consciously or not, can and have been written out of a form of historicity (racism, sexism, nationalism, imperialism) that distorts their universality in basic ways" (Sallie McFague, *Metaphorical Theology: Models of God in Religious Language* [Philadelphia: Fortress Press, 1982], 63).

For an opposing reading that locates Gadamer's sense of morality within the Greek context of φρόησις and παιδεία see P. Christopher Smith, "The Ethical Dimensions of Gadamer's Hermeneutical Theory," in *Research in Phenomenology* 18 (1988): 75–91.

23 Gadamer, *The Idea of the Good*, pp. 104–125.

24 Gadamer, *Wahrheit und Methode*, p. 450/*Truth and Method*, p. 475.

25 Cf. Jacques Derrida, "Violence and Metaphysics: An Essay on the Thought of

Emmanuel Levinas," in *Writing and Difference*, trans. A. Bass (Chicago: University of Chicago Press, 1978), p. 101.

Says Levinas: "To be in oneself is to express oneself, that is, already to serve the Other. The ground of expression is goodness. To be καθ'αὐτό is to be good" (*TeI* 200/*TI* 183). The face is καθ'αὐτό since "the most direct attitude before a being καθ'αὐτό is not the knowledge one can have about him, but is commerce with him" ("Liberté et commandement," p. 270/*CPP* 20–21). Levinas' most sustained discussion on Plato's *Republic* is in this essay.

26 Gadamer, *Wahrheit und Methode*, p. 426/*Truth and Method*, p. 450.

27 Ibid., p. 451/p. 476.

28 Descartes' idea of infinity or God in his third *Meditation* is the idea of perfection because it implies total self-sufficiency and autonomy. Infinity does not present itself as an object for contemplation; it is not a thing or object that is cognitively graspable. Like the Good, the Infinite is beyond all comprehension. Signifying the presence of a prior, radical exteriority, it makes possible our own thought. The idea of infinity is *non*-constituted in Descartes; whereas interiority is constituted by this exteriority of the infinitely other. There is more "objective" reality in the idea of the Infinite than in any other concept; it is the most "clear and distinct" notion we have. It makes it possible for us to conceive other clear and distinct ideas. Infinity is not only an idea or concept; it is one of three variations of substance in Descartes' metaphysics. Nothing positive or negative can be said about infinite substance; only about thinking substance (*cogito*). The finitude of thinking does not limit consciousness from participating in the infinite at all. Inasmuch as thinking substance has a free will, it is infinite. The understanding constitutes the finite aspect of human existence. Humanity is made in the image of God insofar as it has an infinite will, but thinking substance lacks the characteristic of perfection because of its limited, finite understanding. Error arises in consciousness when the will overexceeds the understanding in forming judgments. Only a will that conforms to an understanding of those ideas which are clear and distinct produces truth in judgments.

See *TeI* 40–42, 93–94, 231–32/*TI* 48–50, 92–93, 210–11; Emmanuel Levinas, "Dieu et la philosophie," in *Le Nouveau Commerce* 30–31 (1975): 104–106/*CPP* 159–61; reprinted *LR* 173–75; also see, "La philosophie et l'idée de infini," in *EDE* 171–72/*CPP* 53–54.

29 Emmanuel Levinas and Richard Kearney, "Dialogue with Emmanuel Levinas," in *Face to Face with Levinas*, ed. R. Cohen (Albany: SUNY Press, 1986), p. 25.

30 Whitehead offers a remarkably succinct reformulation of the paradox of the One and Many as the "ultimate metaphysical principle of togetherness." Like Hegel's, his philosophy is predicated on the rationally comprehensible concept of totality. The principle of togetherness spearheads Whitehead's attempt, again like Hegel's, to formulate a "one-substance metaphysics" in order to avoid the cosmological dualism of classic metaphysics which ultimately situates the creative aspect of existence outside the spatio-temporal horizon. This principle is "the advance from disjunction to conjunction, creating a novel entity other than the entities given in disjunction. The novel entity is at once the togetherness of the 'many' which it leaves; it is a novel entity, disjunctively among the many entities which it synthesizes. The many become one, and are increased by one" (*Process and Reality*, p. 21).

For secondary sources on the relation between Hegel and Whitehead see Errol Harris, "The Contemporary Significance of Hegel and Whitehead," pp. 17–28; Brian Leftow, "God and the World in Hegel and Whitehead," pp. 257–67; and Robert Neville, "Hegel and Whitehead on Totality: The Failure of a Conception of System," pp. 86–108, in *Hegel and Whitehead: Contemporary Perspectives on Systematic Philosophy*, ed. G. R. Lucas (Albany: SUNY Press, 1986).

31 Also see Emmanuel Levinas, "De l'un a l'autre: transcendence et temps,"in *Archivio di filosophia* 51, no. 1 (1983): 21–38; and "Hermeneutique et au delà," in *Archivio di filosophia*, nos. 1–3 (1977): 11–20.

32 The theme of height is prevalent in Levinas' work, but for his most sustained treatment of the issue see "Transcendence et hauteur," in *Bulletin de la Société Française de la Philosophie* 56, no. 3 (1962): 89–113.

Chapter 4: IdeoGround

1 I am indebted to H. S. Harris' monumental study on Hegel's early work: *Hegel's Development: Toward the Sunlight 1770–1801* (Oxford: Clarendon Press, 1972); *Hegel's Development: Night Thoughts 1801–1806* (Oxford: Clarendon Press, 1983).

2 G. W. F. Hegel, *Early Theological Writings*, trans. T. M. Knox (Chicago: University of Chicago Press, 1948), p. 258.

3 G. W. F. Hegel, *Wissenschaft der Logik*, Bds. I and II (Hamburg: Felix Meiner, 1951), Bd. 2: 17f; *Science of Logic*, trans. A. V. Miller (New York: Humanities Press, 1969), p. 393f.

4 Hegel, *Phenomenology of Spirit*, § 18.

For an application of the double structure lifted from Hegelian metaphysics see Jacques Derrida, *Glas*, trans. J. P. Leavey and R. Rand (Lincoln: University of Nebraska Press, 1986).

5 Hegel, *Phenomenology of Spirit*, § 55.

6 Derrida, *Writing and Difference*, p. 117. The relation between violence and light is a primary motif in this influential essay, which is perhaps the single most important factor in Levinas' rise to prominence as a philosophical thinker.

7 Emmanuel Levinas, *De l'existence a l'existant* (Paris: Fontaine, 1947; reprinted J. Vrin, 1973), p. 76 (henceforth cited as *DEE*); *Existence and Existents*, trans. A. Lingis (The Hague: Martinus Nijhoff, 1978), pp. 48–49 (henceforth cited as *EE*).

8 Derrida, *Writing and Difference*, p. 91.

9 Hegel, *Philosophy of History*, p. 34.

10 On this question see Piotr Hoffman, *Violence in Modern Philosophy* (Chicago: University of Chicago Press, 1989), esp. p. 149f.

11 Nietzsche, *Werke* 2: 946/*Twilight of the Idols*, p. 470.

12 Hegel, *Philosophy of History*, p. 21; also in *Reason in History*, trans. R. S. Hartman (Indianapolis: Bobbs-Merrill, 1953), p. 27.

13 For Hume, the uncertainty of the causal nexus requires the reexamination of the notions of freedom and necessity. He regards this as an improper pairing of terms. The opposite of freedom is not necessity; it is constraint. Necessity is not the lack or negation of liberty but of randomness. Construed in this way, theories of morality and justice are engaged. The non-contradictory status between the two terms enable one to ascribe "praise and blame" in a consistent manner. According to Hume, there

is no such thing as chance. There are only "necessary connections" or "powers," but any definite knowledge of these connections (or of anything else for that matter) is impossible. Here Hegel differs from Hume. One can only infer these powers through the observation of the repeated conjunctions of similar events. Causation is inferred through custom or habit. There is no innate idea of perfection; metaphysical knowledge is impossible. An organizing principle is needed to order individual lives and society at large. The regulating of the social dimension necessitates the formulation of a notion of justice or ethics, i.e., of praising and blaming. What is important is the establishment of consistent, normative ethical judgments. Defining necessity as regularity (uniformity) and expectation, and freedom as the will to act or not to act, he demonstrates that there is no inconsistency involved with the joining of the two terms. They must be mutually inclusive if it is to be at all possible to make any judgments concerning the ethics of an individual's actions within society. This critique of metaphysics results in a purely atheistic will. Following Descartes' examination of sensually based knowledge, skepticism is extended to the very foundation of knowledge and belief in the West: that of the metaphysically conceived causal nexus. Disregarding traditional problems such as the immortality of the soul on the basis of their hypothetical, speculative nature, Hume engages metaphysics for one last time (or so he thinks) through the analysis of the postulate of freedom of the will. The question of freedom is the only one with any real existential validity; the questions of metaphysics are replaced by those of pragmatic value. Hume's radical skepticism lies at the very foundation of modern and contemporary European thought.

14 Hegel, *Phenomenology of Spirit*, § 110.

15 G. W. F. Hegel, *Philosophy of Mind, Part III of the Encyclopaedia of the Philosophical Sciences* (1830), trans. W. Wallace and A. V. Miller (Oxford: Clarendon Press, 1971), § 462 *Zusätze.*

16 In "The Philosophical Basis of Ethics" (1908), George Herbert Mead adopts a position contrary to the dominant ethical theories of his day, those based on the principle of evolution and on the development of human consciousness via social custom and institutions. But while the individual moral consciousness may be the "most concrete" form or manifestation of consciousness, it does not function as the origin or ground of the social ethic. The force of Mead's philosophy as a whole lies in his situating of sociality as *prior to* the development of individual consciousness. The notion of the "self" is neither a metaphysical nor an epistemological given. Subjectivity is not originary; mind or self-consciousness develops reflexively within the social process (George Herbert Mead, *Mind, Self and Society* [Chicago: University of Chicago Press, 1934], p. 134). Mead breaks with the modernist view of subjectivity as constituting agent of its world by positing a "community moral consciousness, a moral world...[which] goes back into a past that antedates moral consciousness itself" (Ibid.). It is here that Mead moves into close proximity with Levinas, who speaks of an absolutely heteronomous past, a pre-original an-archy whose very seeming meaninglessness is what precisely constitutes ethical meaning. Only when individual consciousness apprehends the limitations of its own rationality does the idea of the Infinite, revealed in the face of the Other, destabilize the domesticity of the self's sense of being at-home and force the self to confront the often repressed truth that it is not alone, and moreover, that it is responsible for the Other, and perpetually

accused in that responsibility. Mead is not espousing, nor is Levinas for that matter, the metaphysical position of a transcendent moral order of which the immanent world is the imperfect reflection. Mead goes to some lengths to criticize this position and to disavow himself of any connection with it; and Levinas will speak of the atheism of the will. But Mead realizes that by positing an antecedent community moral consciousness "it is, of course, possible to make this a metaphysical doctrine" forming "metaphysics upon ethics." However, Mead expresses that he has "no wish to enter this debatable field" and leaves the issue at that.

17 Hegel, *Phenomenology of Spirit*, § 20.

18 G. W. F. Hegel, *Philosophy of Right*, trans. T. M. Knox (London: Oxford University Press, 1952).

19 Jean Hyppolite, *Genesis and Structure of Hegel's Phenomenology of Spirit*, trans. S. Cherniak and J. Heckman (Evanston: Northwestern University Press, 1974), p. 56.

20 See Errol E. Harris, *An Interpretation of the Logic of Hegel* (New York: University Press of America, 1983) for a textual analysis of both the greater and lesser *Logic*.

21 Gadamer, *Hegel's Dialectic*, pp. 79–80. Also cf. Stanley Rosen, *G. W. F. Hegel* (New Haven: Yale University Press, 1974), pp. 64–88.

22 G. W. F. Hegel, *Logic: Part I of the Encyclopaedia of the Philosophical Sciences*, trans. W. Wallace (Oxford: Clarendon Press, 1975), 2: 65–94, for his most developed position on Kant's philosophy.

23 On Levinas' Relation to Kant see Jean-François Lyotard, "Logique de Lévinas," in *Textes pour Emmanuel Lévinas*, ed. F. Laruelle (Paris: Éditions Jean-Michel Place, 1980), pp. 127–50; "Levinas' Logic," trans. I. McLeod, in *Face to Face with Levinas*, pp. 131–58. On the relation between Kant and Hegel see Robert B. Pippin, *Hegel's Idealism: The Satisfactions of Self-Consciousness* (Cambridge: Cambridge University Press, 1989), pp. 6–41ff; and Adriaan Peperzak, "Some Remarks on Hegel, Kant, and Levinas," in *Face to Face with Levinas*, pp. 205–17.

24 Cusanus founds the modern conception of the relation between the finite and the infinite. The "absolute coincidence of opposites" (*absoluta coincidentia oppositorum*) lays the groundwork for the principle that the universe could be understood by mathematical means, that is, in terms of measurement. This concept defines God or the Absolute as the infinite *maximum absolutum* and, simultaneously, the finite *maximum contractum*. Though Descartes is generally regarded as the founder of modern philosophy, that is of its methodology, particularly under the sway of nineteenth century neo-Kantism, it is Cusanus who represents the metaphysical foundations of the modern mind. The *coincidentia oppositorum* challenges the Aristotelian logical principle of non-contradiction and contests the dualism of scholastic metaphysics, that is, the notion of the radical cleavage between the divine and the immanent, with the concept of homogeneous space. The Absolute simultaneously transcends and subtends being; infinite ground is finite limitation. Thus Cusanus unknowingly begins turning the rack upon which God will suffer his death. Epistemology emerges henceforth as the principal concern of philosophy and as the condition upon which all knowledge rests.

See Nicholas de Cusa, *The Layman: About Mind*, trans. C. L. Miller (New York: Abaris Books, 1979). *Nicholas of Cusa on Learned Ignorance* , trans. J. Hopkins (Minneapolis: Arthur J. Banning Press, 1981).

For a development of Cusanus' importance on the history of ideas see Ernst Cassirer, *The Individual and the Cosmos in Renaissance Philosophy*, trans. M. Domandi (Oxford: Basil Blackwell, 1963). Derrida also discusses Cusanus in the context of Levinas' philosophy in *Writing and Difference*, pp. 101–102, 150–51.

25 Though it is unlikely that Luther was familiar with Cusanus, he appears to be very close to both Cusanus and Levinas on the issue of the simultaneous presence and absence of the Infinite in the finite. For all three, God or the Infinite is fully present in human history while simultaneously utterly transcendent. The quasi-sacramental doctrine of consubstantiation, of "real presence," lays out this paradox in theological terms. Luther's indebtedness to Augustine arises here insofar as he maintains that God is closer to everything than anything is to itself. It could also be argued that Hegel is actually more in line with the doctrine of transubstantiation insofar as transcendence is completely overcome in the *Aufhebung* of Spirit; but one could also argue that Hegel adopts the position of consubstantiation insofar as the transcendence of the Godhead is also preserved in the *Aufhebung*. But Luther appears to retain the very element of transcendence that Hegel's totally immanent, albeit abstract, philosophy rejects. Luther attacks the notion of sacramental presence, the *character indelebilis*. The concept of consubstantiation attempts to express in a tangible way (for the believer) the notion of the infinite in the finite without reducing the two terms to a common denominator.

One should resist, though, the temptation to draw too many parallels between such a profoundly Jewish thinker as Levinas and such a deep Christian as Luther. But Cusanus, Luther, Hegel, and Levinas are united in the fact that they are all profoundly concerned with the question of the relation between the infinite and the finite. And certainly to even engage in the possibility of such a question is to find oneself in the midst of speculative thinking, as all metaphysics and fundamental ontology does.

See Edward F. Cranz, "Cusanus, Luther, and the Mystical Tradition," in *The Pursuit of Holiness in Late Medieval and Renaissance Religion*, ed. C. Trinkhaus and H. Oberman (Leiden: E. J. Brill, 1974), pp. 93–102. On the relation between Hegel, Luther, and Lutheranism see John W. Burbidge, *Hegel on Logic and Religion* (Albany: SUNY Press, 1992), pp. 141–53; James Yerkes, *The Christology of Hegel* (Albany: SUNY Press, 1982); and Lawrence S. Stepelevich, "Hegel and the Lutheran Eucharist," in *HeyJ* 27 (1985): 262–74.

26 In leveling or flattening certain hierarchical aspects of the relation between the creator and the created Luther (like Cusanus) is able to assert the radical proposal of the "priesthood of all believers." While he negates the hierarchy of the earthly church, he reinforces the notion of the absolute distance between the human and the divine. But unlike Cusanus, Luther refuses to extend the reformation of certain precepts in the Church to the metaphysical or cosmological plane. This results in an irreconcilable tension and unavoidable nihilism (as in Nazi Germany). Luther prefigures Enlightenment politics by positing a "two kingdom" theology that breaks with the medieval view of the reflection of the heavenly order by the earthly order of things. This, in a nutshell, is the crux of Luther's theology: salvation hinges upon accepting the absolute divine demand, the will of God or, to put it in more Hegelian language, the unconditionality of *Geist*, with an affirming though submissive will. (See Martin Luther, *The Bondage of the Will* [Westwood, NJ: Revell, 1957]). The Reformation

battle cry *sola fide* signifies the place of religion before morality. Ethics is not mere fulfillment of social expectations and laws. As with Augustine, only through the love of God and humanity are the obligations of the law met. Goodness is the cause of ethics and not the consequence. Here Luther and Levinas are very close; and it is at this point that Hegel leaves his Lutheran heritage.

27 Hegel claims that the struggle to the death for recognition only literally occurred at the earlier stages of human history and, as civilization progressed, this struggle became increasingly internalized as *Geist*. Mead will also claim that it is "mind" that internalizes the individual in the social process; mind remains fundamentally social and founds the self. Mind, he says, is the transition from the level of communicative gestures to the level of significant (conscious) symbols, from the level of impulse to that of rationality. But unlike Hegel, Mead is not willing to declare this movement as inherently rational. Both will agree that rationality, like consciousness and language, is developmental; however, for Mead, it is not in accordance with an already present, though initially hidden, logic. Still, Mead's concept of mind bears some similarity to *Geist* inasmuch as it is the medium through which the historical development of self-consciousness occurs through the dialectic of recognition. Socialization involves a reflexivity which is "the essential condition, within the social process, for the development of mind" (*Mind, Self and Society*, p. 134). This reflexivity is contingent upon a unity or totality, as in Hegel, of an objective self which reflects or mirrors, in a manner reminiscent of the Platonic conception of the soul, the totality of the social order. The developmental process of self-consciousness occurs through the behavioral and symbolic interface with the *socius*. Behavior is the product of the symbolic gestural interaction with others. Here Mead is again closely aligned with Hegel. Both Mead and Hegel reject the Cartesian cogito as the irreducible basis for subjectivity. Furthermore, reflection and recognition are the moments in which identity occurs as they are precisely the moments of distantiation and differentiation that allows the dialectic to progress.

28 Hegel addresses this question in an early work, *Faith and Knowledge*, trans. W. Cerf and H. S. Harris (Albany: SUNY Press, 1977).

29 Gadamer, *Hegel's Dialectic*, p. 84.

30 Though the term is most recently associated with Heidegger, it is actually Kant who first coins the term "onto-theology." In *Critique of Pure Reason* (A632; B660) onto-theology is defined as the belief (*Glauben*) that thought can know the existence of the transcendental object "through mere concepts, without the help of any experience whatsoever."

31 Hegel, *Phenomenology of Spirit*, § 177.

The essentially reciprocal constitution of the I and the We is founded, says Levinas, on the structure of command. "This reference from a command to a command is the fact of saying 'we,' of constituting a party. By reason of this reference of one command to another, 'we' is not the plural of 'I'" ("Le moi et la totalité," in *Revue de Metaphysique et de Morale* 59, no. 4 [1954]: 371/*CPP* 43).

32 See Hyppolite, pp. 34–50.

33 Gadamer, *Hegel's Dialectic*, pp. 95, 99.

34 On Hegel's relation to Schelling see Rosen, *G. W. F. Hegel*, pp. 56–63.

Chapter 5: MiddleGround

1 Hegel, *Phenomenology of Spirit*, § 367f.

2 Ibid., § 409. Work, however, need not be interpreted only as the activity of the slave; it also refers to Hegel's own project of writing. Blanchot maintains, for instance, that "culture is linked to the book" which assumes two predominant forms in the West: the Bible and the logic of identity. (All the following citations are from Maurice Blanchot, *The Infinite Conversation*, trans. S. Hanson [Minneapolis: University of Minnesota Press, 1993], pp. 422–34). The two forms are united in their attempt to name the Absolute. Though the book is the condition for all reading and writing, it is also a "ruse by which writing goes towards the *absence of the book*," towards an impersonal exteriority or alterity which is "enclosed" within the book and yet, is more than the book. Writing is a relation established "through the production of the book, between the act of writing and the absence of the work." Hegel's writing is a book-writing in that it understands itself within a teleological framework. Work-writing is a "hesitation" says Blanchot between the presence and absence of the work (non-teleological) that disrupts the spatio-temporal continuum. The difference between *book* and *work* is that the work claims to be unique thus moving beyond the book, "outside its category and dialectic." The work seeks to make itself essential whereas the book, in its highest sense, is the receiver and gatherer of a determinate form of knowledge. But when the book is understood as totality of Work, i.e., when it assumes the form of a work, it promotes itself to a dangerous status. It is not the book that is capable of being inscribed as the Absolute; rather, it is the work which is "already outside everything, but in its resignation, is still designated as absolute. The Work is not bound up with success (with completion) as is the book, but with disaster: but this disaster is yet another affirmation of the absolute." The book can always be signed, but the work knows no single author. Always present in the book and yet unable to be completed, the work celebrates its own impossibility, its own doom. Writing, as that which *actively* produces the absence of the work is "worklessness...the indeterminacy that lies between reason and unreason." Writing disrupts the space-time of the book since it produces the absence of the work and moves toward the absence of the book. As non-absent absence and decentered center, writing ruptures the time of the book (presence) as well as its space (center). Writing, as worklessness, designates the "disjunction of a time and space that are *something other*, precisely that which can no longer assert itself in a relationship of unity." It is at this point that Blanchot's thought moves into close proximity with that of Levinas who stresses that "*a work conceived radically is a movement of the Same towards the Other which never returns to the Same*" (*HH* 41/91; *EDE* 191).

On the relation between Levinas and Blanchot see Paul Davies, "A Fine Risk: Reading Blanchot Reading Levinas," in *Re-Reading Levinas*, ed. R. Bernasconi and S. Critchley (Bloomington: Indiana University Press, 1991), pp. 200–26; and Paul Davies, "Difficult Friendship," in *Research in Phenomenology* 18 (1988): 149–72. Also see Mark C. Taylor, *Altarity* (Chicago: University of Chicago Press, 1987), pp. 247–53 for a reading of Blanchot. Jacques Derrida addresses the question of how Levinas' own work allows the Work to be produced in "En ce moment même dans cet ouvrage me voici," in *Textes pour Emmanuel Lévinas*, ed. F. Laruelle (Paris: Editions Jean-Michel Place, 1980), pp. 21–60; reprinted in *Psyche: Inventions de l'autre* (Paris:

Galilée, 1987); "At this very moment in this work here I am," trans. R. Berezdevin, in *Re-Reading Levinas*, pp. 11–48.

3 Hegel, *Phenomenology of Spirit*, § 444.

4 Ibid., § 439.

5 Otherwise, it could be argued, freedom remains at the negative level that characterizes the freedom associated with the Terror after the French revolution. While this is admittedly not the standard interpretation, this is supported in the *Philosophy of Right* where Hegel maintains that the imagined positive goals of the revolution dissolved into the Terror, into the "freedom of the void" since "such actuality leads at once to some sort of order, to a particularization of organizations and individuals alike; while it is precisely out of the annihilation of particularity and objective characterization that the self-consciousness of this negative freedom proceeds. Consequently, what negative freedom intends to will can never be anything but an abstract idea, and giving effect to this idea can only be the fury of destruction" (*Philosophy of Right*, § 5). Thus is the revolution the culmination of the Enlightenment for Hegel. The inherent non-reconcilable contradiction that is endemic to *Verstand* reaches its political aspirations in a state of discordant anarchy. *Vernunft*, on the other hand, claims to offer humanity the emergence of a new *non-differentiated* State out of the necessary turbulance that the French Revolution ushered in. But Reason, history as Spirit, will run its own course, in its own time. As has been quoted so often, the Owl of Minerva flies only at night.

6 See Allen W. Wood, *Hegel's Ethical Thought* (Cambridge: Cambridge University Press, 1990), p. 127ff.

7 Levinas and Kearney, *Face to Face with Levinas*, pp. 29–30 (italics added).

8 Hegel, *Encyclopaedia*, §§ 501–502.

9 Charles Taylor, *Hegel* (Cambridge: Cambridge University Press, 1975), p. 377.

10 Hegel, *Philosophy of Right*, § 156.

11 On Hegel's relevance to political theory see Schlomo Avineri, *Hegel's Theory of the Modern State* (Cambridge: Cambridge University Press, 1973); and Paul Lakeland, *The Politics of Salvation: The Hegelian Idea of the State* (Albany: SUNY Press, 1984).

12 Hegel, *Philosophy of Right*, § 145.

13 Hegel, *Phenomenology of Spirit*, §§ 484–595.

14 According to Mead, the act, which is not a value in itself but which is always social and gives rise to valuation, arises in the gesture which stimulates in the other, not as imitation but as response, the reflexive gesture which allows the self and the other to function together in the common social situation. The gesture refers to the future by indicating what is to follow. Only the reflexivity of the social act, i.e., the response to the self's gesture by another, gives rise to meaning. Mind and self do not stand as constituting agents or loci of signification. Communication does not occur first through mind. As Levinas maintains, thought consists in speech, and moreover between faces that speak directly to one another. Gestures are meaningless unless directed at and responded to by the other. The vocal gesture is the gesture which affects the self in nearly the same way as it does the other; it is the source of language proper. And yet, depite this eminent place of the phonic, of speech, as that which enables the self and the other to exchange roles and thus constitute societies, there is that prior antecedent moment that must be acknowledged as the ultimate consti-

tuting moment of the subject. For Mead, this is the social; for Levinas, it is the ethical significance of the face which opens up, prior to any affirmative or negative gesture, the very possibility of communication and meaning. This is the point where Mead says "the ethical statement would form metaphysics upon ethics." Thus one could say, along with Levinas, that it is indeed alterity, and not selfsame consciousness, which constitutes ethical subjectivity. Mead echoes this: "Awareness or consciousness is not necessary to the presence of meaning in the social process" (*Mind, Self and Society*, p. 77). But all this is not to say that after the initial constitution of ethical subjectivity by the primal relation with alterity the individual plays no formative role in the process of societal development. In a remark directed towards John Dewey, Mead states that "the individual is no thrall of society. He constitutes society as genuinely as society constitutes the individual." It is at this point that Hegel's theory of recognition comes into play.

15 Hegel, *Phenomenology of Spirit*, § 445.

Tina Chanter notes that while it is generally assumed that Antigone's individual action signifies the embodiment of the divine law and Creon the embodiment of human law, "it is equally true that each law contains the other in a negative way" and thus "both Antigone and Creon are destroyed by their steadfast duty to their own actions, and neither are in a position to fully understand their own ethical stance." See Tina Chanter, "Antigone's Dilemma," in *Re-Reading Levinas*, p. 136.

16 Though Hegel's impact is certainly more evident in Continental thinking, he has exerted a subtle yet powerful influence on Anglo-American philosophy. For example, Mead weds the insights of behavioral psychology with Hegel's dialectic of recognition. His indebtedness to Hegel lies not in the area of metaphysics, nor in Hegel the political thinker, but rather, in Hegel the organic dialectician of the theory of recognition as espoused in the *Phenomenology*, specifically, the theory of the development of self-consciousness through the struggle between self and other. As with Hegel, and contra his contemporary William James, who seeks to ground or define the self in terms of reflexive affectation, Mead says that self-consciousness is "a cognitive rather than an emotional process," the origin and foundations of which are social (*Mind, Self and Society*, p. 173). Yet Mead does not follow Hegel in asserting that the whole of reality, expressed as Spirit, is at base consciousness (p. 77). The concepts of consciousness and mind are "very ambiguous" (pp. 27, 188); they are emergent out of the prereflective state of the social aspect of human existence.

17 Revelation 1: 8 (RSV): "I am the *Alpha* and the *Omega*, the beginning and the end."

18 The reference here is to René Girard, *Violence and the Sacred*, trans. P. Gregory (Baltimore: Johns Hopkins University Press, 1977). Girard forwards the thesis that community is founded on the scapegoat mechanism. Ritual sacrifice (at first of the king or ruler) vented the built-up violence stemming from resentment and hatred within the community. Only by displacing this violence onto an acceptable and neutral victim are the violent tendencies or desires placated.

19 On the relation between mediation, religion, and violence see Georges Bataille, *Theory of Religion*, trans. R. Hurley (New York: Zone Books, 1989), esp. pp. 79–85. Also, Georges Bataille, *Inner Experience*, trans. L. A. Boldt (Albany: SUNY Press, 1988), pp. 108–11; *Visions of Excess*, trans. and ed. A. Stoekl (Minneapolis: University of Minnesota Press, 1985), pp. 105–14.

On the relationship between Hegel and Bataille see Jacques Derrida, "From Restricted to General Economy: A Hegelianism without Reserve," in *Writing and Difference*, pp. 251–77. For an assessment of Bataille's critique of Hegel via Derrida see Kevin Hart, *The Trespass of the Sign* (Cambridge: Cambridge University Press, 1989), pp. 193–98. On Bataille's relation to Hegel and Nietzsche see Taylor, *Altarity*, pp. 115–48.

20 On the relation between Adorno and Hegel with allusion to Levinasian ethics see Drucilla Cornell, *The Philosophy of the Limit* (New York: Routledge, 1992), pp. 13–38.

21 Theodor W. Adorno, *Negative Dialectics*, trans. E. B. Ashton (New York: Continuum Press, 1973), p. xx. Also see Susan Buck-Morss, *The Origin of Negative Dialectics: Theodor Adorno, Walter Benjamin, and the Frankfurt Institute* (New York: Free Press, 1977), pp. 82–85; and Martin Jay, *Adorno* (Cambridge, MA: Harvard University Press, 1984), pp. 21, 63f.

22 Kant defines autonomy as the conquering of the state of immaturity insofar as human beings are responsible for it. Autonomy does not signify lawless subjectivity. The famous Copernican Revolution, the turn to the subject, is, in one sense, the recovery of other forms of reason that the tradition had dismissed as untenable (at best) and of the devil (at worst). Practical reason picks up on the Pietistic emphasis on the will over intellect, yet Kant seeks to mend the old quarrel between will and intellect insofar as he maintains that the essential nature of the human will is the law of reason. However, Kant separates himself from the Greek view that theoretical knowledge constitutes the highest good.

On the notion of autarchy in Kant see Alphonso Lingis, *Deathbound Subjectivity* (Bloomington: Indiana University Press, 1989), pp. 38–58.

23 Of course one need not necessarily interpret Hegel in such a manner. See for instance, Jürgen Habermas, *Knowledge and Human Interests*, trans. J. J. Shapiro (Boston: Beacon Press, 1971).

24 Adorno, *Negative Dialectics*, p. 13.

25 Ibid., p. 183f.

26 Theodor Adorno, "Subject and Object," in *The Essential Frankfurt School Reader*, ed. A. Arato and E. Gebhardt (New York: Continuum Press, 1982), pp. 497–98.

27 Adorno, *Negative Dialectics*, p. 11f.

28 Adorno, "Subject and Object," p. 499.

29 Ibid.

30 Theodor W. Adorno, *Against Epistemology: A Metacritique*, trans. W. Domingo (Cambridge, MA: MIT Press, 1983).

31 Jay, p. 58.

32 Derrida, *Writing and Difference*, p. 79.

Chapter 6: WarGround

1 Hegel, *Reason in History*, p. 25 (italics added).

2 Maurice Merleau-Ponty may have been the first to use this phrase in Part II of his *Phenomenology of Perception*, trans. C. Smith (London: Routledge and Kegan Paul, 1962).

This irrecuperable past origin Levinas terms "an-archy." "But anarchy is not disorder as opposed to order.... Disorder is but another order, and what is diffuse is thematizable. Anarchy troubles being over and beyond these alternatives. It brings to a halt the ontological play which, precisely qua play, is consciousness, where being is lost and found again, and thus illuminated.... Anarchy is persecution" (*AE* 159–60/*OB* 101).

3 See Robert Bernasconi, "Levinas on Time and the Instant," in *Time and Metaphysics*, ed. D. Wood and R. Bernasconi (Coventry: Parousia Press, 1982), pp. 199–217; Alphonso Lingis, "A Time to Exist on One's Own," in *Analecta Husserliana* 6, ed. A. T. Tymieniecka (Dordrecht: Reidel, 1977), pp. 31–40.

4 For a development of this topic see Donald P. Verene, *Hegel's Recollection: A Study of Images in the Phenomenology of Spirit* (Albany: SUNY Press, 1985).

5 Hegel, *Phenomenology of Spirit*, § 19.

6 Hegel, *Wissenschaft der Logik*, 2: 496/*Science of Logic*, p. 835.

7 Hegel, *Phenomenology of Spirit*, § 37.

8 Ibid., § 17.

9 Hegel, *Wissenschaft der Logik*, 1: 128/*Science of Logic*, p. 139.

10 In order to distinguish Levinas' conception of Desire (*désir*) from Hegel's (*Begierde*) a capitalized "D" will be employed when referring to Levinas' usage of the term.

11 Hegel, *Phenomenology of Spirit*, § 167f.

12 Derrida, *Writing and Difference*, p. 93. Also see William Desmond, *Desire, Dialectic, and Otherness* (New Haven: Yale University Press, 1987) for a discussion of the themes in the title. Attempting to retrieve the positive aspects of Hegelian dialectic, Desmond proposes the concept of the "metaxological." This concept focuses on the notion of the "between" in trying to preserve a sense of wholeness or totality without compromising the integrity of radical otherness and origins.

13 On this point Whitehead is very close to Hegel regarding the relation (dialectic) between sameness and otherness in both the empirical and intelligible aspects of the question. But there is a difference in the empirical/intelligible distinction that needs to be brought to light. The infinite, in all its various possible forms of meaning ("concrescence"), is confined to a totality of conceptually grasped relations in Whitehead's metaphysical cosmology as it is in Hegel's speculative dialectics. There is "one subjective aim" that guides the formation of actual occasions. This "actuality is the *totality* of prehensions with subjective unity in the process of concresence into concrete unity" (*Process and Reality*, p. 235). The concept of totality also assumes a privileged role in Whiteheadian metaphysics, and with this concept, the championing of rationality, a position that squarely places him and Hegel within the tradition and not outside of it. Though admittedly a rationalist, Whitehead nevertheless maintains that order emerges and is not foundational, and that all configuration is by decision. Thus does he aim to safeguard the element of the arbitrary and spontaneous in the cosmos much in the manner that Hegel takes recourse at times to the concept of "contingency."

14 On the logic of Levinas' argument against Hegel see Lyotard, "Levinas' Logic," trans. I. McLeod, in *Face to Face with Levinas*, pp. 117–30. Lyotard writes that "Levinas struggles to escape the Hegelian persecution" (p. 121) by attacking "Hegelian alterity so as to show that it is only a caprice of identity" (p. 119).

15 Hegel, *Phenomenology of Spirit*, § 475.

16 Hegel, *Wissenschaft der Logik*, 1: 125/*Science of Logic*, p. 137.

17 Ibid., 1: 159/p. 168.

18 See Edith Wyschogrod, "Derrida, Levinas, and Violence," in *Continental Philosophy* II, ed. H. Silverman (New York: Routledge, 1989), pp. 183–200, esp. p. 191.

19 See Emmanuel Levinas, "Beyond Intentionality," trans. K. McLaughlin, in *Philosophy in France Today*, ed. A. Montefiore (Cambridge: Cambridge University Press, 1983), pp. 100–115; "La Conscience non-intentionelle," in *Philosophers on Their Own Work*, ed. A. Mercier and M. Svilar. Federation internationale des societies de philosophie, vol. 10 (New York: Peter Lang, 1983), pp. 147–57.

For secondary sources see Adriaan Peperzak, "From Intentionality to Responsibility: On Levinas' Philosophy of Language," in *The Question of the Other*, ed. A. Dallery and C. Scott (Albany: SUNY Press, 1989), pp. 3–22; and Craig Vasey, "Emmanuel Levinas: From Intentionality to Proximity," in *Philosophy Today* 25, (1981).

20 See Emmanuel Levinas, "Diachronie et representation," in *University of Ottawa Quarterly* 55, no. 4 (1985); trans. R. Cohen, *TO* 97–120.

21 On Levinas' relation to Buber see Emmanuel Levinas, "Martin Buber et la théorie de la connaisance" and "Dialogue avec Martin Buber," in *Noms Propres* (Montpellier: Fata Morgana, 1976), pp. 23–48 (henceforth cited as *NP*); "Martin Buber and the Theory of Knowledge," in *LR* 60–74. Also, Emmanuel Levinas, *Hors Sujet* (Montpellier: Fata Morgana, 1987), pp. 13–69 (henceforth cited as *HS*); *Outside the Subject*, trans. M. B. Smith (Stanford: Stanford University Press, 1994), pp. 4–48 (henceforth cited as *OS*).

Also see Robert Bernasconi, "'Failure of Communication as a Surplus: Dialogue and Lack of Dialogue Between Buber and Levinas," in *The Provocation of Levinas: Re-Thinking the Other*, ed. R. Bernasconi and D. Wood (London and New York: Routledge, 1988), pp. 100–35.

22 For Levinas' views on the ontological reality of evil see Emmanuel Levinas, "Transcendence et mal," in *Le nouveau commerce* 41, (1978): 55–75; "Transcendence and Evil," trans. A. Lingis, in *The Phenomenology of Man and of the Human Condition*, ed. A. T. Tymieniecka, in *Analecta Husserliana* 14 (Dordrecht: Reidel, 1983), pp. 153–65; reprinted in *CPP* 175–86. Also see, *HH* 80–82/*CPP* 137–39.

23 This is Kojève's contention (*Introduction to the Reading of Hegel*, esp. pp. 3–70). But the danger of his interpretation is that, in its overemphasis on the place and the importance of the *Phenomenology of Spirit*, it promotes a view of subjectivity that lends itself to possible totalitarian manipulation and thus continues the economy of violence that Hegel himself seeks to overcome. "Satisfied" subjecthood is possible only by way of citizenship in the universal homogenous State (which is yet to be realized concretely). In such a political State desire would be placated through universal recognition by the Other, that is, by other citizens. The aftermath of World War II has left a legacy of suspicion that calls such an understanding of the political into question. The Kojèvian interpretation of the State carries with it the specter of totalitarian violence. This relation, violent from its very inception, is precisely what is to be overcome. Is Hegel able to accomplish this? If he is unable, where must thought move in order to transcend or overcome ethical violence and engage in a positive relation with alterity?

See Judith Butler, *Subjects of Desire: Hegelian Reflections in Twentieth-Century*

France (New York: Columbia University Press, 1987) for an overview of the French reception of Hegel; and Vincent Descombes, *Modern French Philosophy*, trans. L. Scott-Fox and J. M. Harding (Cambridge: Cambridge University Press, 1980) for an analysis of the relation between Kojève's interpretation of Hegel and nihilism.

24 Hegel, *Phenomenology of Spirit*, § 195.

25 See Robert Bernasconi, "Hegel and Levinas: The Possibility of Reconciliation and Forgiveness," in *Archivio di Filosophia* 54 (1986): 325–46; "Levinas Face to Face—with Hegel," in *Journal of the British Society for Phenomenology* 123, no. 3 (1982): 267–76.

26 This question is taken up by Cornell, *The Philosophy of the Limit*, p. 91f.

27 Derrida, *Writing and Difference*, p. 94.

28 Ibid., p. 109.

29 Søren Kierkegaard develops the social aspect of this thought in *The Present Age*, trans. A. Dru (New York: Harper & Row, 1962).

30 Cf. Errol E. Harris, "Hegel's Theory of Sovereignty, International Relations, and War," in *Hegel's Social and Political Thought* (Atlantic Highlands, NJ: Humanities Press, 1980), pp. 137–49; Henry Paolucci, "Hegel and the Nation-State System of International Relations," in *Hegel's Social and Political Thought*, pp. 151–65.

Chapter 7: MystiGround

1 Hegel, *Phenomenology of Spirit*, § 90.

2 Edmund Husserl, *The Crisis of the European Sciences*, trans. with introduction D. Carr (Evanston: Northwestern University Press, 1970), esp. pp. 184–86.

3 G. W. F. Hegel, *Lectures on the Philosophy of Religion*, trans. R. F. Brown, P. C. Hodgson, and J. M. Stewart, with the assistance of H. S. Harris, ed. P. C. Hodgson (Berkeley: University of California Press, 1988), esp. pp. 184–88.

4 Hegel, *Phenomenology of Spirit*, § 20.

5 Ibid., § 25.

6 Hegel, *Lectures on the Philosophy of Religion*, pp. 114–15.

7 Ibid., p. 115.

8 Hegel, *Philosophy of Right*, § 11.

9 On the originary status of *Trieb* Hegel says: "It is to be recalled that the beginning, which is *in itself* a concrete totality, may as beginning also be *free* and its immediacy have the determination of an *external existence*; the *germ of the living being* and the *subjective end* in general have proved themselves to be such beginnings and therefore are both themselves *urges*" (*Wissenschaft der Logik*, 2: 555/*Science of Logic*, p. 829).

Like Hegel, Mead too wants to dissolve the mysterious origin of mind. Only the positing of the social interactive process as prior to the existence of mind and self provides an effective alternative to the more religious metaphysic of mystery or transcendent origination. Like Dewey, Mead defines "mind" in terms of function, not as a structure, but as an instrument, a tool. The instrumental function of mind occurs and manifests itself in the "significant gesture," the meaning of which is determined by the response it solicits. When humans are aware or conscious of the meaning of gestures they become significant. One responds to one's own gestures as much as an other does. Through the self-other dialectic one not only comes to recognize the significance of gesture (primarily, but not only, verbal), but also acquires a sense of social role by taking up the role of the other.

10 Hegel, *Philosophy of Right*, § 17.

11 Ibid.

12 "As subjective [the concept] again presupposes an implicit otherness; it is the *urge* to realize itself, the end that wills itself *by means of itself* to give itself objectivity and to realize itself in the objective world" (Hegel, *Wissenschaft der Logik*, 2: 542/*Science of Logic*, p. 818).

Mead will also claim that the self, insofar as it is constituted by its impulses, seeks objects which allow the fulfillment of those impulses. A social self takes unto itself the attitudes of the other through the process of language, which like self-consciousness is developmental. This is the beginning of the individual moral consciousness. What is striking here, with regard to Mead's relation to Hegel, is the role that impulse plays in the constitution of consciousness and self-consciousness. But for both Hegel and Mead, it is the process through which the urges or impulses of the will are satisfied (Hegel) that constitutes the formation of the social self.

13 Thomas Altizer develops the importance of the concepts of *Trieb* and *kenosis* in Hegel's philosophy in *The Genesis of God* (Louisville: Westminster/John Knox Press, 1994), pp. 11–47.

14 Ibid., p. 16.

15 Joseph Flay refers to Hegel's philosophy as a "diremptive totality" in "Religion and the Absolute Standpoint," *Thought* 56 (September 1981): 327; also see his *Hegel's Quest for Certainty* (Albany: SUNY Press, 1984) for an exhaustive index and critical notes on Hegel.

16 Hegel, *Wissenschaft der Logik*, 1: 138/*Science of Logic*, p. 149.

17 Ibid., 2: 504/p. 842; also, *Phenomenology of Spirit*, § 18.

18 Hegel, *Wissenschaft der Logik*, 1: 125/*Science of Logic*, p. 137.

19 Ibid., 1: 128/p. 139.

20 Ibid., 1: 129/p. 140.

21 Ibid., 1: 133–34/pp. 144–45.

22 Ibid., 1: 136f/p. 147f.

23 Hegel, *Encyclopaedia*, § 215.

24 Hegel, *Wissenschaft der Logik*, 1: 145/*Science of Logic*, p. 153.

Chapter 8: TransGround

1 Levinas' philosophy is firmly situated not only in Heidegger but in the phenomenology of Edmund Husserl as well. One of the many shortcomings of this study is that it does not engage Husserl's relation to Levinas. However, Husserl is the sole figure in the history of philosophy to whom Levinas has devoted a full-length study (*Théorie de l'intution dans la phénoménologie de Husserl* [Paris: Alcan, 1930; J. Vrin, 1963]; *The Theory of Intuition in Husserl's Phenomenology*, trans. A. Orianne. [Evanston: Northwestern University Press, 1973]). This is the first published major secondary study on Husserl's work; and there have been numerous excellent commentaries done on Levinas' relation to Husserl, most notably by Derrida in "Violence and Metaphysics" (1964), and it is to these that one should look to for a more defin-

itive reading. Suffice it to say that Levinas is united with Husserl's later thinking, following the critique of transcendental phenomenology by Heidegger and Sartre, in the conviction that the meaning of subjectivity is intersubjectivity. This is not to suggest that he is steadfastly opposed to an operative concept of history or even of the notion of totality, for that matter; just to the notion that being or history constitutes the only possible ground for consciousness. Consciousness, Levinas maintains, is awakened and constituted by and through its relation with alterity. Levinas' view of phenomenology as the latest effort of ontology to assert itself in the history of thought as first philosophy is directed, to bring the question back to Husserl, against the desire, or rather, the *need* to formulate a ground in which meaning can be substantiated in some totalizable way. For Husserl this takes the form of the coherently constituted life-world. In addition, many of the same movements that characterize much of Hegelian phenomenology, which is a very different project from Husserlian phenomenology, are repeated in Husserl's theory of intentionality. Yet there is a tension between Husserlian and Hegelian phenomenology in Levinas that permeates his work, particularly regarding the notions of eschatology and surprise. The notion of "surprise" may perhaps be seen as surprising itself here since Levinas severely criticizes Husserl's notion of the constituted world, that is, the coherence of profiles and operations listed for the formation of the *Lebenswelt.* For Levinas, a crucial commitment is the ideal of the mind, that is, that the constituted world can be disrupted, or that it can have a different coherency than that which we experience. The locus of this disruption is the face of the Other which, as the irruption of the infinite or absolutely other, calls into question the very notion of reality itself. So it is that the novelty or surprise associated with alterity functions as the disruption of, or the counter-example to, the coherently constituted world. But if the *Lebenswelt* can be disrupted, then what else is at stake? This is perhaps one of the most troubling and yet exciting aspects of Levinas' ethical metaphysics. For other sustained discussions of Husserl see *EDE* 7–52; *LR* 11–28; *EDE* 218–22/*CPP* 110–13; *AE* 55–60, 105–11/*OB* 31–34, 65–68.

Secondary sources on Levinas' relation to Husserl include Richard A. Cohen, "Absolute Positivity and Ultrapositivity: Husserl and Levinas," in *The Question of the Other*, pp. 35–43; and Adriaan Peperzak, "Phenomenology—Ontology—Metaphysics: Levinas' Perspective on Husserl and Heidegger," in *Man and World* 16 (1983): 113–27. For a consideration of Husserl's conception of infinity and internal time consciousness, crucial for the development of Levinas' philosophy, see Lingis, *Deathbound Subjectivity*, pp. 11–37.

2 Martin Heidegger, *Identität und Differenz* (Pfullingen: Verlag Günther Neskel, 1957), 35; *Identity and Difference*, trans. J. Stambaugh (New York: Harper & Row, 1969), pp. 45, 111.

3 See Werner Marx, *Heidegger and the Tradition*, trans. T. Kisiel and M. Greene (Evanston: Northwestern University Press, 1971), pp. 85–100.

4 Martin Heidegger, "Was ist Metaphysik?" in *Wegmarken* (Frankfurt am Main: Vittorio Klostermann Verlag, 1967), pp. 1–19; trans. D. F. Krell, "What is Metaphysics?" in *Basic Writings*, pp. 95–112.

5 Levinas discusses the notion of *Geworfenheit* in *EDE* 68–69f, and with regard to the concept of *Entwurf* in *EDE* 83–85f.

6 See Marx, *Heidegger and the Tradition*, esp. p. 208f.
7 Heidegger, *Wegmarken*, p. 8f/*Basic Writings*, p. 102f.
8 Ibid., p. 9/p. 103.
9 Ibid., p. 10f/p. 104f.
10 Heidegger, *Sein und Zeit*, p. 74/*Being and Time*, p. 104–105.
11 Ibid., p. 188/p. 233.
12 Emmanuel Levinas, "Il y a," in *Deucalion* 1 (Paris: Cahiers de Philosophie, 1946), reprinted with some modifications as the Introduction and Chapter 3, § 2 of *DEE*/*EE*; "There Is: Existence without Existents," trans. R. Cohen, in *LR* 30–58; also see, *TeI* 207–209/*TI* 190–91; *AE* 14–15, 253–56/*OB* 3–4, 162–65.

For secondary sources see Philip Lawton, "Levinas' Notion of the 'There Is,'" *Philosophy Today* 20, no. 1 (1976): 69–76; Silvano Petrosino and Jacques Rolland, *La vérité nomade: Introduction à Emmanuel Lévinas* (Paris: La Découverte, 1984), pp. 19–25; Wyschogrod, "Derrida, Levinas, and Violence," esp. pp. 183–86.
13 Cf. Heidegger, *Platons Lehre von der Wahrheit. Mit einem Brief über den "Humanismus."* (Bern: Francke Verlag, 1947), pp. 53–119; "Letter on Humanism," trans. F. A. Capuzzi and J. G. Gray, in *Basic Writings*, pp. 193–240.
14 Heidegger, *Wegmarken*, p. 17/*Basic Writings*, p. 110.
15 Heidegger, *Sein und Zeit*, p. 162/*Being and Time*, p. 205f.
16 Ibid., esp. pp. 118–22/pp. 154–57.
17 Psychoanalyst Jacques Lacan, who was familiar with Heidegger's work, also uses this term in describing the illusory nature of the ego.
18 For an analysis of Heidegger's concept of *Mitsein* see Michael Theunissen, *The Other: Studies in the Social Ontology of Husserl, Heidegger, Sartre, and Buber*, trans. C. Macann (Cambridge: MIT Press, 1986), esp. pp. 167–98; and Fred R. Dallmayr, *Twilight of Subjectivity: Contributions to a Post-Individualist Theory of Politics* (Amherst: University of Massachusetts Press, 1981), pp. 59–71.
19 Heidegger, *Sein und Zeit*, p. 151/*Being and Time*, p. 193.
20 Ibid., p. 123/p. 160.
21 Heidegger, *Wegmarken*, p. 7f/*Basic Writings*, p. 101f.
22 Levinas presents his thoughts on Kierkegaard in two essays: "Kierkegaard: existence et éthique" and "A propos de 'Kierkegaard vivant,'" in *NP* 77–92. On Levinas' relation to Kierkegaard see Taylor, *Altarity*, pp. 185–216.
23 Daniel 5: 27. The meaning of TEKEL in the midrash of the handwriting on the wall (MENE MENE TEKEL UPARSIN). The prophet interpreted it to signal the end of Belshazzar's reign over the Babylonian empire.
24 For an extended treatment on the role of proximity see Joseph Libertson, *Proximity: Levinas, Blanchot, Bataille and Communication* (The Hague: Martinus Nijhoff, 1982).
25 For secondary sources on Levinas' relation to Heidegger see Robert Bernasconi, "Deconstruction and the Possibility of Ethics," in *Deconstruction and Philosophy*, ed. J. Sallis (Chicago: University of Chicago Press, 1987), pp. 122–39; Luk Bouckaert, "Ontology and Ethics: Reflections on Levinas' Critique of Heidegger," in *International Philosophical Quarterly* 10 (1970): 402–19; Steven Gans, "Ethics or Ontology," in *Philosophy Today*, 16, no. 2 (1972): 117–21; Adriaan Peperzak, "Phenomenology—Ontology—Metaphysics: Levinas' Perspective on Husserl and Heidegger," in *Man and World* 16 (1983): 113–27.

26 Martin Heidegger, *The Metaphysical Foundations of Logic*, trans. M. Heim (Bloomington: Indiana University Press, 1984), § 10 [5], p. 137.
27 Heidegger, *Sein und Zeit*, p. 186/*Being and Time*, p. 231.
28 Ibid., p. 263/p. 308.
29 Heidegger, *The Metaphysical Foundations of Logic*, §10 [2–3], pp. 136–37.
30 Caputo points out that in its original context (the Rhineland mystics, especially Meister Eckhart) "*Gelassenheit* meant letting God be God, letting him be—in yourself, in others, in everything—a very non-exclusionary idea.... This idea makes its way down to Heidegger, where it undergoes a wondrous repetition and retrieval—but with one thing missing, the emancipatory tone that announces the liberation of us all" (John Caputo, "Disseminating Originary Ethics and the Ethics of Dissemination," in *The Question of the Other*, p. 61).
31 See Max Picard, *The Human Face*, trans. G. Endore (New York: Farrar and Rinehart, 1930) for a concrete analysis of the face that avoids many of the abstractions arguably associated with Heidegger's and Levinas' renderings. For a response to Picard by Levinas see "Max Picard et le visage," in *NP* 111–16.
32 On the face to face in Heidegger and Levinas see Alphonso Lingis, "Face to Face: A Phenomenological Analysis," in *International Philosophical Quarterly* 19, no. 2 (1979): 151–63; and Lingis, *Deathbound Subjectivity*, pp. 135–55.
33 See Levinas and Kearney, *Face to Face with Levinas*, p. 25.
34 Derrida, *Writing and Difference*, p. 147f.
35 Ibid., p. 136.
36 Heidegger, *Identität und Differenz*, p. 56/*Identity and Difference*, pp. 64, 132.
37 Ibid., p. 45f. For a comparison between Heidegger and Derrida on this issue see Kenneth Itzkowitz, "Différance and Identity," in *Research in Phenomenology* 8 (1978): 127–45.
38 See Emmanuel Levinas, *Transcendence et intelligibilité* (Geneva: Éditions Labor et Fides, 1984); and "Pluralismé et transcendence," in *Actes du congres international de philosophie* (1984): 381–83.
39 Derrida, *Writing and Difference*, p. 114.
40 Ibid., p. 99.
41 Robert Bernasconi develops the importance of the section II ("Interiority and Economy") of *TI* in "Rereading *Totality and Infinity*," in *The Question of the Other*, pp. 23–34.
42 Cf. Roland Paul Blum, "Emmanuel Levinas' Theory of Commitment," *Philosophy and Phenomenological Research* 44, no. 2 (1983): 145–68.
43 Levinas and Kearney, *Face to Face with Levinas*, p. 29. Also, *EeI* 52, 107/*EI* 52, 100.
44 There has always been a conflict between the teachings of the messianic Jesus of the Gospels and the trinitarian Christ of the Patristic tradition. For example, before the destruction of the Temple in Jerusalem and the Diaspora in 70 C.E., there were two major strands of Christian interpretation: the Jewish variant as elaborated in the Letter to the Hebrews, which, though traditionally attributed to Paul is, most likely, by all analyses, not his, and the Pauline-Gentilic hermeneutic as espoused in the epistles.
45 The Levinasian sense of responsibility as substitution is very similar to the infinite obligation that the Jesus as portrayed in the synoptic Gospels places upon his

disciples. The parallel between the teachings of Jesus and Levinas is found, for example, in the midrash of Jesus' confrontation with the Pharisees who, in seeking to trip him up on some theological point, ask him what is the greatest of the commandments. Jesus replies: to love God above all and your neighbor as yourself; in this all the laws and teachings of the prophets are contained. What is remarkable about this answer is that it directly parallels Levinas' insistence that the only access to the absolutely other is through ethical responsibility to the other person, the neighbor, and even more, to the stranger.

46 Derrida, *Writing and Difference*, p. 111.

Chapter 9: DiaGround

1 Maurice Merleau-Ponty, *Signs*, trans. R. Cleary (Evanston: Northwestern University Press, 1964), p. 88.

2 Ibid., p. 96.

3 Merleau-Ponty, *Phenomenology of Perception*, p. 389.

4 Maurice Merleau-Ponty, *The Prose of the World*, trans. J. O'Neill (Evanston: Northwestern University Press, 1973), p. 35.

5 Ibid., p. 14.

6 Maurice Merleau-Ponty, "Philosophy and Non-Philosophy Since Hegel," trans. H. Silverman, in *Telos*, 29 (1976): esp. 79.

7 Maurice Merleau-Ponty, *Sense and Non-Sense*, trans. H. L. and P. A. Dreyfus (Evanston: Northwestern University Press, 1964), p. 63.

8 Maurice Merleau-Ponty, *The Visible and the Invisible*, trans. A. Lingis (Evanston: Northwestern University Press, 1973), p. 94.

9 Ibid., p. 215.

10 Merleau-Ponty, *The Prose of the World*, p. 37.

11 Friedrich Nietzsche, *Die Fröhliche Wissenschaft*, in *Werke*, 2: 78; *The Gay Science*, trans. W. Kaufmann (New York: Vintage Books, 1974), p. 122: "We can destroy only as creators!—But let us not forget this either: it is enough to create new names and estimations and probabilities in order to create in the long run new 'things.'"

12 Merleau-Ponty, *The Prose of the World*, p. 99.

13 Merleau-Ponty, *Signs*, pp. 42–43.

14 Merleau-Ponty, *The Prose of the World*, p. 28.

15 Merleau-Ponty, *Signs*, p. 43.

16 Merleau-Ponty, *The Prose of the World*, p. 38.

17 Merleau-Ponty, *Phenomenology of Perception*, p. 454.

18 Maurice Merleau-Ponty, *The Primacy of Perception*, trans. and ed. J. Edie (Evanston: Northwestern University Press, 1964), p. 13.

19 For a developed appraisal of the relation between the saying and the said see Simon Critchley, *The Ethics of Deconstruction* (Oxford: Blackwell, 1992), esp. pp. 123–30, 162–82.

20 Hegel, *Wissenschaft der Logik*, 1: 132/*Science of Logic*, p. 143.

21 This non-teleological spiralling movement bears close resemblance to the metaphor of the spiral employed in Chapter 2 to describe the dialectic between the visible and the invisible in Plato's analogy of the line. Critchley also addresses this spiralling in *The Ethics of Deconstruction*, pp. 8, 165.

22 Merleau-Ponty, *The Primacy of Perception*, p. 163.
23 Merleau-Ponty, *The Prose of the World*, p. 134.
24 Merleau-Ponty, *Signs*, p. 94.
25 See Merleau-Ponty, *The Visible and the Invisible*, pp. 142–45, 263–64.
26 Merleau-Ponty, *The Prose of the World*, p. 135.
27 "Discourse is discourse with God and not with equals, according to the distinction established by Plato in the *Phaedrus*. Metaphysics is the essence of this language with God; it leads above being" (*TeI* 330–31/*TI* 297).
28 Merleau-Ponty, *The Prose of the World*, p. 133.
29 Gadamer, *Wahrheit und Methode*, p. 348/*Truth and Method*, p. 366.
30 Derrida, *Writing and Difference*, p. 91.
31 Ibid., 142. On the relation between Levinas and Derrida see Robert Bernasconi, "Deconstruction and the Possibility of Ethics," in *Deconstruction and Philosophy*, ed. J. Sallis (Chicago: University of Chicago Press, 1987), pp. 122–39; "Levinas and Derrida: The Question of the Closure of Metaphysics," in *Face to Face with Levinas*, pp. 181–202; "The Trace of Levinas in Derrida," in *Derrida and Difference*, pp. 17–44. Also see John Llewelyn, *Beyond Metaphysics? The Hermeneutic Circle in Contemporary Continental Philosophy* (Atlantic Highlands, NJ: Humanities Press, 1985), pp. 185–206.
32 Derrida, *Writing and Difference*, pp. 146–47.
33 Levinas discusses the relation between skepticism and its refutation in *AE* 260–66/*OB* 167–71.

For secondary sources on this question see Robert Bernasconi, "Skepticism in the Face of Philosophy," in *Re-Reading Levinas*, pp. 149–61; Critchley, *The Ethics of Deconstruction*, pp. 156–69; Jan de Greef, "Skepticism and Reason," trans. D. White, in *Face to Face with Levinas*, pp. 159–79.
34 For a summary of Derrida's relation to Levinas on this issue see Dallmayr, *Twilight of Subjectivity*, pp. 107–15.
35 Derrida, *Writing and Difference*, p. 126.
36 Ibid., p. 103.
37 Ibid., p. 151.
38 Ibid., p. 82.
39 Emmanuel Levinas, "Tout Autrement," in *NP* 68–69; "Wholly Otherwise," trans. S. Critchley, in *Re-Reading Levinas*, p. 5 (italics added).
40 Emmanuel Levinas, *De Dieu qui vient à l'idée*, 2nd edition (Paris: J. Vrin, 1982), p. 270.
41 On the imperative in Levinas, Kant, and Merleau-Ponty see Alphonso Lingis, "The Elemental Imperative," *Research in Phenomenology* 18 (1988): 3–21.
42 Commenting on the Wolf-Man, Deleuze and Guattari note that "we're not far from wolves" (Gilles Deleuze and Felix Guattari, *A Thousand Plateaus: Capitalism and Schizophrenia*, trans. B. Massumi [Minneapolis: University of Minnesota Press, 1987], p. 28). Freud, they maintain, does not recognize what every child knows to be the case, viz. that wolves always travel in packs. Freud misdiagnoses the Wolf-Man's case from the very start because he begins with the classic metaphysical and ontological assumption of the primacy of unity or singularity as foundation or ground and extends that bias into the arena or field of social relations. Freud rein-

terprets the Wolf-Man's dream for him insisting that he did not hear several wolves, but rather, a single dog, that is, the voice of the father. But Freud does not see that "in becoming-wolf, the important thing is the position of the mass, and above all the position of the subject in relation to the pack or wolf-multiplicity..." (p. 29). In other words, he misses the point that subjective identity is constituted by the social or the multiple. Wolves are prime examples of the *schizo* position; their individuality remains intact, though constantly shifting in role, with regard to the pack, to the *others,* through the continual deterriorialization or lines of flight of the pack's movement. The Wolf-Man's human identity, his proper name, is not as secure as his becoming-wolfness. His name is intimately bound with the libidinal assemblage of the social machine, not with the oedipalized family structure of daddy-mommy-me. His madness is the result of being unable to communicate his desire, his need, to become-wild in order to escape his childhood memories of the terror of his family's experience with the Bolsheviks. And even though he is readmitted back into society, his madness never quite dissipates; Freud perhaps even exacerbated it.

On the "wild, lawless otherness" of the Wolf-Man, cf. William Desmond, *Philosophy and its Others: Ways of Being and Mind* (Albany: SUNY Press, 1990), pp. 201–205. Merleau-Ponty takes up the notion of "wild Being" in his working notes to *The Visible and the Invisible,* pp. 165–69.

43 Nietzsche, *Werke,* 2: 959–60/*Twilight of the Idols,* p. 483.

44 Cf. Max Scheler, "Ressentiment," trans. W. Holdheim, in *Nietzsche: A Collection of Critical Essays,* ed. R. Solomon (South Bend, IN: Notre Dame University Press, 1980), p. 250f. Scheler cites two instances of of sacrifice and love towards the Other: one, "from a spontaneous overflow of force, accompanied by bliss and inner calm," and two, as "*escape,* for the inability to 'remain at home' with oneself (*chez soi*)."

45 At the conclusion of a 1923 essay entitled "Scientific Method and the Moral Sciences" Mead writes: "The order of the universe that we live in *is* the moral order.... It has become the moral order by becoming the self-conscious method of members of a human society. We are not pilgrims and strangers. We are *at home* in our own world, but it is not ours by inheritance but by conquest. The world that comes to us from the past possesses and controls us. We possess and control the world that we discover and invent. And this is the world of the moral order" (*International Journal of Ethics* 33 (1923): 229–47; reprinted in *Selected Writings: George Herbert Mead,* ed. A. J. Reck [New York: Bobbs-Merrill, 1964], pp. 248–66). Clearly, Mead exhibits the attitude of the day here, and his indebtedness to the Whiteheadian perspective on history and the evolutionary, imperialistic "right" of conquering peoples is unmistakable. But apart from the obvious difficulties of such a viewpoint, especially in the light of historical retrospection, Mead signals a radical departure from the then and still often espoused Western view that humanity and the world are estranged from one another. Levinas speaks of our at-homeness in the world as a domesticity that is awakened and called to responsibility by the ethical charge or command of the Other. As a result of this arousal, this disruption, the self calls into question the spontaneous capriciousness of its own freedom and begins to construct social custom and institutions. This is the moment when ethics begins its inevitable and necessary slide into the conflictual domain of morality and politics.

46 Edward Casey has been most helpful here in posing of a number of these questions.

47 Levinas addresses the issue of avoiding ontological language in his writing after TI in *Difficile liberté: Essais sur le judaïsme*, 3rd ed.
48 Deleuze and Guattari, *A Thousand Plateaus*, p. 168.
49 Ibid., p. 148.
50 Ibid., p. 170.
51 For an application of the ethical obligation of the face to face relationship *outside* the context of human intersubjectivity (e.g., with animals) see John Llewelyn, "Am I Obsessed by Bobby? (Humanism of the Other Animal)," in *Re-Reading Levinas*, pp. 234–45.
52 Deleuze and Guattari, *A Thousand Plateaus*, p. 171.
53 Ibid., p. 172.
54 This term is used by Edward Casey, *Getting Back Into Place* (Bloomington: Indiana University Press, 1993).
55 Levinas takes up Marcel's philosophy in the greater context of Buber's thinking in *HS* 34–59/*OS* 20–39.
56 Derrida, *Writing and Difference*, p. 95.

Chapter 10: HyperGround

1 Nietzsche, *Werke*, 2: 161/*The Gay Science*, p. 223.
2 For a concrete contemporary scenario of apocalyptic nihilism see George Caffentzis, "The Work/Energy Crisis and the Apocalypse," in *Midnight Oil: Work, Energy, War, 1973–1992* (New York: Autonomedia, 1992), pp. 215–71.
3 "From the Good to me, there is assignation: a relation that survives the 'death of God.' The death of God perhaps signifies only the possibility to reduce every value arousing an impulse to an impulse arousing a value. The fact that in its goodness the Good declines the desire it arouses while inclining it toward responsibility for the neighbor, preserves *difference* in the non-difference of the Good, which chooses me before I welcome it" (*AE* 196/*OB* 123).
4 The death of God theology of Altizer is somewhat similar, albeit contingent upon the necessity of the final death of God in the crucifixion, which is the resurrection of the incarnate body of the world, but which does not simultaneously signal the resurrection and ascension of the dogmatically understood Christ. But Altizer's insistence on the *necessity* of locating an historical moment in which the oppressive transcendence of God is vanquished, or the overcoming of the abyssal modernism that provides the historical ground for the new beginning of a postmodern consciousness, seems perplexing given an understanding of creation as but a moment in continual genesis, though in the light of eschatological possibility and even hope. Must the newness of the world commence with an actual historical event (incarnation and crucifixion) in order to be an actual reality?
5 Altizer, *The Genesis of God*, p. 65.
6 Nietzsche, *Werke*, 2: 974/*Twilight of the Idols*, p. 495.
7 See David B. Allison, "Nietzsche Knows No Noumenon," in *Why Nietzsche Now?* ed. D. O'Hara (Bloomington: Indiana University Press, 1985), pp. 295–310.
8 This term is borrowed from Leszek Kolakowski, *Metaphysical Horror* (Oxford: Basil Blackwell, 1988). The *horror metaphysicus* is the seeming inevitability of even the most radical forms of the Absolute in Western thinking to reveal themselves as

or revert into nothingness.

9 Perhaps in seeking the "truth" of Isis, Nietzsche realizes the illegitimacy of the claim of "male rationality," of the metaphysics of "light," to superiority, and thus the "night" of "female irrationality," breaks through. Derrida says that "the castration or not of λόγος as *ratio* is a central form of this debate around metaphysics. It is also a fight around the poetic (between poetry and philosophy), around the death or the future of philosophy. The stake is the same" (Jacques Derrida, "Of an Apocalytic Tone Newly Adopted in Philosophy," revised trans. J. P. Leavey, in *Derrida and Negative Theology*, ed. H. Coward and T. Foshay [Albany: SUNY Press, 1992], pp. 25–71). The "truth" of the veiled goddess is the emasculation of the rational λόγος. According to some versions of the myth, it is Isis (in others it is Seth) who murders her consort Osiris and then recovers all the pieces of his dismembered body except for one, the penis/phallus, which is devoured by an oxyrhynchus fish.

10 One can undoubtedly find numerous passages in Nietzsche's corpus of writing to defend the thesis that he is inconsistent, to be generous, on the relation between self-overcoming and the overcoming or domination of others. Ophelia Schutte, for instance, provides what is perhaps the most damning recent analysis of Nietzsche on this very point; in fact, it serves as the central thesis of her study: the "unmasking" of Nietzsche's inherent tie to patriarchal domination. (*Beyond Nihilism: Nietzsche Without Masks* [Chicago: University of Chicago Press, 1984]). While many of her points are well taken, especially from the vantage of a literal interpretation of the text, she seems, despite her own preference for a metaphorical reading of the will to power, unwilling to extend Nietzsche's metaphorical and often ironic style to other passages, e.g., the roles of "woman," marriage, politics. But why limit metaphor to essentially the will to power which, in the end, Schutte subsumes under her larger critique of power as domination?

11 See Friedrich Nietzsche, *Der Antichrist*, in *Werke*, 2: 1165; *The Antichrist*, trans. W. Kaufmann, in *The Portable Nietzsche*, p. 569.

12 Jacques Lacan, *Ecrits* (Paris: Éditions du Seuil, 1966), p. 94.

13 On Nietzsche's delerious schizophrenic madness see Alphonso Lingis, "The Irrecuperable," in *International Studies in Philosophy* 23, no. 2: 65–74.

14 Jean Granier, "Nietzsche's Conception of Chaos," in *The New Nietzsche*, trans. D. B. Allison, pp. 135–36. For another perspective cf. Stanley Rosen, "Nietzsche's Image of Chaos," in *International Philosophical Quarterly* 20, no. 1 (1980): 3–23.

15 Whitehead offers an interesting segue into the question of chaos. Though he holds that chaos does not designate an unformed primal pool of forces as it does for Nietzsche, he does claim, borrowing from Plato's reference to the receptacle as the "aboriginal disorder," that chaos is the realm of ideas prior to their hierarchical arrangement by God. Chaos, as otherness, difference, or infinity, is reduced by Whitehead to the sense of non-being, that is, as having no ontological importance. The quantification of the concepts of infinity and chaos *neutralizes* them in a metaphysical sense. But chaos, he states, is not to be construed as lack or defect as is the notion of evil in much scholastic metaphysics. While this is a positive advance from traditional interpretations, it does not go far enough. The radical alterity signified by the concepts of infinity and chaos is not picked up on and addressed by Whitehead; therefore, the extension of this query to the problem of other-being is

never fully engaged and the issue of praxis is ignored or downplayed in an abstract and off-hand manner. Thus the ethical significance of the Infinite is not a problem for Whitehead's cosmological metaphysics, which reduces it to the merely quantitative status it has been assigned in the tradition. But is there an operative notion of a qualitative infinity characterized as chaos? In *Duration and Simultaneity*, Bergson proposes a distinction between the concepts of "qualitative multiplicity" and "quantitative multiplicity." This parallels Nietzsche's claim that what is needed is a "new infinite," one that allows for the *multiplicity* of hermeneutic activity, without closure. And in Levinas, where infinity or absolute alterity is the transcendence of the social multiple over the One, this is expressed as the difference between "radical" and "numerical" multiplicity. The difference, he says, is that a "numerical multiplicity remains defenseless against totalization" (*TeI* 243/*TI* 220).

16 Friedrich Nietzsche, *Jenseits von Gut und Böse*, in *Werke*, 2: 751–52; *Beyond Good and Evil*, trans. W. Kaufmann (New York: Vintage Books, 1966), p. 229.

17 Alphonso Lingis, "The Will to Power," in *The New Nietzsche*, p. 38. Actually, it is probably more accurate to say that Nietzsche's philosophy is not *metaphysical* at all, the term being loaded as it were. Lingis' use of the term "trans-metaphysical" signifies the trajectory of Nietzsche's thought toward the *overcoming* of traditional concepts of being. But as Nietzsche realized full well that one can not absolve oneself from one's tradition or historical context, and hence from its language, one may, with reservation, refer to Nietzsche's "metaphysics."

18 Nietzsche, *Werke*, 2: 127/*The Gay Science*, p. 181.

19 The term is borrowed from Deleuze and Guattari, *A Thousand Plateaus*, pp. 3–25ff.

20 Nietzsche, *Werke*, 2: 127/*The Gay Science*, p. 181. Deleuze and Guattari develop this thought: "Nietzsche's aphorisms shatter the linear unity of knowledge, only to invoke the cyclic unity of the eternal recurrence, present as the unknown in thought. This is as much to say that the fascicular system does not really break with dualism, with the complementarity between a subject and an object, a natural reality and a spiritual reality: unity is thwarted and obstructed in the object, while a new type of unity triumphs in the subject. The world has lost its pivot; the subject can no longer even dichotomize, but accedes to a higher unity, of ambivalence or overdetermination, in an always supplementary dimension to that of its object. The world has become chaos, but the book remains the image of the world: radicle-chaosmos rather than root-cosmos" (*A Thousand Plateaus*, 6).

21 According to Nietzsche, nihilism is the *auto*-devaluation of the "highest values," that is, those values which have been previously coined as absolute. Nihilism is not something new to the twentieth century experience; it makes its debut in the earliest stages of Western thinking. But no one has advanced the thought of nihilism as much as Nietzsche. The precision and intensity of his reflections on the subject are undoubtedly the reason for the often stated though ill-informed claim that his philosophy is fundamentally nihilistic. Foremost among thinkers, Nietzsche recognizes the necessity of the role of nihilism for the overcoming of metaphysics. As the absence of a valuative stance, nihilism is at the very essence of traditional metaphysics or ontology (in Levinas' sense of the term). Faith in the categories of reason, concludes Nietzsche, is the cause of nihilism. The recognition of the value of nihilism, paradoxically the renunciation of all absolute valuation, serves as the basis or foundation for the "reval-

uation of all values," for a new metaphysics/ethics of intersubjectivity.

22 It can be argued though, as Altizer does, that theologically speaking, the death of God is the moment of absolute origination that allows the dialectic of history to unfold in the name of will to power as eternal recurrence.

23 Nietzsche, *Werke*, 2: 250/*The Gay Science*, p. 336.

24 Friedrich Nietzsche, *The Will to Power*, trans. and ed. W. Kaufmann and R. J. Hollingdale (New York: Vintage Books, 1967), § 1062.

25 Nietzsche's thinking is far from being standardly interpreted with regard to his relation to Hegel. This is reflected, for example, in the thinking of two leading figures in French postmodernist thinking, Deleuze and Bataille, who represent polar views on this regard. According to Deleuze, Nietzsche's thought is a direct reaction to Hegel's philosophy, a reaction based upon a thorough familiarity with Hegel's thinking and the overall climate of German idealism. Deleuze certainly has a point here. It is hard to imagine any serious intellectual in Germany at the time, especially one so philosophically bound as Nietzsche, as not possessing a firm grasp on so pervasive an influence. But according to Deleuze, "there is no possible compromise between Nietzsche and Hegel." Though Hegel is rarely mentioned in the Nietzschean corpus, Deleuze contends that Nietzsche's celebrated reversed Platonism is also a reversal of Hegelianism. Deleuze's position sharply contrasts with that of Bataille who maintains that Nietzsche has a lay knowledge of Hegel at best and thus any juxtaposition of their respective positions should be viewed with a wary eye. Cf. Gilles Deleuze, *Nietzsche and Philosophy*, trans. H. Tomlinson (New York: Columbia University Press, 1983), esp. p. 195; and Bataille, *Visions of Excess*, p. 97f.

Also cf. Stephen Houlgate, *Hegel, Nietzsche and the Criticism of Metaphysics* (Cambridge: Cambridge University Press, 1986).

26 Nietzsche, *Werke*, 2: 161–62/*The Gay Science*, pp. 223–24.

27 Altizer, *The Genesis of God*, p. 86. But could not that absolute necessity be embodied in an eternally genetic and differential Godhead which is and has always been identical with the chaotic totality of becoming? Is not Nietzsche's refusal of the Christian God as the essence of No-saying and *ressentiment* a repudiation of *any* retrievable notion of origin and *not* a return to the ground of an original Christianity? It is here that one detects an affinity between Nietzsche and Levinas, who does not abandon the doctrine of creation but merely expounds on the meaning of the indecidability or impossibility of being able to *name* the infinitely other or God. Certainly Nietzsche is "God-obsessed" and perhaps even more so towards the end of his productive years (which may say something in itself), but is it necessarily the Godhead that he seeks to recover in its original conception? Surely not consciously; there is a valorization of "polytheism" which could be interpreted as the differentiation of the divine in the chaotic totality (e.g., see *Werke*, 2: 134–35/*The Gay Science*, pp. 191–92; *The Will to Power*, § 1038). Furthermore, there is no solid evidence in his most "theological" work, *The Antichrist*, that suggests any coincidence of the death of God with the crucifixion. Indeed, he seems to read that event as an unfortunate occurrence, politically instigated and necessitated but without *any* cosmological significance. This is precisely what he chastises Paul for: assigning a metaphysical value to the Passion. Now Altizer claims "it is only with the closure of ancient Israel that Israel could know a truly absolute beginning, just as it was only

an apocalyptic Israel that could know a pure and total ending" (p. 163). But how does one reconcile this with Nietzsche's criticism in *The Antichrist* of the "Jewishness" of later Israel, that very aspect of Israel which made an apocalyptic Christian theology possible? Is Nietzsche's affirmation of the Hebrews synonymous with an affirmation of the apocalyptic here and now expressed as the will to power, and thus his critique of Judaism as essentially synonymous with his critique of Christianity? It is difficult to think of Nietzsche in apocalyptic terminology since such language is so bound with the idea of teleology that he rejects. Nevertheless, Altizer represents the most serious contemporary attempt to determine an absolute origin or genesis in the "light" of the death of God.

28 Friedrich Nietzsche, *Zur Genealogie der Moral*, in *Werke*, 2: 763–64; *On the Genealogy of Morals*, trans. W. Kaufmann and R. J. Hollingdale (New York: Vintage Books, 1967), pp. 25–26.

29 Ibid., *Werke*, 2: 764–65/*On the Genealogy of Morals*, pp. 16–17.

30 Michel Haar, "Nietzsche and Metaphysical Language," trans. C. and L. Welch, *The New Nietzsche*, p. 33.

31 On the difference between traditional (e.g., Hegel) and "effective" (Nietzsche) views of history see Michel Foucault, "Nietzsche, Genealogy, History," in *Language, Counter-memory, Practice*, trans. D. F. Bouchard and S. Simon (Ithaca: Cornell University Press, 1977), esp. p. 155.

32 Nietzsche, *The Will to Power*, § 1057.

33 See Deleuze, *Nietzsche and Philosophy*, esp. pp. 39–72.

34 Ibid., pp. 49–51.

35 Nietzsche, *The Will to Power*, § 619.

36 Deleuze, *Nietzsche and Philosophy*, pp. 50–55.

37 Kant, *Critique of Pure Reason*, A77–79, B102–104. The term "synthesis" refers to the way or manner that the manifold of experience is "taken up or connected" by the spontaneity of thought. In general, synthesis is "the mere result of the power of the imagination."

According to Deleuze, "Nietzsche seems to have sought (and to have found in the "eternal recurrence" and the "will to power") a radical transformation of Kantianism, a reinvention of the critique which Kant betrayed at the same time as he conceived it, a resumption of the critical project on a new basis and with new concepts" (*Nietzsche and Philosophy*, p. 52).

38 In order to preserve meaning, Nietzsche proclaims the need for a "new infinite," not to be found outside the horizon of our existence, but rather, within the world, within the finite sphere, within the horizon of history. The eternal recurrence is this new conception of infinity as the joyfully tragic, non-teleological, creative and destructive movement of the will to power. This "most paralyzing of thoughts" is the precise breaking point of Nietzsche's thought with Hegelian metaphysics. Both Hegel and Nietzsche affirm the formulation of the infinite becoming of finite being, but the eternal recurrence lacks the teleological positivity of *Geist*. The most "heaviest weight" and yet most "divine" of all thoughts, the eternal recurrence lies at the heart of Nietzsche's philosophy as an ethical and cosmological doctrine. It is inseparable from his analyses on nihilism and his theory of the will to power. Nietzsche's conception of the infinite is further similar to the conceptions of Hegel and Levinas inso-

far as it is a formulation of the infinite in the finite. But Nietzsche differs from Hegel in that he rejects the logos structure of dialectical logic. Here Nietzsche and Levinas are in agreement.

39 Nietzsche, *Werke*, 2: 959–60/*Twilight of the Idols*, pp. 582–83.

40 Ibid., p. 161/*The Gay Science*, p. 223.

41 Nietzsche, *The Will to Power*, § 333.

42 Deleuze, *Nietzsche and Philosophy*, p. 40.

43 One overcomes the eternal recurrence by willing its return. Though nihilism is will to nothingness, the question is that of being and not of the nihil. But the two concepts are the same, as Hegel and Heidegger note. A great problem of traditional metaphysics has been the ignoring of nothingness and the tendency to define being only in terms of presence. Nihilism is the impossibility of ever reaching complete nothingness. What does this mean? The realization that nihilism and reversal are the same answers this question on several levels. First, it serves as the recognition of the necessity of nihilism for an affirmative willing of life, i.e., of will to power and eternal return; second, it signifies the impossibility of any closure in the project of philosophy; and third, given this impossibility, it testifies to the inevitability of a plurality of voices and conceptions of "truth."

44 Lingis, "The Will to Power," p. 39.

45 Nietzsche, *The Will to Power*, § 643.

46 Martin Heidegger, "Der Spruch des Anaximander," in *Holzwege*, 6th ed. (Frankfurt: Klostermann, 1980), p. 323; "The Anaximander Fragment," trans. D. F. Krell and F. A. Capuzzi, in *Early Greek Thinking* (San Francisco: Harper & Row, 1975), p. 18.

47 Derrida, *Writing and Difference*, p. 130.

48 See Daniel Berthold-Bond, *Hegel's Grand Synthesis: A Study of Being, Thought, and History* (Albany: SUNY Press, 1989), esp. pp. 113–61, for a discussion of Hegel's relation to Christian and philosophical eschatology. Berthold-Bond focuses, through an interweaving of the major twentieth century interpreters of Hegel, on the ambiguity surrounding his conception of the end of history and the apocalyptic completion of the dialectic and vision of the "new world." The central issue appears to be whether it is possible to reconcile the "epochal" and "absolutist" readings of Hegel's eschatology.

49 As a test of the will see Nietzsche, *Werke*, 2: 202–203/*The Gay Science*, pp. 273–74; as a selective principle see *The Will to Power*, § 1058.

Gilles Deleuze also reads the eternal recurrence as the principle of ethical valuation: "It is the *thought* of the eternal recurrence that selects. It makes willing whole. The thought of the eternal recurrence eliminates from willing everything which falls outside the eternal recurrence, it makes willing a creation, it brings out the equation 'willing = creation'" (*Nietzsche and Philosophy*, p. 69).

50 This position is opposed by Derrida: "History is not the totality transcended by eschatology, metaphysics or speech. It is transcendence itself. If speech is a movement of metaphysical transcendence, it is history and not beyond history" (*Writing and Difference*, p. 117).

51 Despite Levinas' concerted efforts to separate the discourses of philosophy and religion in his writing, they nevertheless mutually inform one another, though it can be argued that his religious reflections have greater bearing on his philosophy than

vice-versa. Be that as it may, the concept of prophetic eschatology guides the corpus of his writing as a whole as it points to the dominant thematic in all of his work, namely, the relation of being to goodness.

52 Merleau-Ponty, *The Prose of the World*, p. 135.

53 Friedrich Nietzsche, *Also Sprach Zarathustra*, in *Werke*, 2: 283; *Thus Spoke Zarathustra*, trans. W. Kaufmann, in *The Portable Nietzsche*, p. 128.

54 Ibid., p. 165/*The Gay Science*, p. 228.

55 Ibid., p. 251/p. 338.

56 Levinas derives much of his conception of command and obedience from the *Republic* 412–21c. "Plato says that qua leader no leader proposes or orders what is useful for himself, but what is useful for the one he commands. To command is then to do the will of the one who obeys" (*CPP* 15).

57 Cf. Thomas J. J. Altizer, "History as Apocalypse," in *Deconstruction and Theology*, ed. T. Altizer (New York: Crossroad Publishers, 1982), pp. 147–77; Derrida, "Of an Apocalytic Tone Newly Adopted in Philosophy," pp. 25–71.

58 Derrida, *Writing and Difference*, p. 153.

59 See Emmanuel Levinas, "Un language pour nous familier," in *Le Matin*, March 1980; "A Language Familiar to Us," trans. D. Collins, in *Telos*, no. 44 (1980): 11–20. Also see Edith Wyschogrod, "Emmanuel Levinas and the Problem of Religious Language," in *The Thomist* 36, no. 1 (1972): 1–38, and "God and 'Being's Move' in the Philosophy of Emmanuel Levinas," in *The Journal of Religion* 62, no. 2 (1982): 145–55.

Bibliography

Adorno, Theodor W. *Against Epistemology: A Metacritique.* trans. W. Domingo. Cambridge, MA: MIT Press, 1983.

———. *Negative Dialectics.* trans. E. B. Ashton. New York: Continuum Publishing Company, 1973.

———. "Subject and Object." *Frankfurt School Reader.* ed. A. Arato and E. Gebhardt. 497–511. New York: Continuum Publishing Company, 1982.

Allison, David B. ed. "Nietzsche Knows No Noumenon." In *Why Nietzsche Now?* ed. D. O'Hara. 295–310. Indianapolis: Indiana University Press, 1985.

Altizer, Thomas J. J. *The Genesis of God.* Louisville: Westminster/John Knox Press, 1994.

———. "History as Apocalypse." *Deconstruction and Theology*, ed. T. Altizer, 147–77. New York: Crossroad Press, 1982.

Arendt, Hanna. *The Origins of Totalitarianism.* New York: Harcourt Brace Jovanovich, 1973.

Aristotle. *Basic Writings.* ed. R. McKeon. New York: Random House Publishers, 1941.

Augustine. *On the Free Choice of the Will.* trans. A. S. Benjamin and L. H. Hackstaff. New York: Macmillan Publishers, 1964.

———. *The Retractations.* Washington: Catholic University of America Press, 1968.

Avineri, Schlomo. *Hegel's Theory of the Modern State.* Cambridge: Cambridge University Press, 1973.

Bataille, Georges. *Inner Experience.* trans. with introduction L. A. Boldt. Albany: SUNY Press, 1988.

———. *Theory of Religion.* trans. R. Hurley. New York: Zone Books, 1989.

———. *Visions of Excess.* ed. and trans. A. Stoekl. Minneapolis: University of Minnesota Press, 1985.

Bernasconi, Robert. "Deconstruction and the Possibility of Ethics." In *Deconstruction and Philosophy*, ed. J. Sallis, 122–39. Chicago: University of Chicago Press, 1987.

———. "'Failure of Communication' as a Surplus: Dialogue and Lack of Dialogue Between Buber and Levinas." In *The Provocation of Levinas: Re-Thinking the Other*, ed. R. Bernasconi and D. Wood, 100–135. London and New York: Routledge, 1988.

———. "Hegel and Levinas: The Possibility of Reconciliation and Forgiveness." *Archivio di Filosophia* 54 (1986): 325–46.

———. "Levinas and Derrida: The Question of the Closure of Metaphysics." In *Face to Face with Levinas*, ed. R. Cohen, 181–202. Albany: SUNY Press, 1986.

———. "Levinas Face to Face—with Hegel." *Journal of the British Society for Phenomenology* 123, no. 3 (1982): 267–76.

———. "Levinas on Time and the Instant." In *Time and Metaphysics*, ed. D. Wood and R.

Bernasconi, 199–217. Coventry: Parousia Press, 1982.

———. "Levinas: Philosophy and Beyond." In *Continental Philosophy* 1, ed. H. Silverman et al. New York: Routledge, 1987.

———. "Rereading *Totality and Infinity*." In *The Question of the Other*, ed. A. Dallery and C. Scott, 23–34. Albany: SUNY Press, 1989.

———. "Skepticism in the Face of Philosophy." In *Re-Reading Levinas*, ed. R. Bernasconi and S. Critchley, 149–161. Bloomington: Indiana University Press, 1991.

———. "The Trace of Levinas in Derrida." In *Derrida and Difference*, ed. D. Wood and R. Bernasconi, 17–44. Coventry: Parousia Press, 1985.

Berthold-Bond, Daniel. *Hegel's Grand Synthesis: A Study of Being, Thought, and History*. Albany: SUNY Press, 1989.

Blanchot, Maurice. *The Infinite Conversation*. trans. S. Hanson. Minneapolis: University of Minnesota Press, 1993.

Blum, Roland Paul. "Emmanuel Levinas' Theory of Commitment." *Philosophy and Phenomenological Research* 44, no. 2 (1983): 145–68.

Bouckaert, Luk. "Ontology and Ethics: Reflections on Levinas' Critique of Heidegger." *International Philosophical Quarterly* 10 (1970): 402–19.

Buck-Morss, Susan. *The Origin of Negative Dialectics: Theodore Adorno, Walter Benjamin, and the Frankfurt Institute*. New York: Free Press, 1977.

Burbidge, John W. *Hegel on Logic and Religion*. Albany: SUNY Press, 1992.

Butler, Judith. *Subjects of Desire: Hegelian Reflections in Twentieth-Century France*. New York: Columbia University Press, 1987.

Caffentzis, George. "The Work/Energy Crisis and the Apocalypse." In *Midnight Oil: Work, Energy, War, 1973–1992*, 215–71. New York: Autonomedia, 1992.

Caputo, John. "Disseminating Originary Ethics and the Ethics of Dissemination." In *The Question of the Other*, ed. A. Dallery and C. Scott, 55–62. Albany: SUNY Press, 1989.

Casey, Edward S. *Getting Back Into Place*. Bloomington: Indiana University Press, 1993.

———. "Levinas on Memory and the Trace." In *The Collegium Phaenomenologicum*, ed. J. Sallis, G. Moneta, and J. Taminiaux, 241–55. Dordrecht: Kluwer, 1989.

Cassirer, Ernst. *The Individual and the Cosmos in Renaissance Philosophy*. trans. M. Domandi. Oxford: Blackwell, 1963.

Chanter, Tina. "Antigone's Dilemma." In *Re-Reading Levinas*, ed. R. Bernasconi and S. Critchley, 130–46. Bloomington: Indiana University Press, 1991.

Cohen, Richard A. "Absolute Positivity and Ultrapositivity: Husserl and Levinas." In *The Question of the Other*, ed. A. Dallery and C. Scott, 35–43. Albany: SUNY Press, 1989.

Cornell, Drucilla. *The Philosophy of the Limit*. New York: Routledge, 1992.

Cranz, Edward F. "Cusanus, Luther, and the Mystical Tradition." In *The Pursuit of Holiness in Late Medieval and Renaissance Religion*, ed. C. Trinkhaus and H. Oberman, 93–102. Leiden: E. J. Brill, 1974.

Critchley, Simon. *The Ethics of Deconstruction*. Oxford: Blackwell, 1992.

Cusa, Nicholas de. *De Docta Ignorantia* (1440); *Nicholas of Cusa on Learned Ignorance*. trans. J. Hopkins. Minneapolis: Arthur J. Banning Press, 1981.

———. *Idiota de Mente* (1450); *The Layman: About Mind*. trans. C. L. Miller. New York: Abaris Books, 1979.

Dallmayr, Fred R. *Twilight of Subjectivity: Contributions to a Post-Individualist Theory of Politics*. Amherst: University of Massachusetts Press, 1981.

Davies, Paul. "Difficult Friendship." *Research in Phenomenology*, vol. 18 (1988): 149–72.

———. "A Fine Risk: Reading Blanchot Reading Levinas." In *Re-Reading Levinas*, ed. R. Bernasconi and S. Critchley, 201–226. Bloomington: Indiana University Press, 1991.

de Certeau, Michel. *Heterologies: Discourse on the Other*. trans. B. Massumi. Minneapolis: University of Minnesota Press, 1986.

de Greef, Jan. "Skepticism and Reason," trans. D. White. In *Face to Face with Levinas*, ed. R. Cohen, 159–79. Albany: SUNY, 1986.

Deleuze, Gilles. *Nietzsche and Philosophy*. trans. H. Tomlinson. New York: Columbia University Press, 1983.

Deleuze, Gilles, and Guattari, Félix. *A Thousand Plateaus: Capitalism and Schizophrenia*. trans. B. Massumi. Minneapolis: University of Minnesota Press, 1987.

Derrida, Jacques. "En ce moment même dans cet ouvrage me voici." In *Textes pour Emmanuel Levinas*, ed. F. Laruelle, 21–60. Paris: Editions Jean-Michel Place, 1980. (Reprinted in *Psyche: Inventions de l'autre*. Paris: Galilée, 1987.) trans. R. Berezdevin, "At this very moment in this work here I am." In *Re-Reading Levinas*, ed. R. Bernasconi and S. Critchley, 11–48. Bloomington: Indiana University Press, 1991.

———. *Glas*. trans. J. P. Leavey and R. Rand. Lincoln: University of Nebraska Press, 1986.

———. "Of an Apocalyptic Tone Recently Adopted in Philosophy." revised and trans. J. P. Leavey, "Of an Apocalytic Tone Newly Adopted in Philosophy." In *Derrida and Negative Theology*, 25–71. Albany: SUNY Press, 1992.

———. *Spurs*. trans. B. Harlow. Chicago: University of Chicago Press, 1979.

———. *Writing and Difference*. trans. A. Bass. Chicago: University of Chicago Press, 1978.

Descartes, René. *The Philosophical Writings*. trans. J. Cottingham, R. Stoothoff, and D. Murdoch. Cambridge: University of Cambridge Press, 1980.

Descombes, Vincent. *Modern French Philosophy*. trans. L. Scott-Fox and J. M. Harding. Cambridge: Cambridge University Press, 1980.

Desmond, William. *Desire, Dialectic, and Otherness*. New Haven: Yale University Press, 1987.

———. *Philosophy and Its Others: Ways of Being and Mind*. Albany: SUNY Press, 1990.

Dussel, Enrique. *Philosophy of Liberation*. Maryknoll: Orbis, 1985.

Flay, Joseph. *Hegel's Quest for Certainty*. Albany: SUNY, 1984.

———. "Religion and the Absolute Standpoint." *Thought* 56 (September 1981): 316–27.

Foucault, Michel. "Nietzsche, Genealogy, History." *Language, Counter-memory, Practice*. trans. D. F. Bouchard and S. Simon. Ithaca: Cornell University Press, 1977.

Friedländer, Paul. *Plato: An Introduction* (Vol. I of three volumes), 2nd ed. trans. H. Meyerhoff. Princeton: Princeton University Press, 1969.

Gadamer, Hans-Georg. *Hegel's Dialectic*. trans. P. C. Smith. New Haven: Yale University Press, 1976.

———. *The Idea of the Good in Platonic-Aristotelian Philosophy*. trans. and ed. P. C. Smith. New Haven: Yale University Press, 1986.

———. *The Relevance of the Beautiful and Other Essays*. trans. N. Walker and ed. R. Bernasconi. Cambridge: Cambridge University Press, 1986.

———. *Wahrheit und Methode*. Tübingen: J. C. B. Mohr (Paul Siebeck), 1972. *Truth and Method*. 2nd rev. ed.trans. and rev. J. Weinsheimer and D. G. Marshall. New York: Continuum Publishing Company, 1993.

Girard, René. *Violence and the Sacred*. trans. P. Gregory. Baltimore: Johns Hopkins

University Press, 1977.

Granier, Jean. "Nietzsche's Conception of Chaos," trans. D. B. Allison. In *The New Nietzsche*, ed. D. B. Allison, 135–44. Cambridge, MA: MIT Press, 1985.

Haar, Michel. "Nietzsche and Metaphysical Language," trans. C. and L. Welch. In *The New Nietzsche*, ed. D. B. Allison, 3–35. Cambridge, MA: MIT Press, 1985.

Habermas, Jürgen. *Knowledge and Human Interest.* trans. J. J. Shapiro. Boston: Beacon Press, 1971.

Harris, Errol E. "The Contemporary Significance of Hegel and Whitehead." In *Hegel and Whitehead: Contemporary Perspectives on Systematic Philosophy*, ed. G. R. Lucas, 17–28. Albany: SUNY Press, 1986.

———. *An Interpretation of the Logic of Hegel.* New York: University Press of America, 1983.

Harris, H. S. *Hegel's Development: Night Thoughts 1801–1806.* Oxford: Clarendon Press, 1983.

———. *Hegel's Development: Toward the Sunlight 1770–1801.* Oxford: Clarendon Press, 1972.

———. "Hegel's Theory of Sovereignty, International Relations, and War." In *Hegel's Social and Political Thought*, 137–49 Atlantic Highlands, NJ: Humanities Press, 1980.

Hart, Kevin. *The Trespass of the Sign: Deconstruction, Theology and Philosophy.* Cambridge: Cambridge University Press, 1989.

Hegel, Georg Wilhelm Freidrich. *Early Theological Writings.* trans. T. M. Knox. Chicago: University of Chicago Press, 1948.

———. *Faith and Knowledge.* trans. W. Cerf and H. S. Harris. Albany: SUNY Press, 1977.

———. *Lectures on the Philosophy of Religion.* trans. R. F. Brown, P. C. Hodgson, and J. M. Stewart, with the assistance of H. S. Harris, ed. P. C. Hodgson. Berkeley: University of California Press, 1988.

———. *Logic: Part One of the Encyclopaedia of the Philosophical Sciences* (1830). trans. W. Wallace. Oxford: Clarendon Press, 1975.

———. *Phänomenologie des Geistes.* Hamburg: Felix Meiner, 1952; *Phenomenology of Spirit.* trans. A. V. Miller. Oxford: Oxford University Press, 1977.

———. *Philosophy of Mind: Part Three of the Encyclopaedia of the Philosophical Sciences* (1830). trans. W. Wallace and A. V. Miller. Oxford: Oxford University Press, 1971.

———. *Philosophy of Right.* trans. T. M. Knox. London: Oxford University Press, 1967.

———. *Reason in History.* trans. R. S. Hartman. Indianapolis: Bobbs-Merrill Company, Inc., 1953.

———. *Wissenschaft der Logik*, Bds. I–II. Hamburg: Felix Meiner, 1951; *Science of Logic.* trans. A. V. Miller. New York: Humanities Press, 1969.

Heidegger, Martin. "Das Ende der Philosophie und die Aufgabe des Denkens." In *Zur Sache des Denkens*, 61–80. Tübingen: Max Niemeyer Verlag, 1969; "The End of Philosophy and the Task of Thinking," trans. J. Stambaugh. In *Basic Writings*, ed. D. F. Krell, 373–92. New York: Harper & Row, 1977.

———. "Der Spruch des Anaximander." In *Holzwege*, 6th ed. Frankfurt: Klostermann, 1980; "The Anaximander Fragment," trans. D. F. Krell and F. A. Capuzzi. In *Early Greek Thinking.* San Francisco: Harper & Row, 1975.

———. *Einfürung in die Metaphysik.* Tübingen: Max Niemeyer Verlag, 1966; *An Introduction to Metaphysics.* trans. R. Manheim. New Haven: Yale University Press, 1959.

———. *Identität und Differenz.* Pfullingen: Verlag Günther Neskel, 1957; *Identity and Difference* (bi-lingual edition). trans. J. Stambaugh. New York: Harper & Row, 1969.

———. *The Metaphysical Foundations of Logic.* trans. M. Heim. Bloomington: Indiana University Press, 1984.

———. *Platons Lehre von der Wahrheit. Mit einem Brief über den "Humanismus."* Bern: Francke Verlag, 1947; "Plato's Doctrine of Truth," trans. J. Barlow. In *Philosophy in the Twentieth Century*, ed. W. Barrett and H. D. Aitken, 251–70. New York: Random House, 1962; "Letter on Humanism," trans. F. A. Capuzzi and J. G. Gray. In *Basic Writings*, ed. D. F. Krell, 193–240. New York: Harper & Row, 1977.

———. *Sein und Zeit.* Tübingen: Max Niemeyer Verlag, 1967; *Being and Time.* trans. J. Macquarrie and E. Robinson. New York: Harper and Row, 1962.

———. "Was ist Metaphysik?" *Wegmarken*, 1–19. Frankfurt am Main: Vittorio Klostermann Verlag, 1967; "What Is Metaphysics?" trans. D. F. Krell. In *Basic Writings*, ed. D. F. Krell, 95–112. New York: Harper & Row, 1977.

Hoffman, Piotr. *Violence in Modern Philosophy.* Chicago: University of Chicago Press, 1989.

Houlgate, Stephen. *Hegel, Nietzsche and the Criticism of Metaphysics.* Cambridge: Cambridge University Press, 1986.

Husserl, Edmund. *The Crisis of the European Sciences.* trans. D. Carr. Evanston: Northwestern University Press, 1970.

Hyppolite, Jean. *Genesis and Structure of Hegel's Phenomenology of Spirit.* trans. S. Cherniak and J. Heckman. Evanston: Northwestern University Press, 1974.

Itzkowitz, Kenneth. "Différance and Identity." *Research in Phenomenology* 8 (1978): 127–45.

Jay, Martin. *Adorno.* Cambridge, MA: Harvard University Press, 1984.

Kant, Immanuel. *Critique of Practical Reason.* trans. N. K. Smith. London: Macmillian, 1932.

———. *Critique of Pure Reason.* trans. N. K. Smith. London: Macmillian, 1929.

Kierkegaard, Søren. *Concluding Unscientific Postscript.* trans. D. F. Swenson and W. Lowrie. Princeton: Princeton University Press, 1968.

———. *The Present Age.* trans. A. Dru. New York: Harper & Row, 1962.

Kirk, G. S. and J. E. Raven. *The Presocratic Philosophers.* Cambridge: Cambridge University Press, 1957.

Kojève, Alexandre. *Introduction to the Reading of Hegel.* trans. J. Nichols and A. Bloom. New York: Basic Books, 1969.

Kolakowski, Leszek. *Metaphysical Horror.* New York: Basil Blackwell, 1988.

Lacan, Jacques. *Écrits.* Paris: Éditions du Seuil, 1966.

Lakeland, Paul. *The Politics of Salvation: The Hegelian Idea of the State.* Albany: SUNY Press, 1984.

Lawton, Philip. "Levinas' Notion of the 'There Is.'" *Philosophy Today* 20, no. 1 (1976): 69–76.

Leftow, Brian. "God and the World in Hegel and Whitehead." In *Hegel and Whitehead: Contemporary Perspectives on Systematic Philosophy*, ed. G. R. Lucas, 257–67. Albany: SUNY Press, 1986.

Levinas, Emmanuel. *Autrement qu'être ou au-delà de l'essence.* Le livre de poche edition. La Haye: Martinus Nijhoff, 1974; *Otherwise Than Being or Beyond Essence.* trans. A. Lingis. The Hague: Martinus Nijhoff, 1981.

———. *A L'Heure des Nations.* Paris: Les Éditions des Minuits, 1988; *In the Time of*

Nations. trans. M. B. Smith. Bloomington: Indiana University Press, 1994.

———. "Beyond Intentionality," trans. K. McLaughlin. In *Philosophy in France Today*, ed. A. Montefiore, 100–115. Cambridge: Cambridge University Press, 1983.

———. *Collected Philosophical Papers*. trans. A. Lingis. The Hague: Martinus Nijhoff, 1987.

———. *De Dieu qui vient à l'idée*. Paris: J. Vrin, 1982.

———. *De l'existence a l'existant*. Paris: Fontaine, 1947; reprinted J. Vrin, 1973; *Existence and Existents*. trans. A. Lingis. The Hague: Martinus Nijhoff, 1978.

———. "De l'un a l'autre: transcendence et temps." *Archivio di filosophia* 51, no. 1 (1983): 21–38.

———. "Dieu et la philosophie," in *Le Nouveau Commerce* 30–31 (1975): 104–106.

———. *Difficile liberté: Essais sur le judaïsme*, 2nd ed. Paris: Albin Michel, 1976.

———. *En découvrant l'existence avec Husserl et Heidegger*. Paris: J. Vrin, 1949; 1967; 1974; 1988.

_______. *Ethique et infini*. Paris: Librairie Arthème Fayard et Radio-France, 1982; *Ethics and Infinity*. trans. R. Cohen. Pittsburgh: Duquesne University Press, 1985.

———. "Hermeneutique et au delà." *Archivio di filosophia*, nos. 1–3 (1977): 11–20.

———. *Hors Sujet*. Montpellier: Fata Morgana, 1987; *Outside the Subject*. trans. M. B. Smith. Stanford: Stanford University Press, 1994.

———. *Humanisme de l'autre homme*. Montpellier: Fata Morgana, 1972.

———. "La Conscience non-intentionelle." In *Philosophers on Their Own Work*, eds. A. Mercier, M. Svilar, 147–57. Federation internationale des societies de philosophie, vol. 10. New York: Peter Lang, 1983.

———. "Le Moi et la totalité." *Revue de Metaphysique et de Morale* 59, no. 4 (1954): 353–73.

———. *Le temps et l'autre*. Paris: Presses Universitaires de France, 1983; *Time and the Other*. trans. R. Cohen. Pittsburgh: Duquesne University Press, 1987.

———. "Liberté et commandement." *Revue de Metaphysique et de Morale* 58, no. 3 (1953): 236–41.

———. *Noms Propres*. Le livre poche edition. Montpellier: Fata Morgana, 1976.

———. "Pluralismé et transcendence." *Actes du congres international de philosophie* (1984): 381–83.

———. *The Levinas Reader*. ed. S. Hand. Oxford: Basil Blackwell, 1989.

———. *Totalité et infini: essai sur l'exteriorite*. Le livre de poche edition. La Haye: Martinus Nijhoff, 1971; *Totality and Infinity: An Essay on Exteriority*. trans. A. Lingis. Pittsburgh: Duquesne University Press, 1969.

———. "Transcendence et hauteur." *Bulletin de la Société Française de la Philosophie*, 56, no. 3 (1962): 89–113.

———. *Transcendence et intelligibilité*. Geneva: Éditions Labor et Fides, 1984.

———. "Un language pour nous familier." *Le Matin*, March 1980; "A Language Familiar to Us," trans. D. Collins. *Telos*, no. 44 (1980): 11–20.

Libertson, Joseph. *Proximity: Levinas, Blanchot, Bataille and Communication*. Phaenomenologica 87. The Hague: Martinus Nijhoff, 1982.

Liddell, Henry George, and Scott Robert (compilators). *A Greek-English Lexicon*. Oxford: Clarendon Press, 1968.

Lingis, Alphonso. *Deathbound Subjectivity*. Bloomington: Indiana University Press, 1989.

———. "The Elemental Imperative." *Research in Phenomenology* 18 (1988): 3–21.

———. "Face to Face: A Phenomenological Analysis." *International Philosophical Quarterly* 19, no. 2 (1979): 151–63.

———. "The Irrecuperable." *International Studies in Philosophy* 23, 2: 65–74.

———. "A Time to Exist on One's Own." In *Analecta Husserliana* 6, ed. A. T. Tymieniecka, 31–40. Dordrecht: Reidel, 1977.

———. "The Will to Power." In *The New Nietzsche*, ed. D. Allison, 37–63. Cambridge: MIT Press, 1985.

Llewelyn, John. "Am I Obsessed by Bobby? (Humanism of the Other Animal)." In *Re-Reading Levinas*, ed. R. Cohen, 234–45. Albany: SUNY Press, 1986.

———. *Beyond Metaphysics? The Hermeneutic Circle in Contemporary Continental Philosophy*. Atlantic Highlands, NJ: Humanities Press, 1985.

Lucas, George R. ed. *Hegel and Whitehead: Contemporary Perspectives on Systematic Philosophy*. Albany: SUNY Press, 1986.

Luther, Martin. *The Bondage of the Will*. Westwood, NJ: Revell, 1957.

Lyotard, Jean-Francois. "Logique de Lévinas." In *Textes pour Emmanuel Lévinas*, ed. F. Laruelle, 127–50. Paris: Éditions Jean-Michel Place, 1980; "Levinas' Logic." trans. I. McLeod. In *Face to Face with Levinas*, ed. R. Cohen, 117–58. Albany: SUNY Press, 1986.

Marx, Werner. *Heidegger and the Tradition*. trans. T. Kisiel and M. Greene. Evanston: Northwestern University Press, 1971.

McFague, Sallie. *Metaphorical Theology: Models of God in Religious Language*. Philadelphia: Fortress Press, 1982.

Mead, George Herbert. *Mind, Self and Society: From the Standpoint of a Social Behaviorist*. Chicago: University of Chicago Press, 1934.

———. "Scientific Method and the Moral Sciences." In *International Journal of Ethics* 33 (1923): 229–47; reprinted in *Selected Writings: George Herbert Mead*. ed. A. J. Reck, 248–66. New York: Bobbs-Merrill, 1964.

Merleau-Ponty, Maurice. *Phenomenology of Perception*. trans. C. Smith. London: Routledge and Kegan Paul, 1962.

———. "Philosophy and Non-Philosophy Since Hegel," trans. H. Silverman. *Telos* 29 (1976).

———. *The Primacy of Perception*. trans. and ed. J. Edie. Evanston: Northwestern University Press, 1964.

———. *The Prose of the World*. trans. J. O'Neill. Evanston: Northwestern University Press, 1973.

———. *Sense and Non-Sense*. trans. H. L. and P. A. Dreyfus. Evanston: Northwestern University Press, 1964.

———. *Signs*. trans. R. Cleary. Evanston: Northwestern University Press, 1964.

———. *The Visible and the Invisible*. trans. A. Lingis. Evanston: Northwestern University Press, 1973.

Neville, Robert C. "Hegel and Whitehead on Totality: The Failure of a Conception on System." In *Hegel and Whitehead: Contemporary Perspectives on Systematic Philosophy*, ed. G. R. Lucas, 86–108. Albany: SUNY Press, 1986.

Nietzsche, Friedrich. *The Antichrist*. In *The Portable Nietzsche*, trans. and ed. W. Kaufmann. New York: Random House, 1954.

———. *Beyond Good and Evil*. trans. W. Kaufmann. New York: Vintage Books, 1966.

———. *The Gay Science*. trans. W Kaufmann. New York: Vintage Books, 1974.

———. *On the Genealogy of Morals.* trans. W. Kaufmann and R. J. Hollingdale. New York: Vintage Books, 1967.

———. *Thus Spoke Zarathustra.* In *The Portable Nietzsche,* trans. and ed. W Kaufmann. New York: Random House, 1954.

———. *Twilight of the Idols.* In *The Portable Nietzsche,* trans. and ed. W. Kaufmann. New York: Random House, 1954.

———. *Werke in Drei Bänden.* Herausgegeben von Karl Schlecta. Müchen: Carl Hanser Verlag, 1956.

———. *The Will to Power.* trans. W. Kaufmann and R. J. Hollingdale. New York: Vintage Books, 1967.

Paolucci, Henry. "Hegel and the Nation-State System of International Relations." In *Hegel's Social and Political Thought,* 151–65. Atlantic Highlands, NJ: Humanities Press, 1980.

Peperzak, Adriaan. "From Intentionality to Responsibility: On Levinas' Philosophy of Language." In *The Question of the Other,* ed. A. Dallery and C. Scott, 3–22. Albany: SUNY Press, 1989.

———. "Phenomenology—Ontology—Metaphysics: Levinas' Perspective on Husserl and Heidegger." *Man and World* 16 (1983): 113–27.

———. "Some Remarks on Hegel, Kant, and Levinas." In *Face to Face with Levinas,* ed. R. Cohen, 205–17. Albany: SUNY, 1986.

Petrosino, Silvano and Jacques Rolland. *La vérité nomade: Introduction à Emmanuel Lévinas.* Paris: La Découverte, 1984.

Picard, Max. *The Human Face.* trans. Guy Endore. New York: Farrar and Rinehart, 1930.

Pippen, Robert B. *Hegel's Idealism: The Satisfactions of Self-Consciousness.* Cambridge: Cambridge University Press, 1989.

Plato. *The Collected Dialogues of Plato.* ed. E. Hamilton and H. Cairns. New York: Bollingen Foundaton, 1961.

Plotinus. *The Enneads.* trans. and ed. S. MacKenna. New York: Burdett, 1992.

Rist, J. M. *Plotinus: The Road to Reality.* Cambridge: Cambridge University Press, 1967.

Ritter, Joachim. *Hegel and the French Revolution.* trans. R. D. Winfield. Cambridge, MA: MIT Press, 1982.

Rosen, Stanley. *G. W. F. Hegel: An Introduction to the Science of Wisdom.* New Haven: Yale University Press, 1974.

———. "Nietzsche's Image of Chaos." *International Philosophical Quarterly* 20, no. 1 (1980): 3–23.

Sallis, John. *Delimitations: Phenomenology and the End of Metaphysics.* Bloomington: Indiana University Press, 1986.

Scheler, Max. "Ressentiment," trans. W. Holdheim. In *Nietzsche: A Collection of Critical Essays,* ed. R. Solomon, 243–57. South Bend, IN: Notre Dame University Press, 1980.

Schutte, Ophelia. *Beyond Nihilism: Nietzsche without Masks.* Chicago: University of Chicago Press, 1984.

Smith, P. Christopher. "The Ethical Dimensions of Gadamer's Hermeneutical Theory." *Research in Phenomenology* 18 (1988): 75–91.

Spivak, Gayatri C. "Displacement and the Discourse of Women." In *Displacement: Derrida and After,* ed. M. Krupnick, 169–95. Bloomington: Indiana University Press, 1983.

Stepelevich, Lawrence S. "Hegel and the Lutheran Eucharist." *HeyJ* 27 (1985): 262–74.

Taylor, Charles. *Hegel.* Cambridge: Cambridge University Press, 1975.

Taylor, Mark C. *Altarity*. Chicago: University of Chicago Press, 1987.

———. ed. *Deconstruction in Context: Literature and Philosophy*. Chicago: University of Chicago Press, 1986.

———. *Erring: A Postmodern A/Theology*. Chicago: University of Chicago Press, 1983.

Theunissen, Michael. *The Other: Studies in the Social Ontology of Husserl, Heidegger, Sartre, and Buber*. trans. C. Macann. Cambridge: MIT Press, 1986.

Vasey, Craig. "Emmanuel Levinas: From Intentionality to Proximity." *Philosophy Today* 25 (1981).

Verene, Donald Phillip. *Hegel's Recollecton: A Study of Images in the Phenomenology of Spirit*. Albany: SUNY Press, 1985.

Whitehead, Alfred North. *Adventures of Ideas*. New York: Macmillan, 1933.

———. *Process and Reality*. New York: Free Press, 1978.

Williamson, Raymond Keith. *Introduction to Hegel's Philosophy of Religion*. Albany: SUNY Press, 1984.

Wood, Allen W. *Hegel's Ethical Thought*. Cambridge: Cambridge University Press, 1990.

Wyschogrod, Edith. "Derrida, Levinas and Violence." In *Continental Philosophy* II. ed. H. Silverman et al, 183–200. New York: Routledge, 1989.

———. "Emmanuel Levinas and the Problem of Religious Language." *The Thomist* 36, no. 1 (1972): 1–38.

———. "God and 'Being's Move' in the Philosophy of Emmanuel Levinas." *The Journal of Religion* 62, no. 2 (1982): 145–55.

Yerkes, James. *The Christology of Hegel*. Albany: SUNY Press, 1982.

Index of Subjects

Index of Names